RAISED!

RAISED!

THE FOURTH "SEASON" OF
OUR FATHER'S EVANGELICAL CHURCH

BRAD BROWN

Copyrighted Material

Raised!

Revised Edition, Copyright © 2024 by Brad Brown.

All rights reserved. No part of this publication may be reproduced or transmitted in any form or by any means without written permission of the publisher.

Unless otherwise indicated, Scripture quotations taken from the Holy Bible, New International Version (NIV). Copyright © 1973, 1978, 1984, 2011 by Biblica, Inc.™ Used by permission. All rights reserved.

For information about this title or to order other books and/or electronic media, contact the publisher:

Brad A Brown
bradbrownauthor.com
BRADSLAND@aol.com

ISBNs:
979-8-9870461-9-7 (hardcover)
979-8-9883647-0-2 (softcover)
979-8-9883647-1-9 (eBook)

Printed in the United States of America

Cover and Interior design: 1106 Design

This book is dedicated to the Cleaver Class (the real "Young and Married" class) of Emmanuel Evangelical Free Church in Burbank, California, who graciously allowed me to be their leader and teacher nearly forty years ago. I was given not only a start; I was given eternal friendships.

As this quartet of books come to an end, every word, paragraph, and sentence has been a love letter to *another* quartet:
Joe, Anne, Hudson, and Samantha.

"*The pleasant surprise in my story,
the sweet refrain in my song.*"

In other words, my beloved "target audience"!

Papa Brad
June 2024

Acknowledgments

A heartfelt thanks to my courageous wife and soulmate, Cindy, who has led the "going not knowing" charge all the way from "Ur of the Chaldees." Your spiritual antenna gets the best reception and bathes the whole family caravan with an appropriate amount of grace, wisdom, and thanksgiving.

And also to my transplanted family, all of whom have been an essential source of inspiration and admiration. Thank you for living such remarkable lives that each and every one is something to write home about!

A special "badge of honor" to my sheriff son-in-law, Nick, who set me up with a triage of emergency terminology and procedures. Thanks to Rick Johnson, who, in generously giving me an *Education of a Wandering Man*, also gave me just the "write" nudge within its pages to crest the hill and finish the race.

My gratitude will always remain utmost for my trio of editors and proofreaders, Margaret Lehman, Linda Osti, and Karen Voorhis, who scrupulously examined every "jot and tittle" scrawled by Ian Block! If his words soar, it is because he had three very good mechanics! And, last but not least, awestruck thanks to a "moving and shaking" Heavenly Father, who, season after season, sees the whole thing through—and everything in-between!

—Brad Brown
Franktown, Colorado
2017

Preface

My childhood in the church was a delight to my spirit and imagination, as they were both nurtured by loving, dedicated, matronly children's workers. Childhood fantasies—even biblical ones—were a protected commodity. The actual running of the church, unbeknownst to me, was handled by an adult population of which, at my standing height, I could see only their kneecaps!

When my own adulthood approached, the complicated inner workings of "big church" were exposed, and a new reality set in—namely, that my whimsical church upbringing had subsisted on the behind-the-scenes vision, meetings, disagreements, and hard work of an adult world. Upon entering that world, after "growing up in the church," I found myself fully grown, first as a youth leader and then as a Bible teacher, elder, and occasional preacher. I was an adult who, from time to time, mentally wandered while silently sitting in church "board meetings" back to a childhood one, only this meeting's "board" was flannel and populated with cloth cutouts of Peter, James, and John.

The particulars of this life transition are true not only in Sunday school but in the school of life as well.

So *Raised!* is just that, a slice from the circle of adult Christian life, after "putting away childish things" in order to successfully navigate through a new world populated by supposedly mature audiences, only to often revert back to the biblical moorings of boyhood, so as to properly "enter the kingdom of God as a little child" one day.

Also, this quartet of books would not be complete without a lost diary! This is a plot device very popular in the Bible:

– An uncovered law book once buried under the rubble of routines, with stipulations reinstated only after the demise of two generations of reprobate royalty.

– A hidden governmental permission slip thought nonexistent found hundreds of miles from the illegal obstruction that so desperately needed it.

– Directions for required religious practices suddenly discovered by an absent-minded, re-established nation unaware of their lack of shelter.

– A secret, grudge-holding scroll containing a passage revealing who's allowed, and who's not, into sacred services, based on a 1,000-year-old infraction.

So a peek into Ian Block's private writings is in good company. Hence, the diary format provides the unique structure of the fourth and final "season" of Our Father's Evangelical Church—a perfect framework by which to describe 11 years of adult . . . Christian . . . education.

This book is also the most personal and autobiographical of the four "fictional memoirs." It is less like doctor Luke writing an "orderly account," and more like mother Mary "treasuring these things in her heart."

Preface

As such, I pray these are pages to ponder by all who desire, in every facet of this life and beyond, to be *Raised!*

—Brad Brown, 2024

"But now at length I have the happiness to know that it is a rising and not a setting sun."

—Benjamin Franklin

I saw a bumper sticker today that said,

"Jesus is coming. Look busy!"

It was one of many plastered all over the SUV idling in front of me, as if the driver considered his vehicle merely a motorized piece of old luggage that needed to account for every spiritual tourist trap he had visited on his life journey thus far.

"Jesus is coming. Look busy!"

I had to think about that one, as I nosed in and out of my tailgating position from behind the SUV plodding along Max Stellar Boulevard during a traffic peak.

For one thing, the message on the bumper sticker is a sloganeering ruse, surely stemming from some theological blunder on our part about the nature of guilt and grace. Another attempt by the human race to perform an "I'm a good person" vaudevillian soft-shoe in order to get away with something.

If margarine of some forty years ago couldn't fool Mother Nature, then surely mankind, on any given day, cannot, and will not, appease the mighty Messiah with such tomfoolery about the ethics of works . . . and faith!

When I finally made it back to the Block Insurance office, I found that my rather lengthy lunch break had produced row upon row of yellow sticky notes—like armored plates on the back of some large, scaly reptile—attached to the surface of my desk. The sloppy stack of files that I had left before the midday meal had grown significantly, as if during my absence there had been an upheaval in the Earth's core beneath my desk, and the mountain of paper was pushed upward by some cataclysmic magma surge. I looked around my office space at the cluttered new Heavens and new Earth that had been created in just under two hours so that I would be fruitful and multiply: *return phone calls, endorse policies, handle claims, pay bills . . . gulp.*

I sat down and came to my senses,

"Jesus is coming. Look busy!"

Busy, busy, busy! I mean, anyone can take out the trash, feed the dog, clean up their room, or go to work. The person who really *wants* to do these things—and can think of nothing else he or she would rather be doing for the glory of God—is rare indeed.

When it comes to relationships—loving your neighbor, giving your cloak to an enemy, picking up the victim by the roadside, washing feet, cheek-turning, taking up crosses, or simply following—are all parts of the compendium of love that Jesus modeled for us more than sufficiently—giving us the power to do likewise—so that we might avoid *another* bumper sticker:

"I love God. It's just His fan club I can't stand!"

That is the two-way street that so often comes between Father, Son, Holy Spirit . . . and Ian Block.

This then, after so many years (and with many fits and starts, both brief and lengthy), is an effort to revive a generation-skipping, lost art of "journaling." It is a series of ongoing, "living life" diary entries, recorded in a now dog-eared, begrudgingly feminine, blue notebook originally purchased back in 1997.

In this book of remembrance are varied recollections of images that span the constantly fluctuating wide and narrow gap between "*Let Us*"... and... "*make man*"

– the original bumper sticker!

Ian Block
April 26, 2005
Monument, California

MENTAL WARD:

Prayers and Observations by Ian Block

"One generation will commend your works to another..."

Psalm 145:4

"Wait for it . . ."

May 4, 2005

"But those who wait upon the Lord will renew their strength, they will mount up with ings like weagles!"

Dr. Clint Banning came to a dead stop during his crescendoing, passionate recitation of the last breath of verse 31, as it was drowned out by the sudden, equally crescendoing chortles, surprised snickers, and guilty guffaws of the packed congregation. Against all Isaianic odds, it was as if he had actually grown weary right before our very eyes and was suddenly about to faint. But he instead produced a sheepish, embarrassed smile of realization, and our under-shepherd joined in with the joyously bleating sheep. While the gaffe was no "THOU SHALT NOT LOVE THE LORD THY GOD" shouted by yours truly, coming from the golden throat of such a spit-and-polished, slick, professional orator like Dr. Clint Banning, it was funny! Very, very funny! Although, I am quite sure that while awkwardly standing there at the podium, our pastor wished at that moment that *he* could just blow away like a fading flower, or fall into the concealing, withering grass from just 24 verses before.

Clint had done such a thorough job of setting up his grand finale of Isaiah 40:31 by carefully explaining that intertwining, crow-sounding Hebrew word for "wait" or "hope," (depending upon your Bible translation), *qavah*. Isaiah had quite a few word choices in the Hebrew lexicon of 550 B.C., but specifically chose the one expression that would define us as all twisted up and bound together with God into such a taut oneness that the knots alone would meet the spiritual and aerodynamic requirements for walking, running, and even soaring.

But then, Dr. Banning's tangled cord of two strands tripped over itself on the potholed Judean runway and . . . crash!

It's amazing what a difference a sudden, sacred scrabbling of just two seemingly innocent letters can make! No matter. For Isaiah—the Prince of the Prophets—there was now a new bird in town!

May 7, 2005

Clint Banning was the sixth in the senior pastor "changing of the guard" I had experienced as an adult at Our Father's Evangelical Church. He was innocently a part of an exhausting, crowded lineup of ordinary, interim pastor pulpit-fill rotation (Why is it always called "pulpit fill"? It sounds like "landfill." Does this kind of trash talk betray what we actually think of our preachers? Perhaps not initially, but, as Benjamin Franklin so wisely quipped, "Guests, like fish, begin to smell after three days"). Nonetheless, the congregation fell in love with his winsome, Socratic speaking abilities, and his hat, as they say, was summarily thrown into the ring.

You were close, Ben—he lasted only three months!

A few years before, by the relentless tractor beam of heredity, I had stepped down from the rung of fifth-grade Sunday school teacher and stepped up to the plate of . . . elder! I had never been one of these before. The last time I was in O.F.E. leadership, we were all just a ragtag bunch of rather randomly selected deacons. But, thanks to Senior Woodpecker Tony Meece, the biblically petrified church bylaws were put through tree mulching, and out popped a completely new pecking order! And I was one of the spraying chips off the old Block that landed in a metal folding chair around the large, rectangular table in the church-board room.

Come to find out, this surprising "promotion" of mine was for the express purpose of providing much-needed representation *of* and leadership *for* Adult Christian Education at Our Father's Evangelical Church. For this, I had been specifically recommended and requested by the current Elder Board at the time. Initially, everything in my fifth-grade Sunday-school teacher comfort zone screamed at the growing pains of my being potentially placed on a stretching rack in the torture chamber of change.

I was presumably to deliver oversight as I paced, overwhelmed, the halls of the Educational Christianity building on the corners of Valentino and Ridgeway Avenues. While I had had prior experience leading and teaching, specifically the "Young and Married" class of my peers, this was an entirely different proposition. I would be speaking to all adult age groups, as a church elder officially overseeing Adult Christian Education, to audiences which—based on their collective Christian walks over the years, and decades of service and sacrifice, trial and error, mountains and valleys, life and death—I, by comparison, had no business attempting to impart my dubious brand of timid, inexperienced wisdom and insight. But, there I was. My ankles and wrists were fastened, the levers were pushed—straining the pulleys and rollers underneath—muscles torn, joints dislocated.

Weakness somehow turned into strength. Gradually. Inexorably. Strrrrrrrrrrretch!

I cast about for a "ram in the thicket." If I must test the teaching waters to see if my supposed spiritual gift would float, then I would first go where I felt most at home, where it all began. I could feel the "pleased as punch" satisfaction from my blessed grandparents as they smiled from their Mama and Papa Bear rocking chairs in that not-so-assisted living in the sky. Looking back down from my gaze at the ceiling, I picked up the phone from our office-bedroom and called Floyd Ames, who had taken over the "Canes and Able" Sunday school class from the late, self-appointed church historian, Frank Petry, and asked if I could stop by their class soon and introduce myself as the new elder over Adult Christian Education (a stuffy, institutional name I would quickly freeze dry into that all-too-common church labeling system, the acronym: A.C.E.).

That's how it all started—where I was most comfortable, in the nurturing, flabby underarms of my surrogate grandparents at O.F.E. I was also determined that, if my first teaching experience fell on deaf ears, they should actually be so. Coward! Be that as it may, this incubator from my past helped immensely to gently launch me into the other demographic solar systems of the remaining Adult Christian Education classes, and to see if my inimitable teaching style actually translated. While I could never be accused of throwing caution to the wind (for fear that "caution" might blow back in my face with the slightest turn of the weathervane), I did, however, channel the teaching method of my beloved mentor and fifth-grade Sunday school teacher, Sid Barrington: the synopsis! Augmented by my cartoon characters—brought to life on both chalk- and white boards—I now had a widespread, tried-and-true recipe for adult retention.

While Maria and I remained tethered to our brainchild, the "Young and Married" class (not so young anymore), I became a "teacher at large" for the Cleavers, Bereans, Crossroads, Lifetime, Sojourners, Koinonia, Harvesters, Faith-builders, Becomers, and Crusaders. Catchy class names that made up a veritable army of God—A.C.E. fighter pilots, all—providing protective cover for the Body of Christ at every level. Their oft-used runway was the backbone of the local Church. My first discipline was to make sure I did not come across as too academic—like some Ivy League emeritus poking his egghead out of a textbook think tank. I purposed to never tell a class what I had learned, but what I had *discovered*. I was not about to give some stale, oral book report on something that might be only remotely interesting to a select few. I would much rather compare hastily written biblical field notes accounting for some exciting bombshell that had blown up in my face while standing together on the same rocky terrain of our life journey together.

May 8, 2005

My eldering started out as routine "pews, weather, and sports" until our current, gracefully aging Senior Pastor Roland Jeffries announced that he and his wife wanted to spend more time with their grandchildren back East and so decided to . . . retire! It seemed that the ink wasn't even dry on the board-meeting minutes acknowledging my elder induction before we were, once again, lighting the torches, releasing the hounds, and forming a search party for that microscopic needle in the towering, ecclesiastical haystack known only to us as Senior Pastor #10.

The chairman of our board, a supernaturally committed Theodore "Ted" McGowan, had been around the church-leadership block so many times and for so many years that he had no idea how to change directions or break his stride. When the chairmanship baton was thrust at his frail frame, beckoning him once again to follow in the now-legendary footsteps made by the World War II boots of the late, great Samuel Caldwell, Ted accepted it with a combination of reluctance and humility. Now, retirement age was looming, as were serious health issues. The former a light at the end of a long career tunnel courtesy of the County of Los Angeles, the latter a grim doctor's complicated radiology report about his liver, no doubt, in part, courtesy of the stressful ups-and-downs of Our Father's Evangelical Church over the years. Before capitulating to his dedicated wife—who was beseeching him to start "taking it easy"—Chairman McGowan wanted to make sure that his beloved O.F.E. was in good hands. So, he would not tender his resignation as Chairman of the Board until a new pastor was in place. Ted was the epitome of grace and placid, spiritual assurance under pressure. He was a humble, walking, talking Enoch who humbly walked and talked with God. The only time I ever saw his pot boil—under all sorts of pastoral management and mismanagement—was when there bubbled to the surface any grumbling from a congregant about not being "fed" from the pulpit. They would receive an uncharacteristic verbal drubbing-down from Ted about the holy smorgasbord served each and every Sunday by whomever was the chosen, apron-clad Pastor-chef. A buffet of all-you-can-eat verses, contextual cuisine cooked to simmering perfection in Pastor study-kitchens, and served on a pentateuchal platter offering such a wide variety of topical morsels and exegetical binges that it rivaled any first-century cruise ship—if there were any. Which is *exactly* the expectation and reputation Chairman McGowan wanted to avoid! He admonished any and all saints who even *thought* they felt their stomachs growling that anyone can get at least *something* out of each service, be it tid or bit.

Resumes began pouring in to our "A-rated restaurant"—the only church in Monument. Word became flesh as the Elder Board invited potential preachers of all shapes and sizes—from whelps fresh out of seminary to seasoned old codgers fresh out of ideas—who lined up behind our lectern week after week. Behind the scenes, we elders were constantly engaged in rifling through cover letters, calling up references, listening to sermon tapes, fielding countless suggestions, visiting other churches undercover, nodding our heads at friend-of-a-friend name dropping, all dutifully passed along to us by the equally frantic Pastoral Search Committee. All the while discerning deep in our hearts and minds Sunday after Sunday after Sunday that the latest oratory offering—whether polemical, exegetical, allegorical, eisegetical, rhetorical, forgettable or diabolical—came from the "sycophantic" lips of yet another in the perpetual interim preaching lineup, who was simply not our guy.

This was taking its toll on the fragile Chairman of the Board. At each meeting of both Elder Board and Search Committee—over which he presided—Theodore "Ted" McGowan's physical constitution was starting to wear thin, as shown by his sunken eyes, softer, slower speech patterns, translucent skin, and labored, shuffling gait. Unfortunately, the entire Elder Board also was beginning to feel like Ted looked. Yet, in spite of all of these rising infirmities, Ted was determined not to succumb to that most dangerous of church-leadership emotions, and one deadly to discernment . . . desperation. And then at last (just in time it seemed), flew in sacred star-power! Dr. Banning was a well-known commodity with the affluence to match. He had many published books to his credit; he was the nationwide go-to guru on youth ministry and a popular adjunct professor right here locally at Vision University in Diamond Bar, California, that competed for new enrollments with my neighboring alma mater, the Antioch Christian Academy.

He sat on many Christian boards, church advisory councils, political action committees, focus groups, and media panels (he even had a nationwide broadcast ministry about the *Culture of Youth in a Post-Modern Age* called, anachronistically, "C.B. Radio"). But, most importantly, he was a longtime friend of a member of Our Father's Evangelical Church.

When the window opened just a crack in his otherwise overbooked-one-year-in-advance day-planner due to a cancellation, supercilious Clint Banning gave grudging assent to his dear friend at O.F.E. and graced the only church in Monument with phraseology flowing with milk and honey. Truth be told, Dr. Banning found the prospect intriguing. After playing itinerant celebrity speaker for most of his adult life, he was attracted to the curious—albeit foreign—notion of a local church environment. An environment that he, a Bible professor, gave sincere lip service to on a worldwide scale, but his renown precluded him from ever darkening the door of one on a consistent basis and experiencing its wonders himself.

He got a good dose of it that very first Sunday—and he liked it! He miraculously carved out time on his prohibitive calendar and informed the disbelieving Elder Board that he would like to come back. Like scurrying, broom-pushing Olympic team members in the winter sport of curling, the toadying board cleared its own calendar to accommodate the illustrious Dr. Banning, vigorously smoothing the walkway themselves of anything conflicting with his miraculous willingness.

He came back again, and again, and again—as often as we could get him. It was apparent that this thing called the Body of Christ, at its most organic, grassroots, love-thy-neighborly level, was a complete unknown to the likable luminary.

And the likable luminary was falling in love.

Better yet, stress levels were plummeting. Criticism was waning. Desertions were diminishing. Why? Because O.F.E. had a crowd-pleaser on their hands!

And then the unthinkable happened. After a few short weeks, Dr. Banning threw his hat (or crown) into the ring to be our next Senior Pastor! By comparison to the other cloying clergy applying, in the eyes of our motley crew, Clint Banning was in a league all his own. Add to this, the church did not have to bankroll any moving expenses, as Pastor Banning's "home base" was already in the area. His Elder Board submission for congregational consideration was a "no-brainer." That same congregational approval was a "shoo-in," his hiring a "piece of cake." Like those flimsy Gates of Hell, no amount of red tape, procedures, bureaucracy, or committees would prevail against it.

It was probably the fastest church decision in church history.

May 20, 2005

Wow! Coronation Day was impressive, as was Banning's entourage (complete with a retinue of bodyguards). The church was packed, as they say, to the rafters. After the harking and heralding accompanied by the requisite fanfare due his celestial arrival, Dr. Banning approached the pulpit of Our Father's Evangelical Church in all his finery for the first time as our new Senior Pastor.

He officially introduced his stunning wife, Danielle—a renowned Christian counselor (who remained oddly aloof and isolated from those women at the church, who wanted so badly to get to know her better. Perhaps her quieter, removed demeanor was a second-nature byproduct from all those years meeting in her office under a cloak of client-counselor confidentiality), along with their beautiful and only daughter, Sutton, who was about the same age as our oldest daughter, Sharayah. It leaked out in bits and pieces over the course of the next few weeks that Sutton Banning was indeed a miracle child, which seemed quite fitting for a child born into such a picture-perfect monarchy.

When she was about seven or eight years old, she began complaining about her back hurting. The first visit to the pediatrician was primarily based on calming their whining daughter down with an official "it's nothing" and prescribing her an increased dosage of children's aspirin. When the pain persisted, another doctor ran a few more tests. Revelations from these required the interpretation and second opinion of a specialist, who determined that it was, in fact, leukemia.

The royal family came crashing down upon itself but quickly dried its tears and re-grouped to muster all of its vast resources to defeat this. More specialists were called in from across the country, and little Sutton herself was flown to just as many—accompanied by either her mother or father as their schedules would permit. Treatment ensued, which weakened the formerly bright and vivacious little girl and rocked her increasingly sallow, cadaverous frame—not to mention the haggard features of her concerned and determined parents. A widespread combing through hospital records commenced from coast to coast in a militant manhunt for a perfectly matched donor for a bone-marrow transplant. The kingdom was turned over from top to bottom, and, at last, he was found and flown in at once. The news of the forthcoming transplant was relayed to Sutton while she was resting in her bed. Her mother pulled back her thinning hair as she listened, with half-lidded eyes, to the news about this next step on their journey. A force-fed smile appeared on her pallid face, a brave indicator that this answer to prayer had registered in her highly medicated brain. When she was well enough, her tainted blood was banished, flushed out in favor of more full-throttled liquid life from a complete, blood type-casted stranger.

The transplant "took," to use an unofficial hospital pronouncement. The ravenous ordeal had rendered Sutton's recovery slow but, thankfully, assured. Over time, the restorative powers became more and more evident, and soon the sweet little girl was seen playing tag, jumping rope, hopscotching, and riding bikes with her friends. Being fearfully and wonderfully made has a long memory, and the lasting gift of that year-long affliction and its eventual subjugation kept right on giving. Sutton grew up into a beautiful, healthy, and highly athletic young lady, as she was thus presented that auspicious Sunday morning to the congregation of Our Father's Evangelical Church.

I liked Clint (as I came to call him), and he me! During his all-too-brief time with us, we actually managed to cram in a few lunches at the Rush More Coffee House. He could expand your horizons just by opening his mouth. I felt for him for as much as I could possibly understand the incredible crucible he shared with his daughter. You never fully forget walking through a valley with the shadow of death creeping into your routine. Thankfully, in this case, there was a victorious outcome. But it can make you wary of the future, even paranoid if you're not careful.

Due to his high demand on so many fronts, Dr. Banning did not occupy the vacant Senior Pastor office on the church campus during the week; many times, he would be rushed from the Burbank Municipal or Los Angeles International Airports (depending on his flight's point of origin), to Monument via private limousine just in time to preach the sermon. After receiving (and accepting) the full slate of resignations from the current O.F.E. staff, and in compensation for his lack of availability midweek, Dr. Banning wasted no time in hiring guns, the best of the best drawn from his widespread connections in and around all of Christendom. These members of his prospective new staff (or cabinet), once approached by either Dr. Banning personally or by an official representative, would give up anything and everything just to be able to "come and follow he"—to serve at the pleasure of such a highly celebrated celebrity. Our Father's Evangelical Church was soon fully operational with brand-new personnel who came gliding into town as needed on Dr. Banning's shimmering coattails. This royal retinue included a new music minister, Dr. Charlotte Rhodes (from Gordon College in Boston); a new children's pastor, Adelaide Ambrose (from the Christian Children Center in Colorado Springs); a new youth pastor, Clayton "Clay" Hanson (from Banning's own Vision University in Diamond Bar); and a new Associate Pastor, honors graduate Grayson Pomeroy (from Harrington Scholastic Temple in Virginia Beach).

During the following weeks, the church exploded. "Lookiloos" from every corner of the Southland made the trek to Monument to hear the famous "new guy." Every Sunday, under the chiseled approbation of the recently completed and dedicated Rudolph Valentino head some fifty feet above, week after week, we were a sold-out movie premiere with an all-star cast that made our city proud. There were not many "conversions," at least not in the Great Commission's way of thinking, but there were many "diversions." Groupies from other competing churches were dropping their plows, not even bothering to look back, say goodbye to father and mother, or bury their dead, in order to see what all the commotion was about.

> *Heavenly Father, I get it now. We need to see ourselves in perspective. We are not unimportant, but we are not all-important, either! Christian celebrity is an oxymoron. The reason you ran interference in that scrape between washed-up judge Samuel and the people about wanting a king, was because You knew that it was ultimately about You. We ignored your warnings. No matter how well-intentioned, mankind is not wired for fame.*
>
> *The only One who should achieve stardom is the One who made them in the first place. The only One to lord over a kingdom is the One whose kingdom is coming.*
>
> *But those neighbor nations, with their kings, sure do look attractive.*
>
> *So do neighbor churches.*
>
> *Father, forgive us. For we know exactly what we do!*

The Elder Board coasted. The royal court of Dr. Banning sported an "I'll take it from here" attitude that reduced our monthly meetings to just dumbfounded testimonies of bystander shock and awe. At least Chairman Ted McGowan got some much-needed rest.

And then, it started once again. The countenance of Sutton Banning was changing. This time it was not caused by the spoils of chemotherapy. Perhaps, from a First Corinthians point of view, it was from something far worse. I had seen this movie before. It had screened at my house a few years earlier. While our church was rejoicing at Dr. Banning arriving on our shores with all of his regalia at just the right place, the right time, Dr. Banning's only daughter was being courted by the wrong crowd. High school will do that to even the best and the brightest. Sutton had not yet fallen in *with*, but was most certainly teetering *from* their temptations. Since her arrival at the church, Sharayah and Sutton were fast becoming close companions. Having been down this wide road already—with the scars to prove it—Sharayah, a soon-to-be graduating Monument High School senior herself—did everything in her power to protect, dissuade, and provide a much-needed course correction for her new friend. But Sutton would not budge and began pulling out the fork in her road. Both her father and mother heard it drop with a clatter to the ground and sent out for reinforcements. First Danielle employed all of her professional-counseling abilities (having successfully delivered many from the *Culture of Youth in a Post-Modern Age*), but these were deflected in a classic "Physician, heal thyself," mother-daughter confrontation that proved patently powerless in the discomfort of their very own home.

Her influential father called out the guards, from every corner of his tremendous power and pull, and money was no object for their priceless miracle of a daughter. But all the king's horses and all the king's men of the Christian marketplace could not provide the necessary reinforcements. But the good doctor had one more trick up his sleeve: Real estate. If you can't take the wrong crowd out of the person, take the person out of the wrong crowd!

Fortunately (literally, a fortune!), Dr. Banning had the high-society luxury and resources to make this happen. Over the years of best-selling wealth and prosperity, O.F.E.'s First Family had second and third homes located around the country. They would transport their beloved Sutton to one of them in Vermont. Danielle decided to move her practice as well in order to accompany her. This left only Dr. Banning to tie up the loose ends, one of which was dangling at the corner of Valentino and Ridgeway Avenues. The Elder Board did not know what hit it when, just three months shy of his inauguration, Dr. Banning tendered his resignation. He softened the blow by promising to fly into California on Sundays to preach for an additional three months. But, as it turned out, his demanding schedule, evidently the result of his shifting priorities, permitted this less and less. Or, so he said. Some in the congregation were relieved by this new arrangement, as they felt that Dr. Banning's once-outstanding sermons were becoming contrived and shallow. Bible-bored messages hollowed out by circumstances, as was their messenger.

In a word, Dr. Banning had panicked. He had lost sight of the family of God—the very Body of Christ—housed in the milieu of the first local church with whom he had allowed himself to fall in love. If only he had consented to let the men, women, and children of the highly experienced, war-torn, seasoned flock at O.F.E. to come alongside his daughter (like those who came alongside my own daughters during their secretive, parent-excluding, wayward years) and himself!

May 21, 2005

Even with all of his world-traveling, widespread experience in all things Youth, he was blinded within his own family by the notion that what was happening to his precious daughter was unique in all the world. No one could possibly walk this lonely journey with him or help him carry the complicated burden marked out solely for him. No one. He truly came to the garden alone. Because no one apparently had his experience, no one was qualified to speak into it. How wrong he was! If he had only bothered to find out that there was nothing new under the sun with the flock at O.F.E., who had *been there, done that!*

Nothing would shock them. Nothing would shake them.

But God's traveling salesman to the churches, Dr. Clint Banning, would not take such a personal risk and mounted up with "ings like weagles."

"Fortified City of Brotherly Love"

June 1, 2005

My older brother Owen and his wife, Penny, are now officially divorced. One could perceive that there was trouble brewing from a few years back. Their son, the embattled Owen, Jr., was now bounced back and forth between meagerly sustainable households of dual custodianship; Penny did her level best as an abrupt single mom, and my brother was on the fast track bellying up to the bar to order a second round of marriage. He retained his home in Los Angeles in the divorce settlement, and Penny moved out and into an affordable apartment in Monument near Max Stellar Boulevard at the bottom of the hill down by the freeway. In addition to a chunk of child support being siphoned off of Owen's second-string coaching salary, Penny's rent was also a bar tab to which he was legally bound by a Superior Court judge to pick up.

Understandably, after the discovery of his marital affair and its chronological age, Penny apparently took Owen for all he was worth. This shook my brother to the core, to say nothing of my parents, who were watching this whole branch of the family pruned before their very eyes from a distance, at their retirement condo up north in Ventura, California. The dulcet sound of the crashing waves that came through the sliding screen door off their balcony was no longer hypnotic and soothing but now provided a pounding soundtrack to their oldest son's little family being dashed upon the rocks. Even the ocean whence the throbbing sound emitted was no longer living up to its peaceful name of "Pacific."

With every iteration of the tide washing in and out, Seth and Nancy were now rhythmically aware that their squeaky-clean public persona of the Block-family dynasty was tainted by what was once quite the stigma in our society—*divorce*. My parents did their level best at damage control via phone calls and email (even making apologies to long-standing friends for the lavish wedding gifts they had presented to the young bride and groom so many years before, that now seemed like such a waste. Refunds and returns were now out of the question (although I'm sure that my sister-in-law, Penny, would have gladly stood in line in order to return my brother for a full refund). But, even with the opening supplications, each rehash of the tragic story as told to others was slowly but surely shifting in Owen's favor. My parents could not abide by any new math that concluded "it takes two."

There had to be a culprit, and it certainly could not have been their son! True, he was impulsive, high-strung, and moody at times. But most of this came from his competitive, athletic bearing, coupled with the stresses of providing for his family in expensive Southern California on such a paltry coach's stipend. In his defense—so said my parents—Penny was far from a magazine-cover-worthy housewife, not better at either "Home" or "Garden." She barely cooked. The house, after the terror, Owen, Jr., was born and capable of mobility, was in

"Fortified City of Brotherly Love"

shambles (even more so, it seemed, when my parents knocked on their door unannounced as a result of a spontaneous trip south to surprise their only grandson). Taking all of this into consideration, is it any wonder that Owen grew frustrated? Penny's parents lived out of state, but, tragically, right after she and Owen married, her mother committed suicide in lockstep with her own mother some thirty years before. As an only child, this—quite understandably—threw Penny into an emotional tailspin, which—quite understandably—left significant emotional scars, which—quite understandably—caused Penny to close up for a time, which—quite understandably—put an enormous strain on her marriage, which—quite understandably—would take some time to repair. The only two not quite understandably sympathetic were—my parents! Even though they knew little, there had to be a devil in the details somewhere. And that, by process of an old math, was none other than their ex-daughter-in-law, Penny. The leap to this absurd conclusion could be rationalized in only two ways, the blinding bond by blood (after all, my father would say jokingly of both Penny and Maria that they were "just a piece of paper," referring, of course, to the marriage certificates they symbolically held in their hands with the Block name on it—which were Penny and Maria's golden ticket into the family fortunes—even though they were "not really family"—just steerage class on the lower deck of a luxury liner with no Block blood actually running through their veins), and the fact that Owen had masterfully kept his long-term affair with Julie Chapman a secret from his parents.

But it was no secret to Penny after she picked up the phone one day when the obstreperous Owen, Jr. was trying to play peaceably at a friend's house down the street. She silenced the ringing receiver by cradling it between her ear and shoulder on the way down the hall to clean the den (an activity my parents would have found impossible to believe). With an industrial-size canister of Lemon Pledge in one hand and a designated towel in the other, she grabbed the phone in one sweeping motion that did not break her stride down the hall. Upon hearing Penny say a slightly out-of-breath "Hello," the female caller on the other end of the line, with an equally slight intake of breath in her surprised, youngish voice, asked Penny, "Are you the maid?"

Woman's intuition graduated Penny Block with honors at that moment.

"No," she said and threw the phone onto the couch, while she took out her shaking fury on every niche of a den that did not know what hit it. The pieces of the puzzle of her suspicions over the past many months, even years, were all falling into place with every swipe of the soiled towel: The late nights at the high school with an overtime game as the excuse. The long weekends away—supposedly to San Diego to visit with a childhood buddy. The appallingly hurtful football-team bowling night that Owen insisted on attending the night of Owen, Jr.'s birth.

But, through it all, Penny was determined to hold her peace and wait for Owen to either repent or back himself into a corner, just like the one she was now scouring with indignation. As it turned out, the current little bubble-headed vixen, that mysterious female voice on the other end of the line—who kept making ensuing phone calls to the house and abruptly hanging up at the sound of Penny's voice, now that the caller realized Owen was not single—was rendezvousing in embarrassingly close proximity, right under her nose!

I must confess that I was impressed that my charming, calculating brother actually kept the whole licentious business under wraps and away from Penny for as long as he did. But my brother was finally caught on the wrong side of the Jordan River, with Moses crunching the Numbers and admonishing, "Your sin will find you out!" The only ones who didn't believe it, or chose not to, were Seth and Nancy Block.

Owen sought the only solace he could devise during the divorce proceedings—the very same solace he had sought as far back as the first sign of trouble in his marriage.

And he married that "solace" just days after the divorce was final.

Maria and I had really enjoyed our relationship with Penny after all these years. We loved her deeply and felt for her predicament as a single mom trying to raise a monster like Owen, Jr., when, on alternate weekends, his father, now "fun uncle" Owen, Sr., was undoing everything Penny tried to instill in her behaviorally problematic son.

Because my parents did not cotton to our fraternizing with the enemy, they looked down their noses at our relationship with the ostracized Penny Block (oddly, she kept her last name until she eventually remarried). To keep peace, we allowed our relationship with Penny to be conducted covertly, as far underground as necessary in order to escape the watchful eye of the Block patriarch and matriarch holding "condo court" up north.

This grew more and more difficult, as the grandparent rescue wagon was arriving quite often in the Los Angeles area in order to enrich (with plentiful and unnecessary gifts with or without a justifiable occasion) and enable Owen, Jr. at the home of Owen and Julie Block.

From my parents' point of view, Owen, Jr. was the victim of dire circumstances as perpetrated by that horrible, irresponsible

Penny. And these dire circumstances had created . . . need. But Owen, Jr.'s bellicose personality—since his squawking birth—had *always* required special attention. It was a span of attention my parents had limited resources toward which to give, which meant that my own two daughters would suffer from a third-generation attention-deficit syndrome.

As a cosmic consequence to all of this, my hilly "Venus and Mars" relationship with Owen, *Sr.* since childhood was becoming mountainous. It had not always been that way. We had once tolerated the occasional rocks thrown at each other—those meteor showers that were a normal part of growing up together as polar-opposite siblings. We even liked each other on occasion. I found my round-faced, muscular, short, curly brown, Julius-Caesar-haired (although flecked with more and more gray these days) brother at times hilarious and entertaining. Wickedly funny (so long as you were not the brunt of his jokes), the charming, debonair Owen Block was truly the life of any party.

Owen was also your go-to guy in any need or emergency, always willing to drop anything and everything and help you in a pinch. In this, he masterfully modeled "loving thy neighbor" without ever opening his own personal door in response to the very One standing there and knocking who had spent thirty-three years promoting the idea. But, of late, our getting together as an entire family was becoming more and more strained. Fueled by the competitive, separating, gravitational pull of parental inequity, Venus and Mars were no longer tolerating differences in order to co-exist. The most scientifically advanced observatory in the world could scarcely spy telescopically our interplanetary passing by one another. There was certainly no astronomical hope for even a brief eclipse! This should come as no surprise. After all, the deep space of the Bible itself is a star-studded panoply of two-boy families with issues. Many of them had all sorts of internal squabbles and got themselves into all sorts of trouble—Cain and Abel, Jacob and Esau, Moses and Rameses, Moses and Aaron, Nadab and Abihu, Hophni and Phinehas, Adrammelech and Sharezer, Joel and Abijah, Peter and Andrew, James and John—a rubber band of brothers.

June 5, 2005

When I asked my father about this Block brand of need-based favoritism toward Owen, Jr.—which was becoming increasingly obvious over the years and one that I could no longer cover for its bare-knuckled imbalance with my girls—he responded regarding his two granddaughters, "They're fine. They don't need us."

This unlocked the new concept that Sharayah and Samantha either had to be incorrigible, like my nephew, in order to capture the attention of their grandparents, or, at the very least, live in a household that was falling apart. Divorce is deafening—stability, silent. Then he added, "They have Paulo and Nicole," referring to my in-laws. Paulo and Nicole had been wonderful grandparents to Sharayah and Samantha. Since their Aunt Angela was childless and lived out of town, my girls were the sole focus of Maria's parents. Unlike my parents, the Ponticellis, subsisting on far fewer available greenbacks—as a result of contractor Paulo Ponticelli's sweaty, blue collar—did not have the financial means to entice the relationships along with their only granddaughters, but had the more-lasting formula of proximity whenever possible and communication however possible. It was not regulated by any circumstantial ups or downs. They remained doggedly consistent and fair-minded. Paulo and Nicole did not try to stop Sharayah and Samantha from growing older—locking them up in only the more comfortable worlds by participating exclusively in the innocent realm of childhood and then taking a proverbial backseat when things got complicated and the teenage years ensued. On the contrary, my girl's grandparents on their mother's side lived life with them however it was presented. Whether that meant getting down on their knees to play imaginative games with them or getting down in the uncomfortable adolescent trenches to simply be with them. This was fortified by phone calls, cards, and letters on any and all occasions that provided that consistent, reassuring note that we were *all* doing life together, no matter where our days or seasons found us or took us.

My father shockingly threw away the key with his final comment: "They're not my problem!" I could perhaps chalk this up to his outlook on philanthropy gone horribly awry; His very own "Midas touch" in the use of his significant wealth which, when applied, apparently fixed everything and gave him a sense of notoriety from the gratitude of those forever indebted to him.

But now he had thrown my daughters under the very bus he had bought and paid for.

"'Problem'?" My daughters had been reduced to a "problem."

My miraculously gentle but admonishing reply to my father was meant to lure him into a new way of thinking—that perhaps deliverance from evil (in Owen, Jr.'s case) wasn't the *only* basis for a deep, abiding relationship, particularly with his two granddaughters.

"They may not need you," I said, "but they want you!" A study in contrast that my parents could not wrap their minds around in either belief or behavior. Consequently, my daughters were more and more sidelined as the years wore on.

If I had listened closely, I would have heard hydraulic hinges purring, as Sharayah and Samantha started to close doors throughout our family, from child-to-parent, grandchild-to-grandparent, doors to hearts—for their own protection. The doors knew instinctively that something was wrong, something was coming, something that would pound on those impregnable doors trying to get at those vulnerable hearts.

Fortified playhouses were becoming fortified cities.

"Tiny Tim"

June 6, 2005

I remember when we first heard the protective door to Samantha's heart of joy slam shut on one particular night. It was the night she received her Timothy Award from the "Approved Workman Are Not Ashamed" program at Our Father's Evangelical Church, better known as A.W.A.N.A. This was quite the feat for Samantha. Not nearly as cerebral as her older sister—who took to memorizing the program's approximately 393 required verses with so much discipline and relish that neither Maria nor I ever had to coach or remind Sharayah to be prepared each Wednesday night. In the car on the way to church, she would rattle off entire passages that were "due." Young Timothy and his Award had nothing on her. She was determined to receive it and did.

On the other hand, four years later, it seemed that Maria and I both spent hours with the more distracted and carefree Samantha on just coaching her to utter the words, "Jesus wept!"

The O.F.E. gymnasium was filled with parents holding cameras and children wearing their military-gray uniforms, festooned with epaulettes, ribbons, and pins of the award-winning cadet. Many of our friends from the "Young and Married" class were there, beaming with pride at the equally astonishing accomplishments of their sons and daughters. Paulo and Nicole were on a much-needed mini-vacation, so my parents gave themselves permission in the always-competitive grandparent arena of besting one another to jump into the void and show up. This seemed a perfect fit, however, as my mother was a stalwart aficionado of the AWANA Program. As far back as I can remember, she was an AWANA Commander at Our Father's Evangelical Church and even continued in the same capacity upon arrival at their church up north. There were hundreds of changed lives—especially those of young girls—as a result of my mother's influence and steadfast volunteering as one of the "approved" women who "are not ashamed."

And now, her second granddaughter was getting the coveted Timothy Award! (Owen, Jr., of course, was setting his sights on the more worldly Heisman Trophy.) The ceremony was a wonderful celebration of youth for Christ. We were all very proud of Samantha's well-deserved distinction, given the uncharacteristic grit, patience, and determination it represented. After a punch-and-cake celebration in the gymnasium with all of our church family and friends, Maria had planned a second, smaller gathering at our home for just our family in order to celebrate more intimately Samantha's achievement in the same tradition as had been done for Sharayah. When we walked out to our cars (with Samantha struggling to hold the coveted but unwieldy "golden cup" in her arms), Maria called over to my parents, "See you at our house!" To which my mother flatly responded, "We're not coming."

"What?" Maria queried.

"It's been a long day, and we're very tired. So we're not going to make it tonight."

As my parents were shutting their car doors in the O.F. E. parking lot, Samantha went running over to the passenger-side window, beseeching my mother to roll it down. At this distance, I could not hear the conversation, but I knew that my brokenhearted younger daughter was all but begging her grandparents to come to her party, as they had for her older sister four years earlier. My heart sank, as I saw Samantha slowly back away from the car as the reverse lights went on. The car backed up and sped away, leaving Samantha still standing there, like some rejected street urchin in a Dickens novel, stock still, clutching her award in a grip of humiliation and hurt.

My mother's influence had affected yet another young girl's life at AWANA.

Maria and I would look back on that night as the night Samantha changed. Her joyful spirit seemed sucked out of the playful inner space that was her soul. Later that night, when I went to kiss her "Goodnight" in her room, she was already in tears. Not tears from some temporary loss or misunderstanding, but tears from a dreaded finality that had come: grief, loss, abandonment. My little "Bud" was clutching something to her chest. It was not the Timothy Award, which had been tossed in her closet, cursed by association, never to be openly displayed. Rather, it was a very wrinkled, tear-stained letter.

"What's that, Honey?" I said softly.

"It's a letter from Papa," she sniveled, smoothing the wrinkles lovingly out upon her chest. As my parents opted for the names of the more traditional "Grandpa" and "Grandma," this was a term of endearment uniquely applied to Paulo Ponticelli. He alone was "Papa" Paulo. (My mother-in-law had to settle for the ridiculous title of "Ya-Ya." When you least expect it, truly out of the mouth of babes comes that cooing, gurgling sound that suddenly forms a permanent name change, one that attaches itself to an adoring grandparent like a plastic dart shot through the air and affixing to the forehead of that same, tolerant grandparent, who is now stuck with it for the rest of their lives!)

The handwritten letter was simply a random one, full of love and encouragement and about the day's events (they often reminded me of the rambling letters my Grandpa Colby used to send me when I was on staff at the Cheyenne Christian Conference Center). Papa Paulo could not have known when he casually wrote this particular letter—like so many of his meandering epistles in the past—and mailed it to Samantha, that it would not only wipe every tear from her eyes but would also save her tender heart.

It was kept under her pillow for weeks thereafter.

I shut the door to Samantha's room that night, still hearing her sniffling. I wondered as I walked downstairs; What were my parents thinking? Did they have any regrets? Were they even wondering about my little girl's entreating face in front of the glass of the closing passenger-side window, rising like a fatal water level inside a disabled submersible?

Perhaps not. Perhaps they were just that tired and, after the long drive home, went right to bed. Little did they know as they put their gray heads down on their pillows that their grandchild landscape was forever being altered. The shape of things to come would look very different, much of it by glaring absences. Holidays, graduations, weddings, and the birth of their great-grandchildren now hung in the balance, and the scale was precariously tipping.

"Pomp and Difficult Circumstances"

June 17, 2005

As I write this, it is very late at night. Sharayah's graduation day was a long, exciting, and exhausting one! Our first daughter to graduate from Monument High School, and the fourth generation in the Block family to do so. The event was held on the football field, with the bleachers full on both home and visitor sides with proud parents, grandparents, and every shape and size of friends and relatives. It was a beautiful June day in southern California—a little on the warm side, considering the chilly "June gloom" that greeted the citizens of Monument that morning. But the sun that had burned off the coastal fog with blazing, midday vigor started to sink west into a lazy retirement for the evening, allowing afternoon sea breezes to occasionally brush by our sweat-glistened faces, as we fanned ourselves with commencement programs.

While sitting there on the sunny side of the grandstands, leaning into the prepared woman next to me, who was holding up a large umbrella, in order to borrow her shade, I was getting more and more nervous. Not for Sharayah poking her eye out (or one of her friend's) with the cardboard corners of the square, tasseled cap, or tripping over her gown when she walked up onto the makeshift platform at the fifty-yard line to receive her diploma from the school principal, but something far more foreboding and nerve-wracking. It had all started with a *second* phone call from my father this morning.

"Your mother and I have been talking." He started his *first* phone call without even saying "Hello," when I answered the phone at our home on Chestnut Street the night before Sharayah's graduation.

"Is Penny coming to the party?" A few weeks ago, Sharayah had asked Maria and me if she could have a graduation party at our house after the ceremony. We heartily agreed. High-school graduation was a big deal and ought to be celebrated as such. Upon our enthusiastic consent, Sharayah had sprung through the hallways of Monument High School during the last fleeting days of school, inviting all of her friends to the party (deftly pre-empting the potential of other graduating seniors planning parties of their own). There were more than fifty people on the list! It was to this party that my father was referring. More specifically, to that ostracized ex-daughter-in-law who had had the unmitigated gall to take their beloved oldest son to the cleaners in court and who, despite a declaration of profound disloyalty from our entire branch of the Block family, had somehow made it onto Sharayah's invitation list.

"Yes," I answered confidently. Of course, Aunt Penny was coming to Sharayah's graduation party. They had developed a deep relationship over the years. As a matter of fact, Sharayah could not picture her graduation party *without* the attendance of Aunt Penny. On the other hand, Uncle Owen and the new Aunt Julie were not invited (nor was her miscreant cousin, who, as he grew older, only engaged in more sophisticated forms of miscreant behavior). To Sharayah's way of thinking, these relationships had gone by the wayside, growing increasingly distant over the past few years, and had no supportive, congratulatory initials carved in her current milestone.

This was exactly the underlying point in my father's mercurial pronouncement.

"Well, if Penny is coming to the party, then we're not coming." I had to let this sink in. What came rushing to the surface within moments from my plumbed depths was a methodical, bullet-point-driven, 45-minute tirade which I had apparently been rehearsing in my mind. For the past few years, as new situations were experienced and tolerated, the information was catalogued. If and when that moment arrived when push would come to shove and I was forced to defend my "not my problem" daughters against the foibles of favoritism, I would be ready. And that moment had arrived! Admittedly, it was likely more flesh-fed than Spirit-led. But there was no stopping it. Protective father Ian Block's historical review, as he saw it, came gushing out like a fire hydrant of mistreatment and abuses, driven by the intensified water pressure of festering time. When I had finished, my dad was silent. The line went dead. How could this be? Whatever happened to those great father-son conversations between us, when my father would bestow all sorts of sage, "elderly" advice on how to handle every facet of leadership issues in the church? Something had come between us, and it was a misunderstanding that was growing bigger by the day.

Ashen-faced, I hung up the phone and walked down the hallway to tell Maria what had just occurred. The only news for her was what had been said on my father's end of the line; my side of the conversation could have been heard all the way to the Monument City Hall. She immediately suggested we commit this whole ugly situation to prayer, and we bathed it accordingly.

This morning, I drove to the Block Insurance Agency in a state of preoccupation. I was conflicted, ashamed, sad, hurt, angry, defensive, resolute, and all of the above on my oldest daughter's graduation day. Cap and gown had been exchanged for sackcloth and ashes.

The first phone call I received at the office was the second from my father in as many days. Evidently, even though it was thrown, I had given him food for thought last night. In an effort to run interference between our family and my mother (who was not about to be in the same room as "that Penny person"), my father, sounding somewhat deflated from a feeling of culpability, stated that he would like to at least make a singular appearance at Sharayah's graduation party, a halved representation of both him and my mother. After I had hung up with him, I immediately called Maria to relay this news, and we both agreed—wisely or unwisely—not to tell Sharayah until after the graduation ceremony, at which my parents were not in attendance. When we did, she was understandably furious. The bus she had been thrown under time and time again was now backing up over her, on this, of all occasions. How dare her grandparents pick *now* to take a stand for Uncle Owen and make their point against Aunt Penny!

Sensing permanent family damage, I called my father in an attempt to head him off at the pass. The way Sharayah was feeling presently (however justified), my father showing up at her party, no matter how well-intentioned, would not be a good idea. In spite of the bed that he and my mother had made over time, I simply wanted to spare him from being short-sheeted. There was no answer on the other end of the line.

After the ceremony, we all caravanned to our house in our Honda Odyssey van—Maria, myself, Samantha, "Papa" Paulo, "Ya-Ya" Nicole, and our graduate! The parking on both sides of Chestnut Street was jammed, as was our humble abode, pleasantly populated with people, it seemed, from every relational corner of Sharayah's eighteen years of life. Some people I had not seen for quite some time, including many of our own generation who had had much positive influence in our oldest daughter's life: Lorne and Candice Carlson, Sam and Betsy Morley, Dennis and Patty O'Connor (who willingly made the long drive from their home up north). Even Sharayah's O.F.E. small-group leader, Beverly Anderson, was in attendance. And, so it seemed, every high school-aged kid currently living in Monument and beyond decided to drop by! So did my father, with a case of soft drinks cradled in his arm, his own unique brand of olive branch. It was a sweet gesture, even courageous. But it was too late.

He engaged in careful, forced small talk with Paulo and Nicole, and held court with the other adult chaperones in attendance (who had been conscripted by Maria and me the minute we realized that the number of young-adult invitees was mounting and that we would be sorely outnumbered by caps and gowns). He was trying to be the life of his own separate little party with monologue "conversation" punctuated by his usual colorful word pictures. It was a delay tactic against the inevitable, when Seth Block would have to congratulate the guest of honor.

Although quietly played out, the attempt was a humiliating disaster of epic proportions. Sharayah had deliberately avoided any contact with my father throughout the entire evening, which was quite easy to execute, as the house seemed to be still standing only with the support of its wall-to-wall people. This also made it difficult for my father to make his move as well. When he finally tried to hug the Block family's fourth-generation graduate from Monument High School, Sharayah twisted her body and spun her upturned face in the opposite direction, dissolving my dad's well-intended hug into a brief, ineffectual arm across her shoulders. Sharayah left the room without saying a word, leaving my dejected father standing there alone.

I was quite conflicted then and there. While I could not abide by the inhospitable, disrespectful rudeness my daughter had displayed at that moment, I couldn't blame her, either. My father looked around, embarrassed at the smattering of people who had witnessed this brush-off from his granddaughter, and said sheepishly, "Well, I guess I'd better be going." I came into the room just as he was headed for the front door, saying "Goodbye" and sincerely thanking him for coming. Maria hugged him and thanked him for coming as well.

With that, he left.

August 24, 2005

Last Father's Day, knowing that Dad would not appreciate a phone call at this sensitive time (that was how the game was played), we opted to give him a gift from all four of us and a card that expressly thanked him again for coming to Sharayah's graduation party and also for the generous case of soft drinks. We had a feeling they would not be home (for some reason, on both Father's Day and Mother's Day, my parents performed artful disappearing acts from the family), but we made the Sunday drive to Ventura anyway to personally place the gift and card on their front porch. There was no response.

We sent gifts for my mother's birthday the following month.

There was no response.

My adoption process had begun.

"Put Out to Pastor"

August 31, 2005

As expected, the roustabouts that jumped onto the circus train to follow Dr. Banning to Our Father's Evangelical Church jumped off just as quickly. Once again, their dumping departures landed on the laps of a flummoxed Elder Board, requiring them to scramble to fill the vacated Cabinet positions. The only hireling from the previous performers who decided for some reason to stick it out was our Associate Pastor, Grayson Pomeroy. The Board was grateful for the assistance, because so many of Dr. Banning's fan base, thinking that the greatest show on Earth was over, started looking for the next empty lot where the circus might come to town. I had been through this sort of "transition" before, but, the older I got, the more piqued I became at the flighty, migratory bird brains that always flew south for the winter, or should I say flew south to the Floridian winter quarters of the circus!

In the meantime, it having been only been a couple of weeks since the big top dog had left town, I dressed as a circus Ringmaster (complete with a whip and chair), and let the Koinonia class have a synopsis full.

All that was missing was the "Casey Junior" train theme from Disney's *Dumbo* playing on the calliope.

"Put Out to Pastor"

"The 'Bethel Wild Beast Bungalow' was the greatest zoo in all of newly captured Samaria. The curator, an Israelite simply known as 'the Priest,' was one of the best lion-tamers in the land. The only problem was that the lions kept getting out of their cages at night, stalking Bethel and the surrounding towns, mauling and devouring everyone who didn't go to church! (Rumors were circulating as to whether this was a persistent mechanical malfunction or a deliberate Samaritan safari by the Priest!) This was not only emptying the pews week after week, but fewer and fewer non-eaten people were coming to the zoo at all. So, the Priest closed it down, re-opening a new church on the property now called the 'King of Beasts Bible Bungalow.'"

"Open your Bibles to 2nd Kings, Chapter Seventeen."

I first met Grayson Pomeroy and his wife at Dr. Banning's house for a special "Kick- Off Meeting." Dr. Banning was introducing his new crack team of church leaders to O.F.E.'s Elder Board. When I was introduced to Associate Pastor Pomeroy, it was "like" at first sight. He had a wide range of folksy charm that he drew upon from his deep, Virginia roots. He was well-traveled (mostly in the south), well-educated (working on his doctorate from Vision University under the tutelage of none other than his advisor and former boss, Clint Banning), a devoted family man with a plucky wife (Caroline), and four well-mannered, delightful kids.

What was most surprising was the entire family's adaptability to all things Southern California. They acted as if they had, in fact, been born here, or even better! Those of us born in this neck of the woods tend to take the entertainment nerve center for granted. We have been raised in the shadow of movie-studio water towers, grown accustomed to star-sightings and the routine re-routing from neighborhood street-closures due to the filming of a television show, movie, or commercial.

Those of us fortunate enough to have been born in Monument proper have had the extra, added benefit of a 100-foot head of Rudolph Valentino staring down at us every waking minute as we go about our lives. The frontage of our own civic museum is a mock-up of a movie set that most of us drive by on a daily basis. We ho-hum natives rarely take advantage of our world-famous location. We have seen Hollywood and Vine, cruised Rodeo and Mulholland Drives, climbed to the "Hollywood" sign, made out at the Griffith Park Observatory, vicariously placed intimidated feet into cement prints of Golden Age celebrities in the courtyard at Grauman's Chinese Theatre. For us, the tourist attraction novelty has worn off years ago. We also fail to take advantage of the ticket booth of amusements at our fingertips: Disneyland, Knott's Berry Farm, Universal Studios, La Brea Tar Pits, the Hollywood Wax Museum, the Cinerama Dome. And rarely do we take advantage of this worldwide hub for the arts: The Pantages, Greek, and Amanson Theaters, the Disney Concert Hall, and Dorothy Chandler Pavilion. Nor do we take advantage of our astounding geographic location (which the Spaniards knew intuitively to be uniquely beautiful and diverse some 300 years ago, when they first settled in what they called "*Vista Pacifica*"). Escapes to the beach, the mountains, the forests, the desert, are all theoretically within a couple hours' drive from our homes, although 'round-the-clock traffic clogging every freeway artery in every direction has taken care of that enticement. But the six Pomeroys? They made us natives restless and ashamed. Not jaded by commonplace familiarity, crowds, or inconvenience, they took advantage of every opportunity, every entertaining square foot the Southland afforded. They never stopped, and they loved every minute of it. It's as if they had always been here. The only dead giveaway was that wide-eyed, folksy charm, which was a refreshing contrast set against our cool, aloof, California individualism and benumbed appreciation.

Now that Clint Banning had flown the coop and O.F.E. was, once again, running around in circles like a chicken with its head cut off, country-boy Grayson Pomeroy used all of the farm tools at his disposal to quell the cackling and to come alongside the other "hands." In this case, the "hands" were an exhausted Elder Board that was all "done-in" from eating crow, led by a depleted Chairman McGowan, who was just simply "done." With some remote help from his dissertation advisor—our raptured, previous Senior Pastor Banning—Associate Pastor Pomeroy helped to cobble together a list of willing, nomadic preachers from both near and far who would come at Sunday dawn to roost at the corner of Valentino and Ridgeway Avenues and provide our flock with their own, early morning *cock-a-doodle-doo* wake-up call. Although not a dynamic orator himself, Pastor Pomeroy had some preaching experience from his previous church and did enjoy "feeding the chickens" at O.F.E. on occasion with his own brand of clucking grain. But his deep passion was pure pastor, and he was a consummate one. It was in his spiritual DNA. It oozed out of his pores. There was not a single member of Our Father's Evangelical Church who did not like Grayson Pomeroy and his Norman Rockwell family. Attached to anyone singing his praises was usually a companion, "bedside manner" story of how Grayson had visited, advised, helped, or comforted them in an hour of need. While I am no church historian (not like our own hoary resident chronicler of old, the late Frank Petry), I would confidently say that, in my nearly fifty-year-old estimation, Grayson Pomeroy was the best pastor Our Father's Evangelical Church had ever encountered. This made for many delightful lunches that Associate Pastor Pomeroy and I would enjoy, once I introduced him to the town's most-popular watering hole, The Rush More Coffee House.

September 7, 2005

In spite of this late date, it was still a beautiful, warm summer day in California. The southern portions of the Golden State did not fall in line with either vernal equinoxes or calendar proclamations. The high temperatures of summer could linger well past what the Indians would call theirs, and even heat things up during what Christians call Christmas. Today was just such a day, with only a few scudding clouds providing large, shadowy Dalmatian spots that were scampering across the white pavement of the restaurant parking lot. It was on this outdoor disco dance floor that a smiling Grayson and I shook hands and casually strode through the glass double doors of our restaurant of choice, making our way to our traditional empty booth in the back, with Rudolph staring us down about a half-mile up the road. Without any agenda, we let the conversation drift like a lazy river. The Rush More Coffee House was our water park, and Grayson and I were bobbing along on inner tubes, moving with a current set at "nice-and-slow" in the peaceful canal that circled around the fringes. We paddled through small-town small talk with not a care in the world for the water slides, wave machines, and splash zones that made up the inner circle of potential subject matters with both deeper depths and height requirements. It was abnormally crowded at this much-later portion of the traditional lunch hour. We waved to Beverly Anderson and her husband, Tom, said "Hello" to Donna Prichit (our retired church secretary) and her friend Bernice, and gave a cordial nod to Tristan Holbert, who was entertaining a bunch of guys from his work, before we got our feet wet.

"Grape," Pastor Pomeroy was saying. "That was my nickname all through childhood."

"Grape?" I asked.

"Yup. Came from my elementary-school days. You know when the teacher called roll, using your first name and the first letter of your last? I had already shortened my name to 'Gray,' which was easier to yell on the playground or baseball diamond. The first time I said 'Here,' or 'Present' in response to a teacher calling out a garbled 'Gray P.?' it was finished! 'Grape,' it was!"

"I can only imagine the jokes!" I responded after swallowing a mouthful of my usual club sandwich.

"Oh, yeah! When I was really mad, I was 'Grape of Wrath.' When I was in a bad mood, 'Sour Grape.' When I was accused of something I never said, the tattletale would always begin with, 'I Heard It Through the Grapevine.' What's up with that? I mean, most of us were not even born when that song first came out!"

Point well taken. A good gossip gathers grandiloquent grist, I thought, in the key of "G." And even though the joke was a couple of decades old, Pastor Pomeroy could now be called a "California Raisin." Although I am not so sure about his singing and dancing capabilities.

"But the worst was the one from the junior-high locker room."

"Which was?" my concupiscent curiosity piqued.

"If I was ever accused of not 'making it' with a girl, I was a 'seedless Grape'!"

"Wow! Kids can sure be cruel! I remember all of the 'chip off the ol' Block' nicknames I had to tolerate. There was a time when I actually heard someone say to me—"

The water started sloshing in our peaceful canal. I stopped speaking. Grayson became uncharacteristically tense as he shot his head back and forth in the restaurant, looking for clues as to why our entire booth was moving. The restaurant grew quiet in a moment of silent observance and not-so-silent anticipation. I looked up, questioning. The lamp above our booth was swaying, in concert with all of the other lamps over all of the other booths lining the outer perimeter of the restaurant. Like so many clock pendulums swinging in unison. Time told.

I had my answer.

"Earthquake," I said succinctly. And a little too nonchalantly, considering country-boy Grayson's deer-in-headlights face.

"No kidding!"

"Yep. Have them all the time. They are either an aftershock from some previous tremor. Or, according to seismologists, it is just the San Andreas Fault relieving some pressure. Or . . ."

I took a bite of my sandwich.

"Or?" Grayson baited.

"Or, it is a precursor to something more, a harbinger of the end times!" I said this with the sinister voice-over doom-and-gloom of a code-cracking, prophetic thriller.

"How do you live like that?" he asked, as he looked up at our booth light to confirm that the uneasy rolling sensation had stopped.

"You get used to it," I said. "Even the prophet Amos ranted and raved for two years under the pressure of an upcoming earthquake. But it is sure a whole lot better than tornadoes and hurricanes!" I posited.

"I'm not so sure about that," answered Pastor Pomeroy, who had been through both. In an effort to settle his nerves, I changed the subject from derogatory nicknames and our state falling into the ocean to . . .

"Grayson—'Grape!' (I smiled at him), you and I are becoming fast friends."

He nodded vigorously, smiling back. He was chewing.

"I am concerned that, typically, associate (and youth) pastors are only in that position because they are just buying time until they get a real 'call' to be a senior pastor. To be honest, I am hesitant to pursue this relationship much deeper for fear of you skipping town on me at the first call to a senior-pastor position."

I regretted speaking so cavalierly about such a serious subject as obedience to a sobering, supernatural call of an all-powerful Sovereign, but our budding relationship was beginning to matter and would eventually need to be weighed against any such itchy feet from God. Grayson graciously played along, genuinely sensitive to my insecurities. "You mean like the Man Upstairs ringing that great triangular bell in the sky and yelling, 'Come and get it!'"

I laughed. "Yeah. Something like that." But my smile quickly dissipated. "And there you go! . . . like all the rest," snapping my fingers for effect.

Now *he* laughed. "No way, Ian! I have known from a very early age that I am cut out to be an Associate Pastor. It's my gift. It's what makes me tick! I am not interested in all of the headaches and sermon prep required for a Senior Pastor. I don't want to be cooped up in an office all day. I like being out with the folks. And I like being the wingman, the support." He paused to see if I was convinced. He sensed some equivocation, so he leaned into the table.

"I'm not going anywhere!" he said emphatically. "I like it here! And I love my job at, what do you people call it? Oh yes, 'O.F.E'! Yes, I came because of Clint Banning, but I am staying because of the people. And that includes you!" I smiled, reassured. But Grayson was not so reassured on an earlier subject. When it came time after lunch for us to leave, as he stood up, even though it was hanging quite still by that time, he steadied the lamp above our booth.

"Fear Factor"

October 1, 2005

"If you utter worthy, not worthless, words, you will be my spokesman."

—Jeremiah 15:19

In typical Grayson Pomeroy fashion, the next time he and I were scheduled to have lunch, he decided to "change it up" by suggesting we meet at the commissary of the Warner Brothers Studio in nearby Burbank. Among his many, widespread connections, he had met a neighbor across the street from the house that he and Caroline had recently purchased (with a little help from their friends at O.F.E., another testament to the deep stakes that the entire family had put in the ground during their great California Land Grab of 2005). Of all things serendipitous, this neighbor, who worked in the Accounting Department at the Studios, had given Pastor Pomeroy a standing invitation to come on over any time and have lunch in one of the great historical, celluloid hubs of Tinsel Town.

This came as no surprise to me. Grayson Pomeroy and his family were well-connected within minutes of arriving on the shores of the West Coast. As a pastor, he did not garner favors from well-to-do parishioners. He didn't have to! The parishioners did all the garnering! As a result of some wonderful, kind gesture or word that came so naturally to Pastor Pomeroy—and that could have just as easily been done in his sleep—the recipient would want to return the favor. The "bead exchange" would oftentimes be linked to the most unique, enticing commodity that the working-class denizens of Monument and beyond could offer someone from the backwoods of back East, namely, Hollywood! So it was not surprising to hear from Grayson about his latest lunch on the backlot of Universal Studios or in the other commissaries at the Walt Disney Studios, Paramount Studios, and 20th Century Fox. He was always posting on one-year-old Facebook: pictures of his walking through Disney's Animation Building, standing by the famous "Mickey Avenue, Dopey Drive" sign, posing with arms outstretched like Charlton Heston's Moses under Paramount's celebrated, arched main entrance, walking down New York Street at 20th Century Fox, or asking Jay Leno for a selfie while holding up his backstage passes to NBC Television Studios for "The Tonight Show" taping. I swear on a stack of movie scripts that the "G" in "MGM" stood for Grayson!

But that's not all! There were the infield box seats given up by a grateful season-ticket holder for a big game at Dodger Stadium. It seemed that every time Grayson Pomeroy sat down in any entertainment venue, it had a box around it—jazz festivals, raceways, theaters, and concert halls. You, yourself could pull not just a few strings, call in not just a few favors, mortgage your house, clear your schedule, and sit your family down in the most coveted seats not available in any store for the most anticipated event in Los Angeles, and there, five rows in front of you, like the Von Trapps, or the Rockefellers, would be the six Pomeroys.

"Fear Factor"

This particular Warner Brothers "connection" with our well-connected Associate Pastor could not stay for lunch, as he was forthwith called back to the desk of his demanding job. This left Grayson and myself to finish lunch and then wander around the Warner Brothers Studio backlot, as if we owned the place. Our conversation rabbit-trailed to all sorts of interesting subjects, and not all church-related. This heightened the element of surprise as we were walking (moseying) by the propped-up exterior façade of a western saloon (after just turning the corner from a mock-up of Pennsylvania Avenue and the White House portico—such is the life in the Dream Factory), when Grayson turned to me and said,

"For someone who has taught nearly every age group at the church for so long, why haven't you ever preached?"

This caught me off-guard, and I nearly fell into a nearby horse trough. The question had been raised before, repeatedly by Milton Derringer during his tenure at Our Father's Evangelical Church, and my excuse was always the same: Because I had such a high regard for the pulpit and held it in even greater esteem than the other "mini-pulpits"—those makeshift music stands of the Sunday-school classroom—I just did not feel qualified to stand in such a gap, whether my tongue had been touched by the burning sensation of coal-cleansing or not. Milton Derringer's response was always a rather frustrated, "Nonsense!" But his approach seemed too assertive, even programmatic, like it was simply the next logical thing to happen, the next obvious, upward ladder rung for Ian Block, calling or no.

The question, as posed by Grayson Pomeroy, was another matter entirely. I started to give my party-line response, but my words became weightless from overuse, and the flimsy sentences fell apart on my lips and scattered into the air like so much chaff, joining the dust devils and tumbleweeds of the deserted, dirt street of the western movie set through which we were now strolling.

From vast experience, Grayson detected what was happening: A classic case of conviction, waiting for just the right moment to latch on, and that moment was now. It was just a question when first asked, purely conversational, but my halting response served notice to Pastor Pomeroy that this area of obstinacy in my soul had been worked on for nearly a decade. Our surroundings could not have been more appropriate. Through Grayson's discerning eyes, there was evidence of a lifelong trail of curlicued shavings on the boardwalk around me, *soul sawdust* as carved by *The Great Whittler,* and I was now ready to be unveiled, like a wooden Indian in front of a cigar store. Pomeroy knew instinctively that it was time. But he allowed for my stammering to continue until my awkward silence made room for the prompting of God.

"Ian, it is time for you to preach at Our Father's Evangelical Church!"

October 3, 2005

I don't remember much of our backlot conversation after that. Under the helm of Grayson Pomeroy, I am sure it was winsome and full of delightful, lazy-river tributaries. But, as much as I attempted to smile and play along, my preoccupations made this difficult. Without any compelling diversions, all I could picture while Grayson was talking was a dreamy possibility of myself standing at the podium of Our Father's Evangelical Church, opening my mouth, and nothing coming out. I even allowed my drifting mind to entertain that classic remedy for public speaking jitters—picturing the audience in their underwear. This only served to exacerbate the problem. Now, an appropriate opening line addressed to looms of fruit was all the more impossible to devise!

Once back at the office that afternoon, my imaginary pulpit debut spanned out into all sorts of nightmarish scenarios: From everyone walking out (the result of some grandiose theological error on my part), to no one showing up in the first place (the result of advance notice about my soporific sermon from a sneak preview of the press-ready church bulletin). Or, worst of all, a worship center filled to standing room only—and *I'm* the one in my underwear! I tried to force my mind to pivot from these musings with the pressing insurance matters 'round about me, but any time there was even a brief moment of silence in the din of doing business, there appeared the Ian Block of my mind, clad only in tighty-whiteys, barking heresy to a crowd that was at once laughing and fleeing, like juvenile delinquents during a fire drill.

After dinner, I told Maria about Grayson's proclamation, hoping to extract some sympathetic camaraderie about the absurdity of it all. Her response gave me an instant cold sweat that continued its pumping of beaded perspiration well into the darkest hours of the oncoming night: "Well, it's about time!"

I was licked. The voice of God had decided to use Grayson Pomeroy and Maria Ponticelli Block as His mouthpiece. It was then that my mind frantically went racing into an imaginary metal filing cabinet in search of a topic. But, to my horror, I found that the drawer pulled out on its track with only a hollow rattle because it was completely empty. The imagined black letters on the label taped to the front of the vacant drawer was an exercise in the obvious: "Never Been Done Before!"

October 6, 2005

On my drive down Chestnut Street toward the office, I thought of that old adage for a novelist, "Write what you know," and wondered if it could be as squarely applied to a preacher as well: "Preach what you know." The second night of cold sweats confirmed my suspicions and ratified the subject matter, as the title for my first sermon came into view: "The Fear Factor."

I did not call Pastor Pomeroy at the church just yet, for fear of committing too soon. Rather, I wanted to do a little homework on the subject and see if I could actually come up with not only a headline but an outline as well. God met me at every chapter, at every verse, at every commentary, at every concordance. It wasn't long before I had too much material! In a bold Holy Spirit moment that I could only call *spiritual suicide*, I took a terrifying leap of faith and decided that "The Fear Factor" needed to be a two-part sermon, if for no other reason than my own personal fears could not be contained in just one forty-minute episode! I phoned Grayson Pomeroy and agreed to preach at the church at his request, but that my subject matter now required two weeks. I was hoping that this doubled-down calendar monopoly would make fitting me into his ongoing task of "preacher-cobbling" a virtual impossibility. But my attempt at sabotage was thwarted by two words: "No problem!"

I was still licked. So, I hit the books. After first dropping the crutches of synopsis and cartoon, I decided to prepare like I would any other Sunday-school lesson. Once completed, I would then convert the lesson into what I thought would be acceptable sermon fodder. My preparations were actually humming right along, with a microscopic vote of confidence, when one evening, in our office-bedroom, the phone rang. It was Grayson.

"O.K., Ian, you're all set. We have you scheduled for two consecutive Sundays, beginning September 11th."

What? I thought. I felt the beaded perspiration of cold sweat making a victorious comeback. I was going to preach on the fourth anniversary of the worst terrorist attack in our country's history!

Talk about adding fuel to the fire. But Pastor Pomeroy sensed my trepidation and responded, "I can't think of a more appropriate subject matter, Ian. It is no coincidence that you came up with this idea! And you are just the right person to encourage the congregation at—what do you call it, again? O.F.E.!"

The next two weeks were filled with both crusader and coward ups and downs, along with a gargantuan amount of anticipation. Which just as accurately described the growing size of the butterflies and moths that, thanks to the nourishing chrysalis in the cocoon of my stomach lining, were now as gigantic as any on the silver screen of a Japanese monster movie, no longer terrorizing Tokyo, but my central nervous system!

I informed my old roommate from the Antioch Christian Academy, Malcolm Davis, of this absurd twist in my life's great adventure. He reassuringly said that he and his wife, Daniella, would make the trip from their home in Los Angeles to be there. They would not miss it for the world! I would have missed it for a whole lot less, but I thought it best not to rain on the parade of Malcolm's sincere encouragement, especially his oft-repeated one-liner, "Never fill the unknown with a negative!" At present, I was siphoning pessimism out of the void with mustered determination, like a stranded sailor desperately bailing out a rapidly sinking dinghy!

RAISED!

October 11, 2005

On the morning of September 11, 2005, I arrived at the church after a precarious drive, due to difficulty breathing, even though the distance from our house to God's was quite short. Getting out of my car, I tried to avoid social contact with any well-wishing O.F.E. members in order to capture some solitude and to think and pray while I walked. But it seemed that the whole congregation at Valentino and Ridgeway Avenues were right there with me. We were all in this together, shoulder-to-shoulder, as they cheered for their homegrown boy during his very first sermon. It seemed that, before I knew it, I was standing behind the pulpit at Our Father's Evangelical Church, looking out at a very crowded congregation, both of us fully clothed! As predicted by so many who had been down this road before, as soon as I said, "Good morning! Please open your Bibles to . . ." the Japanese monster movie was over.

It also seemed that, before I knew it, I was speaking my closing line,

"So let's stop quibbling! Say 'Yes' to God no matter what He may be asking. Let's leave our burning bushes behind and let's go part some Red Seas!" (Looking back over the past years, this was probably more of a "Do as I say, not as I do" application. By comparison to so many in the congregation that morning, I was what Charles Spurgeon would call a "featherbed warrior," who hadn't even parted the sea in his bathtub!)

But, before I knew it, it was finished, and I was stepping down off the platform, going back to my seat in the front row next to a beaming Maria, Sharayah, and Samantha. I had done it! Though Part Two still loomed a week away, the potential of a disastrous delivery had lost much of its bite.

"Fear Factor"

"Never fill the unknown with a negative!"

It appears that my first sermon had gone well and, miraculously, was well-received.

I went home that afternoon with a new thought: For all of the numerous "Fear nots" in the Bible, I was, at least for the moment, more "not" than "fear"!

> *"But if I say, 'I will not mention his word*
> *or speak anymore in his name,'*
> *his word is in my heart like a fire,*
> *a fire shut up in my bones.*
> *I am weary of holding it in;*
> *indeed, I cannot."*

—Jeremiah 20:9

"Silent Night"

November 4, 2005

Today, I finished taking down my award-winning, family-friendly Halloween decorations on Chestnut Street. After yet another banner year attracting hundreds of cute little trick-or-treaters to our porch, I realized with my traditional, annual shudder that Christmas was coming . . . fast!

We had not a stitch of communication with my parents in an effort to patch up the outspread rip in our relationship. No one was in the mood to darn rent stockings—Christmas or otherwise. But, what was at first an understandable "going into our corners" for a cooling-off period now had an aura of foreboding. With Christmas came complications. Hence, for the sake of my family (who did not see the yule logjam coming since it had just turned November), I summoned up the strength to call my father in Ventura just to see if he would answer the phone. After that, who knew? While the phone was ringing and ringing and my anticipation growing and growing, I thought back to a much-different epoch in time-space history, when I told my kibitzing mother as a joke that I was too shy to call the girl I wanted to take to the senior prom. Not wanting me to miss out on an important high-school memory, she took the bait and actually called her on my behalf. Since I had already asked the girl (who was in on the prank), she informed my mother that she already had a date for the prom. Dejected, and not being able to resist, my meddlesome mother asked who her date was. "Your son!" the girl answered with a big smile!

I wished someone were making this call for me right now—even my own mother!

"Hello," my father miraculously answered, albeit guardedly, Caller I.D. having tipped him off.

"Hey, Dad!" I feigned energy and excitement at hearing his voice.

"Yes."

Captain Kirk called for "Shields up!" Or was it Nehemiah yelling, "Walls up!"? (In the cupbearer's case, the answer "How high?" came from Shallum, who, ironically, fortified his section with the help of his daughters.)

"We need to talk." I got right to it, since I could sense that my glad-handing was not even cracking a smile on the other end of the line. With that, I delicately convinced my father to drop by the Block Insurance office the next time he and my mother were in town, so that we could, I said safely, "catch up." He seemed to become agreeable to the idea. Truth be told, after the indignity he had experienced at Sharayah's graduation party, I think he wanted his day in court. As a matter of fact, he and my mom were going to be in town in a few days to see Owen, Julie and Owen, Jr. (surprise, surprise), and he thought it a possibility that he could make it. I thanked him as I hung up the phone. I got a chill as I sat there, staring down at the cradled receiver. What had I done?

"You better watch out. You better not cry."

November 9, 2005

I have prayed hard over the ensuing days.

Specifically, "praying the Psalms." Moreover, I have spent ample time in that great scriptural M.R.I., Psalm 139: 23-24. My heart has been searched, my anxious thoughts known. But even so, I am tempted to offend my eyes by wandering to the *preceding* verses showcasing David's *other* heart and thoughts. The psalmist throws caution to the wind—even with God able to track him down quite easily anywhere in the world and beyond—just to share with him a precious thought or two. In an effort to show tender togetherness with God, David implores Him to slay the wicked, those "bloodthirsty" ones the "sweet psalmist of Israel" considers his archenemies and for whom he has nothing but hatred and abhorrence. I can only imagine that, when David volunteers for his spiritual M.R.I., the report comes up with a suspicious spot or two.

To that end, I have prayed hard over the ensuing days.

JOURNAL "ISM": The prayers of the desperate seldom involve making contact with all three members of the Trinity—soliciting the combined forces of an approachable Father, Son, and Holy Spirit. The reason they are so rarely called upon in triplicate these days is due to a "gap theory" more gaping than the billion-year Band-Aid often affixed between Genesis 1:1 and 1:2. We mentally leave the Trinity high and dry after the Spirit returns from water-brooding, as they all confess to having had a hand in imprinting their image upon a human with the little word "Us." The Trio's image doesn't show up again for thousands of years, when the Father thunders "Pleased!"

"Silent Night"

while His Son gets dunked in the Jordan River, which is all dovetailed by the Spirit cooing upon Messianic shoulders. But in the 1,400-page biblical middle, it seems we can only picture a cantankerous Father drowning humanity, plaguing Egypt, generating genocide, raising and deposing kings, permitting slaughter, allowing for murder, and giving an "R" rating to behavior rife with sexual escapades, all the while speaking through the mouthpiece of maniacal prophets. This, with only an occasional "theophany" by a suspected Son to soften the blows with good news, a rescue or two, and birth announcements for mothers as good as dead. It is hard for our politically correct minds to be wrapped around a Trinity getting all down-and-dirty with the mayhem and misdeeds of the Old Testament. But there they are! By the time the Son of God is staring down Pontius Pilate, who is asking, "What is truth?" while he is looking right into the face of it, what we really see is a political puppet cowering before a seasoned veteran who is flanked by His two highly decorated partners, all holding red-letter pens in the creation-redemption story. Whether coming to push, shove, nudge, or needle, you want *all Three* in your camp!

November 10, 2005

When my father walked into my office, I noticed immediately that he had aged, with the liver spots to prove it. His lean, father-on-"Dennis-the-Menace" look was still intact but now slightly bent, as the graying "Henry Mitchell" standing in front of me now looked like he was returning to a T.V.-showcast reunion after forty years of re-runs. He sat down without saying a word.

"So, how have you been?" I started. He waved his prognosis aside, looking absently around my office without surrendering to eye contact.

"Your mother couldn't come. She is babysitting Owen, Jr." I read between this line a passive-aggressive newsflash from my mother. She had stayed behind at Owen and Julie's to babysit Owen, Jr., who was now far too grown-up for it. The excuse was feeble, but the point made was not, nor was it well-taken. Once again, she had not only chosen my brother's family over my own but had brushed off an opportunity for us to see each other after five long months, even if just to renew an old acquaintance. Instead, she sent my father as her emissary.

"O.K. Well, I'm sorry she decided not to come." After all these months, I could not avoid a tone in my voice that spoke more condescending irritation than unassuming disappointment. Without knowing it, I had turned potential reconciliation into a not-so-diplomatic negotiation. My father suddenly leaned forward, looked me straight in the eye (crow's feet and all), pointed his finger at me, and laid out the terms of our agreement.

"You need to honor me!" he pronounced petulantly.

I sat back, astonished at this ambush coming out of a very far-left field of the Bible. But, from my own stored-up hostility, I quickly recovered and, too, loaded my dueling pistol with a Bible bullet of my own.

"And you need to stop exasperating me!"

There. Two shots fired from both Testaments. Although not simultaneous, they hit their marks and made each of us feel like we had got one in. We both blew away the puerile steam now trailing upward from our smoking guns. And, with that, my fulminating father launched into a veritable diatribe—word pictures and all—a negative retrospective of their second son, from childhood to the present. But from an opprobrious angle I had never heard before. It was a whole new plot twist, whose main character was a whole-new-incorrigible and difficult-to-raise, me! The pauses were anything but pregnant. But when I sensed breath intake, simply for refueling, I got my edgewise word in.

"You don't say any encouraging word about me!"

"No. That's not my job!" My father apparently no longer felt at home on that range.

> *"The parents have eaten sour grapes,*
> *and the children's teeth are set on edge."*

What had happened? Since the deafening silence post-Sharayah's commencement soirée, Maria and I had been asking that question of ourselves nearly every day. After all, no misunderstanding, no matter how metastasized, materializes in a vacuum. Perhaps this sudden turning stemmed from some father-son childhood-upbringing issues between Colby and Seth Block that the grave had now rendered unresolved (I was certainly one of the two guilty parties in my father's observance of his own father's favoritism toward me).

Or perhaps a series of competitive Colby-Seth father-son deacon issues, fomenting and cropping up later in life, had now rendered my father as "never good enough." I knew that, when my father and I were on better terms, on the rare occasion of a vulnerable moment, he would actually confess to me that his father had never told him that he loved him. This then gives self-esteem no foothold whatsoever and makes any vibrations in the delicate father-son-becoming-a-man balance all the more devastating for both. Did Colby Block know any different? Might he just be imitating his own father, Adam? Who, in turn, was imitating his own father, Pete? And where is the Father God in all of this? (I wonder whether Moses was thinking of either Amran or Pharaoh when he broke out in song while stepping over dead bodies and broken chariot wheels, shortly after his feet were dry from Red Seawater, proclaiming that God was not only his, but his dad's, as well!) Or maybe this could all be merely the aging effects of being beat up by the castrating school of life: Owen's divorce, health issues, not being as active in ministry any longer—which was the only life he knew—and a whole host of other "life-beaters."

Or, maybe this sticky wicket was all just the headliner of those seven sins that the Lord hates so much that He wanted it: Dead or Alive! *Pride*. Either offensive or defensive, it can slip in and fill any vacuum of misunderstanding.

A few months earlier, just prior to the leaves on the maple trees planted all over our town showing their true colors, I was "Pole-Vaulting Through Proverbs" in the Sojourners class at Our Father's Evangelical Church. This very subject of pride cameth literally before the Fall. I actually procured a pole used precisely for this type of track-and-field event. I could barely fit it diagonally into the Sunday-school room. But once I was able to hold it high in the air, I recited the following:

> *"Jumpin' Judah! Ever since she was a little girl, the Queen Mother was the highest Asherah pole-vaulter in the Middle East! Is it any wonder that, way back when, King Rehoboam loved his bouncing bride more than all of his other eighteen wives and sixty girlfriends? Even as a senior citizen, Grandma Maacah was still winning gold medals for raising the bar and soaring with the gods. It was not until her royal grandson played a trick on her by chopping up her pole with*

"Silent Night"

an ax and hiding the evidence by burning up the pieces right before the big Kidron Valley Track Meet, that her leaping legacy came to a screeching halt. It was said that little Asa was green with 'grandma envy.' After all, he had very bad feet and couldn't jump over any high places."

"Turn to 2nd Chronicles, Chapters 15 and 16."

Years later, the eyes of the Lord were flashing to and fro throughout the Earth—like a light on top of an ambulance—in order to defibrillate any committed heart that may need strengthening. But first, they bored a hole into the prideful, self-reliant, grown-up King Asa's plans, as he mortgaged his house in Judah and stole from the church treasury in order to buy off the pagan king of Aram so that he could stick it to his estranged "older sister," Israel.

The prophet Hanani had to remind Asa that God always wins a staring contest.

Which was exactly what my father and I were left with—a staring contest. After all was said and done, there was nothing more to say or do. Wasting life to prove a point. He left after more than an hour's attempt at our laying down our independence, our pride, and beginning to understand one another. Is it any wonder the last sentence that inaugurates the four hundred years of painful silence between Old and New Testaments grapples with father-son issues?

Lord, even when the lines form on my body and spirit, baked in hard and intractable in life's kiln, please allow me to be easy to honor for my children. When I am finally called home to you, may my children need to recover from only my absence, and not my legacy.

I called Maria and gave her my most accurate rundown of our enervating conversation. She thought this little kerfuffle an answer to her many prayers as it was, in her estimation, an historic first step at communication for family members who have been severely handicapped, and who had thus operated at various stages of dysfunction in this arena for multiple generations. While I appreciated her spiritually considered, positive outlook, I was hoping for more. To that end, I sulked a bit.

"Better not pout, I'm telling you why . . ."

December 26, 2005

With decades of Christmas Eve tradition behind us, Maria had bought gifts for my parents, brother, new sister-in-law, and nephew, in anticipation of our annual celebration, which had started many years ago, when my parents lived in Monument, and had continued when they had moved to their retirement condo in Ventura.

This was always an evening every one of us enjoyed—especially Sharayah and Samantha. The food-consuming and present-opening was a masterpiece of supreme creativity and heartfelt generosity on behalf of my mother. She even went so far as to type up clues on an old Remington typewriter, roll them up into little scrolls, and stuff them into helium balloons. She would then make her children and grandchildren leap into the air to try to grip one of the wriggling strings dangling from the ceiling, like so many jellyfish tentacles, pull it down, and pop the attached balloon in order to discover, from the exploded latex, the paper trail to where the next gift was hidden. This was much easier to devise in the house on Vista Street, but my mother still made it work wonderfully in the smaller condo confines.

But, as the days crept ominously closer to Christmas Eve, the uninvited silence spelled the same fate for us. We were uninvited. We tried to manufacture a new Christmas Eve tradition on the spot with "Papa" and "Ya Ya" Ponticelli at the Block home in Monument, all the while knowing that the food was flowing, balloons were popping, and the wrapping paper flying at the Block home in Ventura, just an hour's drive to the north. But I suspected that both very distant households felt a pall as dark as the ninth Egyptian plague, as we each tried our hardest to portray stiff upper lips in the light of the birth—of all people—of the Prince of Peace!

February 23, 2006

Well, Christmas morning was better because, favorably, it, too, was attached to a long-standing tradition—just the four of us.

It was a wounded but bonded foursome of Maria, Sharayah, Samantha, and me who exchanged gifts and determined to build fond memories that particular Christmas. But to no avail. It was a relief to take down my award-winning Christmas decorations and move right into Presidential birthdays.

Forlornly, Maria took the overextended family gifts back to the stores whence she had first purchased them, testament to a peace offering not being accepted. But she was determined to "grow through this and come out the other side," as she stated. I had to hand it to her. In spite of this complicated Christmas, her faith, hope, and love were unassailable. She gave it all back to God, to Whom I also had to hand it to these days, because now . . . the government wasn't the only thing on His shoulders.

"Comeback Kid"

March 6, 2006

The absence of the "innkeeper and his wife" from our extended family Christmas play did not come without its price. As a matter of fact, a healthy down payment had already been laid down at Samantha's Timothy Award ceremony and Sharayah's graduation parties, respectively. Being four years older, however, it seemed that Sharayah bore a significant brunt of the abandonment issues, standing as it were, as a point person in front of a phalanx of denouncement—the number-one bowling pin—since her relational investment with my parents had had 1,460 more days in which to germinate and take root. In a word, Samantha went underground. Sharayah erupted.

Maria and I had found ourselves in that parental no-man's-land: those few years after high school when your children no longer rise up and call you blessed, but go out to find themselves and come back with some very interesting souvenirs! We knew that their grandparents' "forsaking the gathering" had been a huge body blow to both Sharayah and Samantha, which resulted in them both having to live in the tension of a new reality that produced, in spite of their individual coping mechanisms or because of them, a bite to their behavior. And, falling over the precipice of the safety and familiarity of high school, Sharayah bit off more than she could chew. She wanted to "get out of the house," as she said, with no uncertain finality and shrillness, as it now represented both directly and indirectly much pain for her. She was college bound. But she was also bound by the non-negotiable notion that her parents would not pay for any sort of higher education unless it answered to a Higher Power, namely, a Christian school.

As Sharayah wanted to blaze her own trail, my alma mater of the Antioch Christian Academy—no matter how convincingly I could sing its praises—was out of the question for the sole reason that it included a fatherly residue that would, once again, plunge her into a "churchy fish bowl," as she put it, stunting her from growing into her own individual self. With that argument in tow, she found a Christian university in the Orange County area that, while not our first choice, did seem to provide a respectable liberal-arts education with an acceptable undercurrent of required biblical education. In our estimation, the price for God-learnin' in this case was enormous, even absurd. But, Maria and I cooperatively pulled out the inside linings of all clothing articles blessed with pockets, smashed porcine financial institutions to fiduciary smithereens, and hand-swept the underbelly of couch cushions like five-fingered metal detectors, in search for that lost coin—a widow's mite—that could be included in the collection plate going toward the seemingly insurmountable scaling of Mt. Tuition—and we had just five short months in which to do it!

October 15, 2006

Maria basement-bargained with Sharayah for dorm-room supplies, with nothing flying into the shopping cart that had not survived the mother-daughter dispute over "cute" versus "cool."

"Comeback Kid"

Although not far from her home in Monument, it was still an emotional, page-turning moment saying "Goodbye" to my far-too-grown-up-far-too-soon little girl on a balmy evening in Orange County in her newly decorated dorm room, after meeting her chatty roommate from Arizona.

Our Honda van was now quite empty and quiet as Maria and I drove home, secluded in our own thoughts, of which I would still give a penny for as part of the collection to bail us out of that debtor's prison called "Student Loan."

An emancipated Samantha thoroughly enjoyed the run of the house, no longer living in the shadow *of*, nor sharing the bathroom *with*, her older sister. We savored every occasion, as she entered and excelled as a freshman at Monument High School, all the while knowing with equal satisfaction that Sharayah was right where she belonged, at college. It seemed that we could not keep up with Samantha's social life. Never letting an irritating thing like homework get in her way, she jumped into every high-school activity imaginable. Our triangular conversations around the dinner table left Maria and me breathless—joyful jaunts of note passing, cute guys, who liked who, and the next upcoming game or event.

In the topsy-turvy world of daughter-raising, now Samantha erupted, and Sharayah went underground.

Because it was so uncharacteristic, Sharayah's distancing was the first clue (once again, her singular, communicating plumb line to the family was not handwritten letters, but loving and clumsy emails from "Papa" Ponticelli). Nor was her countenance in play, as her lack of proximity made facial indicators too intermittent to be of any value. She came home only for the first couple of weekends, when I could gently press her on her grades and gauge the potency of her college-level biblical education—a line of questioning to which I felt more than justified, as I held the purse strings to this whole operation. But soon, her weekend homecomings started to dwindle under the excuse that she was "doing stuff with her friends" (but with friends we oddly never met). Only after a week or two did we realize that her weekend occupations were not with her friends, but her "friend." And it was a he.

Mitchell was his name. I never caught his last name. Although I could think of a few myself (much to the chagrin of my always-respectful, conscientious wife). I was told that he was "hot," from San Diego, and had withdrawn from the college Sharayah was attending after only the first couple of weeks (in order to enroll in a reputable business school closer to home with a program that supposedly included an apprenticeship in a Fortune 500 company), and went back home with a priceless prize—the heart of my disillusioned, angry, and vulnerable daughter.

November 9, 2006

I came home from the office today, and Maria sat me down on the living-room couch as if I was to be scolded for something. She was white-faced with knowledge. With the double barrel of spiritual discernment coupled with a mother's cunning, Maria had first pieced together the whole weekend-excursion thing, and had squeezed a confession out of Sharayah over the phone. "Excursions" was putting it mildly. She was shacking up with Mitchell!

"Really?" I asked of Maria, shell-shocked!

"Not again!" I ranted.

One more weary lap around the track of Psalm 46:

"God is within her, she will not fall!"

—referring to our child-rearing escapades, compliments of Sharayah's rebellious teenage years some time back. But the stakes were much higher this time!

Jesus closed the generation gap at Camp Pharisee when he held a flashlight up to his face and told a spooky story around the campfire about those seven demonic squatters who get the word from their comrade—the first evicted tenant—that his former rental property is now spic-and-span, all soul-swept and ready for occupancy! In no time, all eight had forfeited the cleaning deposit and trashed the place. The landlord is helpless in obtaining a court order or suing for back rent.

For Pete's sake, Satan may prowl around like a roaring lion, but first he dressed up like a big, red dragon, stalking the maternity ward at St. John's Hospital on 12th Street in the town of Revelation, walking back and forth in front of the glass partition, swinging his great tail from side to side, ready to devour the infant just as soon as he heard the words, "It's a boy!"

Or in my case, "It's a girl!"

November 21, 2006

I grabbed Grayson Pomeroy for an emergency lunch just before the Thanksgiving holidays. The Rush More Coffee House was bedecked in gimcrack fall leaves, ears of corn, gourds, pumpkins, little wax statues of musket-toting Governor William Bradford, and all sorts of pilgrims and pilgrettes. But they were not to be outdone by a bow-and-arrow-shouldering Squanto, accompanied by all sorts of Indians and papoose-laden squaws. Running from them all were a whole army of papier-mâché turkeys adorning every table. Of course, each waiter and waitress endeavored to hard-sell ("Let's talk turkey!") the highly acclaimed "turkey dinner with all the trimmings" on the menu. They were sorely disappointed by Grayson's Caesar salad and my club sandwich, hardly appropriate for even a casual picnic on Plymouth Rock!

Since my first sermon debut, I had been asked occasionally by Pastor Pomeroy to preach at O.F.E. (I was now part of a preaching rotation team that included not only Pastor Pomeroy but also our old missions pastor and Santa Claus thief, Forrest Ripley, fellow-musketeer Patrick Hamilton, and other capable teachers at the church—taking the edge off what seemed to be the longest interim period in our church's history). While each time the external presentation seemed to get easier, I was having an increasingly difficult time in justifying my internal qualifications, or lack thereof. What with my father thinking I had "dishonored" him (which Grayson put to rest in one counseling session), and now my daughter "playing house."

"There is a cost to her freedom," he had said after I unpacked our situation and brought him up to speed on all things Sharayah.

"What?" I said.

"There is a cost to her freedom, Ian. If she wants to act like an adult, then she now has adult responsibilities. And that includes money management." He said this with a look of intensity I had not seen before—as if he were rehearsing for one day with his own four kids.

"I feel like Maria and I are paying for her . . . well, you know! It is hard to reconcile that as good stewardship!"

"Because you shouldn't have to. Look, Sharayah is a great kid. She's smart. I have no doubt she will get through this quickly. Don't put yourself in a position of having to choose between stewardship and fatherhood. Don't make her pay for this that way. That will only hurt your relationship, perhaps even permanently.

Just calmly send her 'the bill.'" There was a wry smile to this—not against Sharayah, but against the demonic squatters! Over lunch, Grayson had poured into me all the knowledge he possessed on the subject at hand, and he then hammered home his point by sliding our bill over to my side of the table, with an even broader smile, "There's a cost to your wisdom!"

There was. At least for Maria and me. We discussed it that very evening and decided that, since we were, in fact, hemorrhaging from bankrolling Sharayah's college "experience," we had a say. We would cut off the monetary oxygen supply of her weekly hooking up with Mitchell.

December 30, 2006

We told her as much when she came home for Thanksgiving, which was probably not a good idea. It threw the household into such an awkward state of strain and irritation that, sadly, we were all glad when the long weekend was finally over. I was tormented throughout, furtively casting glances across the table (ironically with no appetite) of our bountiful feast at my quiet, despondent Sharayah, who had disengaged in an effort at self-protection. I wanted throughout the day to just walk over and hug her tightly, protectively, thankfully! But a league of historical inmates from the Block family of time immemorial were at once whispering and screaming into my wounded ears their own stigmata of disfiguring passive-aggression and other tricky, hobbling coping mechanisms that had served them so badly over epochs of family dysfunction, from which they knew no better. I emerged from the internal clamor and discord lamely fearing that any affectionate display toward Sharayah would be interpreted as condoning her behavior, when, in actuality, it would have spoken volumes to the contrary. Forgiveness is the mightiest sword, they say. But, instead, my lack of eye contact, accompanied by deft avoidance, served only to stack up for Sharayah a mound of evidence proving that I was, in fact, joining the ranks of my parents (and beyond) in pronouncing her as irredeemable and expendable. That, if pushed to a limit unknown to her, Maria and I would one day walk away from our firstborn. I never felt anything so opposite in all my life, but by my not wanting to risk saying anything judgmental and impetuous—and making matters worse—I was giving an alternate impression that was just what Sharayah had feared all along. In so doing, I had allowed one of our favorite family holidays to be held hostage for us all.

Pilgrims and Indians were not getting along this year.

To say nothing of the smelly shepherds with angel burn and wise men looking for their bright morning star a month later! But stiff upper lips were had by all as we ignored the cattle that were lowing and exchanged our own, devalued brand of gold, frankincense, and myrrh.

February 15, 2007

Sharayah was not willing to abide by our stipulations for continuing to finance her extra-curricular "education," but neither could she afford the cost to her freedom.

By the early part of her second semester, she had dropped out of school and returned home. My fatherly instincts breathed a sigh of relief, as Maria gradually confirmed to me that her live-in partner was now out of the picture.

I never did meet Mitchell. But if I ever did, I hoped it would be in a back alley!

"Comeback Kid"

JOURNAL "ISM": Every time I pictured a most satisfying scene of the head of Mitchell served on a platter in the righteous indignation of my fertile imagination, it would always end up fading into the shadows with that darn sunset going down on my anger! "Never do anything in anger," Maria would warn. But even though the Apostle Paul had a thing about getting under the sheets while being hot under the collar, King David's fourth try as a balladeering psalmist advises his silent audience to chill out for a while and see how things turn out in the morning. Both might prove to be wise counsel, provided there is no barking dog in the mix.

His name was Fluffy. He belonged to a sweet little ol' German lady named Gerta, who lived next door to us on Chestnut Street. Gerta had lost her husband, Larry, a few years earlier to a heart attack, and was now living alone in a rather large house which they had built together and in which they had lived comfortably for the past forty years, raising their three children. One of their daughters lived nearby and came over frequently to care for her mother in spite of her steely, Germanic resolve and supreme self-sufficiency. Her daughter thought that Gerta needed a companion and pressed the idea of getting a dog for months. Finally, Gerta caved, and, on a day I never saw coming, Fluffy arrived. He was small, white, and, eponymously fluffy! He was also blessed with an obnoxious, spoiled-brat-of-a-bark, if it could be called that. It was more like a yap that never grew up.

Freed from the moral confines of her regimented husband, Gerta also loved to gamble. Not recklessly—or so she said with her thick German accent—but strictly for recreational purposes. So, she was off on numerous weekends, taking a designated senior-citizen bus that left the depot outside of Union Station in Los Angeles bound for the MGM Grand, Caesar's Palace, or

Bally's in Las Vegas. She had been going on these excursions for a few years now, and it was part of the Chestnut Street routine to have her house vacated and subjected to our highly efficient neighborhood-watch network. It was frankly hard to tell the difference between her occupation and absence. While quite friendly and loyal, she was a very quiet lady who kept to herself most of the time, puttering in and out of her family home. But now things were different. When the bus pulled away from the City of Angels terminal, filled to capacity with matronly widows, who bounced along toward the City of Sin, there was left behind one Fluffy!

Alone and unsupervised, Fluffy occupied his time by testing the resolve of every neighbor within earshot with his yap—a perfectly torturous combination of screeching brakes on a diesel truck and fingernails on a chalkboard, with maybe the "bugling" of an effeminate bull elk thrown in for good measure. Since Gerta's house was a one-story, and ours two, our bedroom window looked right down on her backyard pool—complete with covered porches, a barbecue, firepit, chaise lounges, umbrellas, rafts, beach balls, and gamboling Fluffy, who would stop to stare up at us with call-of-the-wild defiance and houndtrack to prove it. Since his master was usually up all night playing slots, he thought that he, too, should adopt the same nocturnal working hours.

On one unseasonally warm night last Spring, when Gerta had roared away in a trail of bus exhaust for one of her last excursions before the high desert started to fry for the summer, we had all of our upstairs windows open by necessity. This gave our ears a ringside seat for the canine cantata that would bark unsupervised—from dusk till dawn—from the backyard deck of the pool of the unoccupied home. I tried to muffle the noise by turning my head to one side on my pillow so that only my partly deaf ear (a loud indicator that I was rapidly approaching 50) was exposed to Fluffy's sinister serenade. Oh, to be Malchus right about then!

Since I could not sleep, I tried to keep sanity by mentally escaping the audio assault in any way that I could. I recalled a synopsis that I had performed for the Cleaver class some months back. I had come into the room wearing a Mickey Mouse hat that I had purchased from a recent trip to Disneyland. I had had it specifically embroidered in the traditional gold cursive with the name "Malchus" on the front (much to the quizzical eye of the Disney cast member working the stitching machine), and, before arriving at Our Father's Evangelical Church that Sunday morning, I pulled off the right plastic ear!

"Malchus could hear a pin drop! Or, rams in a thicket at five-hundred yards. He was the greatest asset of his boss, the high priest, because he could hear the sneaking footfall of anyone—be it friend or foe—from any direction! Malchus himself learned to greatly appreciate this valuable gift of his. He never lacked for food, and he could not have an enemy. But one morning he came into work all bleary-eyed—apparently from being up all night—with the collar of his tunic askew and caked in dried blood. When the high priest asked Malchus what had happened, he incoherently murmured something about an olive garden and a sword-swinging big fisherman who had obviously skipped fencing class, recalling the night while cupping his hand protectively over his repositioned right ear. The high priest was even more puzzled when Malchus came to work the next day wearing a T-shirt that said,

RAISED!

'He who has ear to hear, let him hear!'"

"Turn to John, Chapter 18."

Even one of Malchus' relatives was all ears when they heard the story. With Mafia-like malice, this loyal member of *mi familia*

blasted the Apostle Peter a few hours later with a third and final courtyard accusation that sent the cock crowing for dear life.

After a full night's sleeplessness, the rhythmic yap of Fluffy became a ticking bomb, and I snapped around dawn. I sat up in my bed with a glazed, bug-eyed look on my face, like Dracula rising from his coffin. I pivoted and slid my feet to the cold floor. Maria, also understandably awake, sensed the commotion and asked me what I was doing. Like all serious vampires, I said nothing. I got up and walked robotically out of our bedroom (with no reflection as I glided by the oval mirror), down the hall, down the stairs, and out the back door. I opened our garage door, walked deep into its recesses, and grabbed the barrel of my weapon of choice still propped up where I had last left it when we first moved to the house. It was my very own genuine, "Red Ryder" BB gun from Jean Shepherd's *A Christmas Story*, and it was loaded. Like a demon-possessed Ralphie, I slowly, methodically lifted the extension ladder from its support brackets, walked out of the garage with it under one arm and my "Red Ryder" BB gun under the other, walked with plodded, method-to-my-madness steps into our backyard, adjusted the extension ladder for the desired height, and leaned it up against the wall partitioning our property from Gerta's. Dressed in just the shorts I had worn to bed and unconcerned about the chilly, early morning air, I climbed up the ladder, which gave me full access to the roof of Gerta's covered porch and a perfect vantage point from which to see Fluffy, just sitting there, smugly yapping like some defiant, rabid New Yeller, not the least bit tired from the entire night's recital.

I stood there, in full view of the neighbors as the rising sun caught the ridiculous-looking figure of my scrawny, scantily clad body, standing there on top of the roof, pointing my gun at my target hellhound twenty yards across the pool, a target that actually looked from a distance like the jerking head of a dust mop.

I leveled the BB gun so that Fluffy was directly in my line of fire—caught in the crosshairs of the dreaded "Red Ryder"—steadied the barrel, and fired. The report interrupted the still morning hours and echoed up Chestnut Street, rousting sleeping bird flocks from trees and bouncing off the canyon walls, as it made its way back to check on the fate of its quarry. Fluffy had been hit squarely in his hindquarters. He yelped like a dog who had just had his limbs severed and ran into his outdoor crate. He did not so much as peek his head out to see Clint Eastwood standing in his underwear on top of the covered porch, blowing on the barrel of his trusty BB gun, slowly turning around to the soundtrack of *The Good, the Bad, and the Ugly,* and vanishing from sight like a *High Plains Drifter* as he descended the ladder. Once back on our property, and just as mechanically, I lowered the ladder back to its pre-extended size, scooped it under my arm, walked back to the garage, hung the ladder back in place, and propped "Red Ryder" into its gun rack. I closed the garage door, shuffled back into the house like some pound-of-flesh satisfied zombie from *Night of the Living Dead*, walked upstairs, down the hall, and into our bedroom, slipping quietly back into bed. Just as soon as I lay down with my glazed eyes still wide-open, staring at the ceiling, Maria bolted up. "What have you done?" She had heard the shot. Probably so did all of Monument.

"It's quiet, isn't it?" I justified, in a creepy monotone.

"Where's Fluffy?" Maria asked, slightly panicked at the sudden quiet.

And then, in sync with the sun, it dawned on me. What had I done? Isn't shooting someone's pet a felony or something? I suddenly woke up from my hypnotic stupor of vengeance, put on my clothes and rushed over to the outside gate of Gerta's backyard. Opening the gate, I ran over to Fluffy's crate to see if he was still alive. I felt not a bit of compassion but was rather inspecting the pooch to save my own skin. He was shaking, terrified to see the shooter up close and personal. But he was still sound, with maybe some soreness in his hindquarters. But he never barked again. My satisfaction was instantly dissipated when I realized that it was a Sunday morning, and I was teaching Sunday school in an hour for the Harvesters class on, of all things . . . anger.

When I sleepwalked into the classroom that morning, I did not perform a synopsis.

I was one.

March 22, 2007

Now that Sharayah was back home, Maria wasted no time in coming alongside and nurturing her back to spiritual health. My wife had to enroll in the higher education offered at the school of forgiveness as well. Then one night in bed, when, once again our routine, end-of-the-day "pillow talk" was interrupted by yet another "conflict conference" about what to do next in the proper, delicate balance of providing guidance and direction for our oldest daughter, Maria had an epiphany of sorts. She and I were not the only students at Forgiveness U. Both Sharayah and Samantha were seated right next to us in the very same classroom, each having to deal with the other's culpability in the great realization that forgiveness (like its sinister twin "un"), is a community event of giving and receiving with systemic effects throughout the entire organism called "family." We would choose that mightiest of swords to become a scalpel with which to lance the wounds and begin the process of genuine healing for all four of us: Maria and I forgiving each other for oftentimes diametrically opposed, first-time parenting techniques (particularly in times of a first-rodeo crisis). Sharayah forgiving us for some of those very same first-time, blundering techniques. Samantha forgiving her older sister for hijacking the family dynamic in such a distracting way during her high-school years. And, most important of all, each one of us receiving the cross-shaped forgiveness from the Father that lifts us out of all levels of generational dysfunction as "bought and paid for" members of His family.

But none of this happened overnight.

Sharayah was still acting out in ways that indicated she was not yet ready to capitulate to any divine wooing. As before, she found local friends from that underhanded, welcoming club known as the "wrong crowd." Only this time they were much older, and their self-destructive behavior was proportionately more sophisticated. It seemed to me that they could not co-exist for any conversation or activity without first being lubricated at alarmingly slippery levels with that inhibition-killing intoxicant known as alcohol. At the request of Maria, and because of Sharayah's deep, if not nostalgic respect for her, Beverly Anderson was asked to give our daughter a call. Even though she no longer attended O.F.E. with us, Sharayah had a special place in Beverly's heart, and she made a phone call to our daughter shortly after Maria's request. As Beverly reported to us later, still loyally keeping a high level of confidentiality with Sharayah, our daughter was cordial but unresponsive. This quarry was difficult to bag. Sharayah was not rebellious this time, which was quantifiable; she was apathetic, which had no shadow, and worse yet, was understandable given her circumstances. I wondered what the great Dr. Banning—the go-to guru for all things Youth Culture—would suggest. Probably whisking Sharayah off to some desert island in Tahiti where "wrong crowd" could not venture to swim. But, alas, we had not the resources and were thus forced to deal with the situation firmly sequestered in the foothills of Monument, California.

While not as exotic, this was right where God wanted us to heal. When asked by close friends, O.F.E. members, and acquaintances how Sharayah was doing, we would succinctly respond that she was "working on her testimony."

Aren't we all?

June 6, 2007

One late Saturday morning, we heard Sharayah yelling from inside her bedroom. She had been driven home by some friend late the night before (in a nose-to-nose horse race with her curfew), at 11:54 p.m., to be exact. But who's counting? Only her worried parents, who maintain, as part of their job description, countless late-night waiting vigils before being able to go to sleep themselves, knowing their children are now safely tucked in bed. My suspicions were that lilting, Bible-based lullabies were not likely ringing in Sharayah's head that night. More like a bawdy chorus line of "Ninety-nine Bottles of Beer on the Wall."

Upon entering her room, we discovered that, under the influence, she had left her purse at the restaurant bar in nearby Pasadena the night before. This included her driver's license, clearly indicating the address to our house, as well as her full set of keys, which provided the final invitation to come on over any time to Chestnut Street, stay for a while, and take anything not nailed down when you left. Since a locksmith could not be engaged until the following Monday, Maria gave Sharayah a passionately pointed lecture.

"You think your sin is your own private business, young lady, but then you realize that, all along it has been waiting to blow up into a community event, *our* community, affecting every one of us!

She had said this with a firmness born out of great frustration. Whether Sharayah caught the portent of her words was unclear. Maria's actions, however, were crystal clear in their intent. She was securing all of the windows in our house and propping chairs in front of all of the doors. Maria reported later that night during our "pillow talk" session that she had actually seen a spark of regret and remorse in Sharayah's face for the possible peril in which she had put our whole family. It was a start.

Sharayah was saved by the skin of her teeth by a Good Samaritan, or Pasadenan, who did not think the found purse a keeper, searched for the owner's cell phone number within, and called. Maria drove weeping-loser Sharayah over to Pasadena for a quick retrieval, where the reward money offered was humbly refused. Sighs of relief accompanied the drive home, but only temporarily. Unbeknownst to our oldest daughter, God had enrolled her in a crash course at Forgiveness U. Literally.

One night a few weeks later, on the stretch of freeway at the bottom of the hill, a car suddenly stopped in front of Sharayah, whose reflexes were dozing from a long day of odd nannying jobs that she had patched together, and she plowed into the car, which caused the car behind her at once to plow into her. We received a phone call while out to dinner and came rushing over. By the time we arrived, Sharayah's car had already been towed from the freeway via the Valentino Avenue off-ramp and into the Union 76 gas station across from the Monument Hospital at the bottom of the hill.

Sharayah was a bucket of more tears when we ran over to make sure she was all right. She was quite shaken, but sound. Her car, on the other hand, not so much. It was an obvious total loss to my trained, insurance-agent eye, with a little help from the inflated white airbag now occupying the driver's seat (like some cruising Pillsbury doughboy, the steering column plunged so far into its billowy stomach that it looked like biblical Eglon, king of Moab, whose folds of fat thoroughly engulfed the judgmental sword of left-handed Ehud), and the widening puddle of radiator and brake fluids that were dripping from the accordion that was once my daughter's car. But at least my little girl was safe and sound.

After a thorough vital organ and soft-tissue examination and x-rays, the urgent-care doctor at the Monument Hospital recommended weeks of bed rest for the back pain with a neck brace to boot. Like the last days of the Apostle Paul, Sharayah was now under house arrest, and Maria was the guard to which she was chained. It was during this slow, but sure, convalescence that God got our oldest daughter's attention once and for all. While no one gets a diploma from Forgiveness U.—at least not on this terrestrial ball—Sharayah did get to go to the head of the class. Over the next few weeks, Sharayah showed encouraging signs that she was, in fact, healing, not only physically but psychologically and spiritually as well.

Even so, the loving guard attached to her leg had wonderful plans for her life. Maria had been pressing the idea of a major remodel to the upstairs of our Chestnut Street home, complete with a master bath. Both girls would be out of the house soon—so she said—and it was time that we made the upstairs more of our own. It seemed like only yesterday that we had redecorated both of their childhood rooms into something more adult. Now, they were to be houseguests.

Accordingly, in preparation for the imminent arrival of a regiment of hard-hatted construction workers, each day Maria and "Neck Brace" would pack up box after box of non-essential valuables to prepare a way. Each evening after work, I would be greeted by a barricade of sealed boxes blocking the landing at the top of the stairs, a subtle hint that, if I wanted access to our bedroom, I had to first haul them downstairs to the garage. The lazy part of me wanted to slide the boxes to the side, clearing a path so that I could just squeeze through. But I knew that this would only postpone the inevitable well into the evening, when I just might convince myself of being too tired to move the boxes at all. To help both my procrastination and resignation along, I made sure that my feet were comfortably reclined in my den chair downstairs, the T.V. turned on to my favorite program, and a drink in one hand and the remote control in the other. Even so, I knew the box barricade upstairs posed a potential risk to Sharayah and all of her expensive medical care. I could not have her possibly tripping over one of the ignored boxes during the dark of night, no matter how much my slothfulness stretched that powerful promise,

"God is within her, she will not fall."

"The Gala"

December 27, 2007

Dear Diary: Where have you been? It was probably on some random afternoon eight months ago when Maria or Sharayah unknowingly shoved a feminine-looking blue notebook into the next box with an assortment of other books, knick-knacks, and tchotchkes. Little did they realize that this would bring my journaling to a screeching halt. Once I discovered that the notebook was missing, it had already been subsumed in a veritable fortress of cardboard that was irretrievable.

Or, maybe it had dodged the packing frenzy altogether and had just been misplaced somewhere. I had little time to mourn either fate, however, as I was soon swept up in a bedlam of plastic tarps, pounding hammers, drywall dust, coils of orange extension cords, and the high-pitched squeal of table saws. Two months after the promised completion date (something to do with delays in both obtaining the necessary permits from the City of Monument's persnickety Building Department and scheduling the required inspections that punctuated the project) and thousands of dollars over budget (something to do with an unforeseen cost increase of materials, labor, and fees that the project—bid way back when—could not possibly have foreseen), our new, remodeled second story, complete with a sparkling new master bath, was completed on Chestnut Street.

December 28, 2007

"You turning fifty yet?" I looked over from where I was standing out in front of our house. I was admiring the completion of my award-winning exterior Christmas decorations out in the front yard (ignoring the episode from the previous afternoon, when Maria had kindly stated that it looked like "Christmas had thrown up all over the lawn!"), as they were now set against the backdrop of our freshly painted home. The voice was Harley's, a neighbor from across the street who had sauntered by, walking his dog. We had often talked before, as we seemed to coincidentally run into each other at this exact same time in the morning throughout the week, when I was leaving for work. I guess that we had logged enough safe, neighborly acquaintance conversations over that same period of time with each other to be frank on occasion.

"No, not yet," I answered as I broke from my gaze at the mechanical reindeer, who was leaning too far to the right, and stared at my neighbor in mock surprise. I then realized that this subject had already been broached before during our good-morning chats, when Harley admitted that he had turned fifty just a few months prior.

Getting into my car, I did some quick calculations and realized, like Pentecost, that my big 5–0 was, in fact, fast approaching. It became a preoccupation throughout my entire workday.

"What do you want to do? Do you want a party?" asked Maria that evening, when I had told her about neighbor Harley and my ensuing contemplations. She had known all along.

Although I was becoming more and more introverted by the year and didn't want to put Maria to any trouble, I surprised myself by answering quite matter-of-factly, "I want to have a party!" I'm not sure if this was simply a subconscious attempt to right myself after my father had pulled the proverbial rug out from underneath my family and craving the affirmation a birthday bash of this potential magnitude would provide. But I never wavered on the idea. It seemed to be propelled primarily by need rather than want.

"Well, then," she said with a smile, "a party it is!"

January 10, 2008

The whole concept really gained momentum once the Christmas-decoration boxes were safely stowed in the garage for another go-round with the annual calendar. It was then, as well, that Maria could begin to ratchet up her focus on the myriad of party details, the first of which would be the attendees, and this job she quickly delegated to the future guest of honor, namely me.

"Ian, can you give me a list of everyone you want to invite? I need to have an idea of how many people might be coming." At her request, I went right to work on compiling a list of the people who had bought permanent houses on both sides of my memory lane—a road-of-life walk that meandered backwards all the way to my very first human encounters. When Maria received her morning briefings on my swelling invitation list, she realized that her next responsibility—securing the location—was going to be complicated. All of our friends' houses were simply not big enough to handle a social gathering of this size and scope, even the friends who were blessed with very large houses. Out of options, Maria jettisoned her original, but now-impossible, idea of a homey atmosphere, and embraced a more-industrial setting to put my cast of thousands under one roof.

"How about the church gymnasium? It could handle your list! I mean, it has a colder feeling than a home, but we could decorate it up. What do you think?"

I thought it was a great idea and told Maria as much. At that point, she went dark with the details.

"O.K., that's all you're going to know about the party. Just get me the current names and addresses of everyone on your list so that we can be ready to send out invitations in time." And she submerged. I was now floundering around in that euphoric cloud of suspicion and anticipation experienced by anyone who finds themselves the direct object of a surprise, no matter how many clues have been revealed along the way. But, thankfully, I had a job to do, one that required a mammoth effort of sleuthing, digging, questioning, and research over a period of nearly fifty years, and I was a one-man show.

February 28, 2008

"How's 'The Gala' coming?" my daughters would ask me at the dinner table. It was how they were describing—with tongue firmly planted in cheek—my upcoming, highly promulgated, 50th-birthday party. But their tagline gained even more popularity once I revealed the numerical value of my growing guest list for "This Is Your Life."

"You know, the party with 150 of your closest friends!" they quipped. I would argue, with futility, that they were *all* close friends! At least to the extent that they had all played a part in making me who I am today. This received another roll of the eyes around the dinner table from the three women in my life, and deservedly so. Good-natured mockery gently poking fun, like little thorns in the flesh, and keeping me from any closet conceit—that unwelcome souvenir that gets caught up from too many trips to the third heaven of my paradisiacal past. Regardless, I created an ever-widening file expressly for my one job, the gathering and containing of the current names and addresses of my 150 closest friends as I obtained them—invitees to what was printed affectionately in black felt-tipped pen on the label at the top of the file, "The Gala."

One Saturday morning, like a bear in a bee hive, I had shoved myself into an upstairs closet, hindquarters protruding, pawing through dusty Manila envelopes full of even smaller old Christmas card envelopes, trying to further my genealogical research (without the aid of Utah) by using return addresses as clues to the possible whereabouts of one of my closest friends, from whom I had not heard in more than thirty years. During my rifling through these postal Ghosts of Christmases past, I repositioned my wedged shoulders in the cramped quarters and spied on another shelf my missing journal! "There you are!" I said to no one in particular. How it ended up here was anyone's guess, but it had survived the upstairs remodel with only a thin coating of dust to show for it, fortuitously making the blue cover look a little more weather-beaten and thus more masculine! I stopped what I was doing and quickly got to work on bringing my journal up to speed.

February 29, 2008

As the day of the party drew closer, the introvert in me would awaken during the night watches and yell into my inner ear, "What have you done, Block?" The party idea that originally produced that warm, fuzzy feeling was now drenching me with a cold sweat. I remembered teaching a series combed from the banks of the Chebar canal, "Zeke's Wheelhouse," to the Faithbuilders class, and a portion of it was just asking for a synopsis. I came into class wearing a party hat and recited the following:

"The en-'graved' invitations were out! On March 17, 585 B.C., to cure his loneliness, Pharaoh was throwing a party from down-under like no other! Temperatures were rising as whole wayward nations burned with anticipation as to whether they would receive the coveted, gold-leafed envelope, embossed with well-known Egyptian calligraphy and hieroglyphics announcing 'Sheol's First Annual Uncircumcised Terrorist Ball.' R.S.V.P.s came pouring in from notorious 'mighty ones' such as Meshech and Tubal, along with the Assyrians, Edomites, and Elamites. Even the Sidonians, and Chiefs from way up north decided to drop in! But in spite of the swashbuckling, performing sword fights, the 'wailing and gnashing of teeth' karaoke, and the open, 'dry bones' bar, Pharaoh found his little soirée to be the pits!"

"Turn to Ezekiel, Chapter 32."

But soon my emotions turned from ignoring Malcolm Davis's admonition of "never filling the unknown with a negative" to "*Vive la France!*" as the English responses to Maria's *repondez s'il vous plaît*—R.S.V.P.—from the secretly mailed invitations began to trickle in. Maria allowed me to be privy to this information if for no other reason than to occupy myself with the simple task of putting a "Yes" or "No" by a particular name—taking attendance in my bulging "Gala" file. When the

"The Gala"

tally was complete, I gave a self-satisfied, if not smug, smile to the three women around the dinner table. It was going to be a "Gala" after all! And, according to my records, the gymnasium at Our Father's Evangelical Church was, in fact, going to be filled with 150 of my closest friends!

I received the birthday card the next day. Oddly, it was mailed to the Block Insurance office and not to our home on Chestnut Street, giving it the air of official notice rather than cordial greeting. I recognized the writing on the front immediately as my mother's. I looked down at the card for a few moments, waiting for the strange sensation to pass. This was the first card of its kind to be exchanged between my parents and our family since the lines of communication were cut nearly three years before. Even after all we had been through, I was honestly wondering if my parents would surface for this milestone in my life, and here was their response, lying there on my desk, staring at me, daring me to open it and dive into the process of reconciliation.

I opened it expectantly, in full readiness to accept this olive branch from Hallmark and to start repairing this relationship. The card was sweet enough, with a three-way foldout covered with humorous prose and cartoons about turning fifty. But it was the little narrow slice of white paper tucked inside that was the game-changer. Back in the day, my father had always taken it upon himself to type notes to family members in all of the cards my mother would dutifully purchase and send for birthdays, Halloween, wedding anniversaries, and graduations. His notes were characteristically crisp, pithy, and loaded with spelling and grammatical errors. So, this was an expected, even welcome, gesture of normalcy and goodwill. But he apparently did not proof his words to see if they were at all sullied by any channeling of the emotional hurt and anger he was still harboring at the time. It was all a simple, obligatory routine for him. So, he did not detect what might be read between the lines, especially from the commensurately wounded perception of his hurt, angry, and vulnerable son who was about to pass the half-century mark.

"Dear Ian,

I was going to write a letter with a lot of information on this day. But gave it more thought and realized that was a long time ago and no one really cares about what went on. Fifty years is a long time and you have had a life filled with support and Love from us and your family. Choices are made along the way some influenced by other but choices nevertheless. Some choices get a response and that can be either good or bad. Our role has been and always will be the protection of our family. So enjoy your 50th try and realize you did not get where you are today without help. Dad"

It took a few minutes for the subtle or not-so-subtle, passive-aggressive incongruity of the affectionate, comical card and the abrupt, denunciatory note inside to sink in, all to the deflating hissing of hopeful expectations being dashed to pieces. At the very least, the right mom did not know what the left dad was doing. Either way, the tone of the note was not compensated by the tone of the card and cut deep into emotional flesh that had been quite tenderized by the passage of time as commemorated by this occasion.

I left early from the office, taking the card with me. As I had done numerous times in the past, I would set aside this incident and endeavor to clear my head by running it off. I had a wonderful jogging route, with just the right amount of distance and uphill challenges. Usually this type of rigorous exercise and its companion endorphin injection helped immensely to relieve stress and clear my dolorous head (like King David's runner, Ahimaaz, the fleet-footed positive thinker). But not today. The paper content of the birthday card hung onto my ankles like 10-pound weights that dragged down my pace until I came at last to a despairing halt and limped back home, willing myself to hold back tears. Maria suspected nothing as I gave her a forced smile and went directly upstairs to shower and change. But I got only as far as the tiled floor of our new master bath before I sat down and sobbed, with the card in its envelope sitting in my lap. Since there was no sound of running water coming from upstairs, Maria became curious. She found me sitting there, tears streaming down my face. I handed her the envelope. She read the card, and then the note, sat down next to me, put her arms around me, and softly said, "Oh, Honey." Sensing the uncharacteristic absence of both of their parents from the first story of our Chestnut Street home around dinnertime, both Sharayah and Samantha came into our bathroom in sequential order. Both read the letter and note, and soon all four of us were sitting on the bathroom floor, arms around each other, crying.

Sometimes the cold, hard tile of the bathroom floor of our lives can become holy ground.

Sometimes it is right where God, Who should be enough, wants us to be.

Sometimes it is right where God, Who is enough, wants us to stay.

RAISED!

March 2, 2008

The calendar date of "The Gala" finally arrived! Maria was absent most of that day in order to attend to all of the last-minute details pressing upon her and her secret army of our gracious, solicitous friends. That evening, once every one was dressed, the four of us made the trip together to Our Father's Evangelical Church and its completely transformed gymnasium. Maria and her army (including the dynamic decorating duo of Sharayah and Samantha—truly chips off the ol' "birthday boy" Block) had worked their wonders. The entire ceiling of the gymnasium looked like a helium-balloon convention—a cavalcade of color, movement, and dangling strings. The fifteen round tables positioned throughout the hall were festooned with colorful Disney-themed centerpieces (an homage to both my childhood and that of my two daughters), complementing the vivid kaleidoscope of red, blue, yellow, and green balloons bouncing on the ceiling. The place was dazzling. The look of astonishment and appreciation on my face said it all. Then my invitation list began to take human form as the confluence of all of my "worlds" over the past five decades materialized and began populating the round tables.

I was whispering to Maria about how she had truly outdone herself when the call of "Ian!" carried with it a voice from far back in my past that gave me pause before I turned my head around. I would have recognized him anywhere, tattoos and all!

"Glen!" I yelled. It was Glen Tollockson, my fellow conspirator in sitting on the girls' side in the 2nd Grade Department at Our Father's Evangelical Church under the watchful eye of Superintendent Doris Mackintosh! I hadn't seen him since the fourth grade, in 1967. He was still lanky, if not slightly stooped,

"The Gala"

and his brown hair had thinned and grayed with time. We shook hands vigorously in a grip of elation at seeing one another again after so many years. We did our best to quickly catch up in the growing din and conversational sidebars of other arrivals to the party.

"You still live in Tucson?" I asked.

"Yes!" he smiled back, with the proper amount of nostalgia and chagrin. I had always wondered about this first "scattered seed" to come in and out of my life, and the disparate journey God was taking each of us on since we had been first connected, seemingly at random, as two precocious (or so we thought of ourselves) little boys.

Maria came over and, after hugging Glen, gently grabbed my arm to turn me around. She leaned into my ear and said, "There's Tom and Jean!" We both excused ourselves from Glen and went to greet our old junior-high leaders, Tom and Jean Worrell. Tom and Jean looked older as well but still had that spark so crucial to effective junior-high ministry. They were soon joined by Sam and Betsy Morley, who went off on their own reminiscent conversation as a foursome. Speaking of foursomes, I spotted former Senior Pastor Milton Derringer and his wife Amber "talking shop" with current Associate Pastor Grayson Pomeroy and his wife, Caroline. I saw my "first kiss" Tammy Wyngate, got to briefly discuss our church's interim situation with Chairman Ted McGowan, was interrupted by a Santa Claus joke from Forrest Ripley, and then I was hugged from behind in a "Guess who?" manner by none other than "rabbit killer" Paula Henson from my Cheyenne Christian Conference Center days. I spotted Peter Grant, no doubt sharing the latest developments from his benign testimony to a gourd-faced Terry Cronklin. I waved to Tristan Holbert and his wife, Tina, who had glanced my way while talking to Troy Cobb (with hair that was still stuck in the '70s) and Donna Pritchit, was kissed on the cheek by Daniella Davis, my best friend's wife, found myself singing a few bars from "In Him Was Life" with Trent Farrell and Santiago Alvarez, after they had both snuck up behind me and yelled "THOU SHALT NOT LOVE THE LORD THY GOD!"—a jab from my colossal blunder at the First Congregational Church, while male voices were yelling and waving to me from the far side of the gymnasium. It was Nathan Raab, Kenneth Ball, and Patrick Hamilton, members of the forty-year-old "Three Musketeers" from our fifth- and sixth-grade Sunday-school days! Like the hundreds of balloons banging into one another on the ceiling at the slightest variation of temperature and air currents, my worlds were colliding below, and it was leaving me overwhelmed and euphoric!

Maria guided me to the "table of honor" facing the erected platform and podium before dinner. Around our table, in addition to Maria and myself, were Sharayah and Samantha, Paulo and Nicole Ponticelli, Maria's sister Angela, and our ex-sister-in law, Penny Block. Since every chair was occupied around our table, it distracted from the glaring absences of my parents, brother, new sister-in-law, and nephew.

After a sumptuous buffet dinner catered by an Italian Restaurant in nearby Burbank, Maria went to the podium to begin the program. She first asked for the lights to be dimmed, and a retrospective slide show on the life and times of Ian Block commenced, accompanied by Elton John's 1972 jukebox jingle, "Crocodile Rock."

Moving the panegyrical program along "by the testimony of two or three witnesses," Maria then introduced the other Three of our original Four Musketeers, who came up onstage, all wielding plastic swords. After the applause—with the other two grinning from behind like Cheshire cats—blond-haired Nathan Raab talked about my leaving a legacy. When he finished, that was Patrick Hamilton's cue to introduce the next generation of Musketeers: Sean, Leonard, Alex, Robert, Todd, Jacob, Mark, Geraldo, and Leon (also waving plastic swords), all of whom I had taught when they were in the fifth grade, and all nearly unrecognizable as mature, strapping young adults. With a dramatic, swashbuckling flair, all twelve of them took a bow to more applause, and the legion of Musketeers descended the platform.

Right on cue, Dennis and Patty O'Connor came to the podium and told the story of our first meeting at the 4th of July party at their old home on Ocean View Street.

They were followed by a fulsome Lorne and Candice Carlson, who told not only the hilarious story of the "Great Painting Scam," but also that of our miraculous reconciliation more than a decade ago, all to the sound of sniffing and scuffling for tissues from both laughter and tears.

Malcolm Davis—sporting a "Monument Valley" T-shirt in commemoration of a recent wild West road-trip adventure we had taken together—joined the speaker lineup with the story of our first meeting as college roommates at the Antioch Christian Academy, and his part in the "Eiffel Tower Plot"—the engagement of Maria and myself.

Finally, up came my two beloved daughters. Sharayah spoke for the two of them, while Samantha stood by her side, encouragingly rubbing her back in order to give her older sister what she later described as "love and stuff." Sharayah gave a tribute that I will never forget for as long as I live. It was from a devoted, loyal, adoring daughter, who knew only too well that life has its share of ups and downs, but none of these were going to hinder the relationship she had with her daddy. She communicated a prescient understanding that "it is not easy to be a Block these days," as her fatherless father carried much on his protective shoulders. Those in the gymnasium that night who knew of our undulating father-daughter journey over the years could only marvel at the grace of an almighty God on display before their very eyes. I would wholeheartedly agree if only I could have seen through the grateful tears of my own.

Before cutting the magnificent cake, depicting a batter-and-frosting Matterhorn mountain ride at Disneyland—*and* what truly seemed like a cast of thousands singing back at me an affectionate laudation of "Happy Birthday to You"—I collected my composure long enough to stand at the podium and look out appreciatively at 150 of my closest friends. I thanked them all for making this a night to remember, and then, on the spur of the moment, I borrowed a line from my 40th-birthday party, a blink-of-an-eye decade before, a line that was just as true then as it was now, perhaps even more so:

> *"Here's to fifty years of the abundant life,*
> *'cause that's exactly what it's been!"*

"Second Degree Murder"

March 13, 2008

Yesterday I received a phone call from Chairman Ted McGowan asking if I would be so kind as to drop by the P.S.C. meeting (Pastoral Search Committee) tonight for a few minutes at the beginning portion of what was looking to be yet another long, drawn-out, interim season. He did not divulge the reasons behind the request, and I didn't press him, but agreed.

Gaining entrance to the boardroom at Our Father's Evangelical Church (where the Search Committee also met), even as the Elder overseeing Adult Christian Education, I was still frequently flooded with a bank of memories from bygone deacon days—of so many late-night meetings, so much strategic planning, and the never-ending drumbeat of tragic issues with which to deal, some on the spur of the moment, others that dragged on for months, even years. But I was most taken aback by that seat planted firmly on the forest green carpet at the far end of the table and the decisive board meeting from my past, when my much-younger self had warred with the conflicting examples of his deacon father and deacon grandfather—and almost walked out.

Fortunately, that particular seat was taken by another this night. When I sat down, Emilio Paas, a perfect example of the biblical model of organically hiring from within—our old head church custodian, now an even-older Elder and P.S.C. member—asked me,

"Did you feel the tremor just now?"

"No," I responded. I had been in my car, en route to the church for the past few minutes.

"Well," Emilio continued, "Grady was just praying, and the whole table started shaking." He was referring to Grady Storm, a seasoned church transplant from the Living Waters Fellowship just east of Monument, who found himself on our Elder Board after a few years, and, after a few more, the P.S.C.

"We're thinking about having Grady pray before every meeting if he can get a response like that from God!" The rest of the committee members laughed as if strained, the half-hearted sounds in keeping with the debatable theology.

Pressured by the lengthy agenda staring up at him from his clipboard, Chairman McGowan got right to the point as it pertained to me.

"Ian, since you have started preaching as an Elder at our church, many of the members have inquired of some of us on both the Elder Board and Search Committee, if you are being considered for the Senior Pastor position." This surprise revelation made me feel equal parts edgy and awkward. I looked over at Grayson Pomeroy, who was seated across from me at the table, our Associate Pastor—a standing, non-voting member of the Elder Board—who wanted to sit in on this particular meeting of the P.S.C. He was also a fellow member of the highly successful preaching-rotation team (so successful that I think at times the sluggish progress of the Search Committee for God's man took a back seat to God's men. Perhaps there was more to this model for a biblical, organic church than meets the eye) and instigator of the whole idea in the first place! He smiled at me reassuringly, an indication that he bore no ill will at my being singled out in this way. After all, my first sermon was also his idea in the first place!

"The committee was wondering if you are considering this position," Chairman Ted continued, "and wanted to hear from you directly on the subject."

I sat there, silent for probably far too long, weighing this new information about the public response to my preaching. Then I stammered, "I have not thought about it, until now."

"You have been well-received in the Sunday school classes, Ian." It was Grady Storm, energized by his opening prayer and its earth-shaking response from the Almighty. "And the positive feedback is over a wide spectrum of age groups."

"We are receiving a lot of resumes from other churches and seminaries in the area," Ted again. "Which this Search Committee is reviewing. The question is," (Right to the point, Ted. That's what made him such an admirable Chairman of the Board and protected most elder meetings from seeing midnight.) "Are you at all interested?"

Before I could respond, Townsend Stevens interjected, an officious new Elder, now doubling as new bloodhound for the P.S.C. I had only spoken to Elder Stevens casually on occasion, so he consequently and innocently did not know my history.

"What is your education, Mr. Block?"

Mr. Block! I had not heard that kind of distancing formality since the doctrinally frigid O.F.E. Pastor Tony Meece.

"Umm, I have a degree in Speech Communication, and a minor degree in Biblical Studies and Theology from the Antioch Christian Academy. The Bible degree was required for everyone graduating from the school." The postscript to my answer came out weak, sounding as if I would not have taken a single Bible class had they not been required.

"Do you have any graduate education?" Elder Stevens again. I came to find out later that he was the representative spokesperson who reported to the Elder Board all of the "sluggish progress" of the Search Committee.

"No," I answered flatly. Hearing the voice of my father over a quarter of a century ago, and agreeing that I did not think that the ink was yet fully dry on my first degree, or degrees, as it were. They were both still much in use at the corners of Valentino and Ridgeway Avenues.

"The Search Committee really wants to consider only potential candidates with graduate degrees. Particularly a Master of Divinity," continued Elder Stevens.

Chairman McGowan looked a little rattled by this hot-off-the-press job description from the Search Committee's town crier. He did not want to monopolize my time or the committee's with a frivolous conversation when I was not qualified in the first place!

"Would you be willing to continue in your education, Ian?" asked Chairman McGowan, apparently trying to save face and stay on point.

Once again, I looked over at Grayson, who nodded encouragingly. "I've never thought about it."

There was silence around the table. The committee was obviously waiting for more. "But I can consider it."

I counted ten sighs around the table and an "excellent!" under someone's breath. Their precious time consumption with me had now been justified. "Mr. Block" would consider their proposal. Ted McGowan stood up while he thanked me for coming. He walked over and shook my hand to usher me out. I got the cue and stood up as well. It was a cordial send-off from the committee that had given me not only food for thought but also a heavy meal reminiscent of medieval times that engorged one to the point of painful groaning.

Maria was engaged in her usual multi-tasking of watching television reruns and reading an inquiring magazine in the living room when I returned quite early, uncharacteristic for both Elder and P.S.C. meetings.

"That didn't take long," she said, not even looking up from the latest celebrity uncovered to now be an alien.

"Well, it was only the preliminaries," I said as I took off my coat and threw it over a chair. I sat down opposite her and, using my right toe as a shoehorn, popped off my left loafer and then gave the job transfer to my left toe and sent my right loafer tumbling onto the floor. The familiar sound of audacious and abject laziness raised Maria's nose from her magazine to join up with her eyes in an imperious look of "how"; her forehead took up the cue by raising her two eyebrows, "dare" and "you."

I saw her look and knew at once what it was pronouncing, so I ignored the non-verbal scolding and pressed on. I gave her my own minutes of the P.S.C.'s meeting with her husband. She turned the T.V. off and listened intently. When I had finished, she responded, "I think a Master's Degree is a good idea. It's the perfect time in your life to take on this challenge. Our kids are grown. We are financially capable of handling the tuition. Even if nothing pans out at the church, I think God is preparing you for something." I just sat there, attentively, anticipating more pearls of wisdom. But she was quite finished. Her pearl of great price, "Thus saith the Lord," was the assumed, unspoken finale. Her head sank back down like the setting of the sun after it had used up all of its enlightening rays, and she returned to that world-famous singer, who, it had been recently discovered, had had her vocal cords removed at birth and had been lip-synching her way to stardom.

I went to bed that night with a sizable bug in my ear—thanks to the intuitive entomology of my wife.

March 18, 2008

The first free moment afforded me the next morning at the Block Insurance Agency found me on my computer, searching for seminary possibilities. My search did not take long, however. As a matter of fact, it ended where it had begun, with the extended, welcoming hand of my alma mater's graduate school, the Antioch Christian Academy School of Theology.

Here they offered a Master's Degree program in Theology, with a curriculum and schedule that was quite conducive for a middle-aged, out-of-town commuter like myself. My short-list decision about a potential school was made in short order. I would return to my scholastic roots.

April 21, 2008

The more we floated this idea out to our close friends over the next few weeks (after both Sharayah and Samantha enthusiastically jumped on-board with the whole prospect), the more it was validated—especially those who had witnessed my ministry trajectory at Our Father's Evangelical Church over the years, first as a teacher and now as a preacher.

I made a phone call to the Antioch Christian Academy School of Theology the next day, completed an application online, drafted my cover letter ("My dear Theophilus"), and scheduled an appointment with an enrollment counselor for the following week.

July 9, 2008

Right after all the red, white, and blue bunting and streamers of all shapes and sizes, along with "Old Glory," were "independently" placed back in the garage, my appointment at the Antioch Christian Academy School of Theology arrived on a bright Tuesday morning. It was windy that day. Dried palm fronds were ejected from their lofty perches and were strewn about the streets and sidewalks like so many dinosaur bones. After a kiss, and harder-than-normal hug from Maria, I went out to my Honda Civic all dressed and prepared for my interview, tilting my overly hair-sprayed head in such a way as not to go against the wind. I got into the car, turned the ignition key, and received for my efforts that ominous clicking sound that indicated Eveready was anything but.

When I walked back through the front door, a surprised Maria turned my way. "Forgot something?" she asked.

"Car battery's dead. I am not going to make the appointment." It was at that moment that Son of the Morning got in a headlock with the Daughter of Paulo Ponticelli.

"Ian, don't you see? Satan is using anything he can to prevent you from going to seminary. This is another one of his tricks! He's trying to kill your calling." She raised her voice so that the pointy ears of the Angel of Light would be ringing in the netherworld.

"Call the school, and tell them you'll be a little late. Get the battery fixed and *go*! You can do this!!" Her declaration of war was at once flattering and convincing. Did my prospects for seminary really shake the gates of Hell? And if so, hadn't I better finish the job and kick them down? They would prevail if I just sat there, immobile, with a dead car battery! After I called a very understanding school to explain my predicament, war parties on both sides of principalities and powers were having a knock-down, drag-out brawl over the phone and also above the auto-parts store in Monument, as I purchased a new battery, replaced the old one, and was zipping down the freeway with time to spare for my re-scheduled appointment at the Antioch Christian Academy School of Theology.

The meeting went well, and I was encouraged. The flexible scheduling, the donor-decreased tuition, and even the transfer of an abundance of units from my prior Bible degree at A.C.A. all seemed to point to something divinely doable. But when the official meeting and tour of the seminary were concluded, I needed to answer perhaps the most important question for myself. Was this return to the same piece of educational real estate after thirty years a harkening back to my safe and familiar past, or was it really part of an adventurous, challenging future? I did not want to live in the former—I wanted to be prepared for the latter!

I walked over to the adjacent cloisters of the undergraduate-university campus, which was relatively deserted for the summer break. I thought this advantageous, as it would give me time to walk around the school, with its plentiful old haunts, alone with my thoughts and prayers undisturbed. But my contemplations were no match for the blast from my past that was exploding around every corner that I turned, in every window that I looked, on every narrow street that I walked. Like some character in an imaginative children's story, I had jumped through the looking glass into the pages of my very own, living, breathing college yearbook!

"Second Degree Murder"

I passed "Barney's," the collegiate coffee bar, now closed for the summer (whose namesake was the most encouraging missionary in Antioch), and stood outside next to the large plate-glass windows of the now-empty cafeteria. I saluted to the reflection in order to deflect the sun and pressed my nose against the glass. I could see the rows of long tables still in the same configuration of that same, eventful night. I could see our table. By "our," I mean the inmates of our upper floor in the dorm that was our makeshift fraternal clubhouse. We came into the dining hall each evening at the same prescribed time, howling like a herd of wild beasts gathering around a kill.

We had become famous (or infamous) for a rousing rendition of the closing number from the "Tiki Room" at Disneyland, complete with Tahitian war chants and pounding on the long, rectangular table like so many mesmerized South Sea gods. This would always receive thunderous applause throughout the cafeteria—until the night in question, when a rival dorm had had enough of our floor-show notoriety, and one of its most nettled members tossed a French fry at our table. It was our own Doug Fuller, from Lincoln, Nebraska, who took the bait and responded to this provocation that had been brewing for quite a few nights of successive "Tiki Room" performances and encores. He stood up, brandishing a bowl of green beans in his hand, and yelled at the antagonistic table in question, "I'll take you all on!"

That is all it took for the dam to break.

Within seconds, flying food—mashed potatoes, salad lettuce, chunks of meat, spaghetti noodles, chicken legs, condiment packets, catsup containers, pickles, slices of cheese, sugar cubes, onion peels, crockery, plastic plates, cups, saucers, knives, forks, and spoons—all filled the cafeteria sky with culinary projectiles, arching over each other like rounds of opposition artillery on some Civil War battlefield. The majority of the student body dove for cover, especially those prim Protestants who had actually dressed for dinner with the assumption that it would be civilized. They were cowering under tables with their hands over their heads like elementary school children in the 1950s during a nuclear-war drill. I have never seen anything like it. It was glorious. But, alas, it was not without its punishment. We, the perpetrators, were summarily admonished and required to perform cafeteria-cleanup duty for weeks. But as our entire floor vacuumed, washed dishes, mopped, and polished during after-hours in the cafeteria, we did so with satisfied smiles on our collective faces. After all, it was a small price to pay for being able to tell our children and grandchildren that we were a part, nay, the *instigators*, of the Great Antioch Christian Academy Food Fight of 1981!

All this, while receiving a quality Christian education!

I entered my old brick dorm, ascended the stairs, and walked down the hallway of our upper floor. The old, frayed carpet was still there, greeting my feet. As was the chipping paint, the dull, yellowed fluorescent lights, and that same musty smell that had settled in from decades of steam escaping from the improperly ventilated showers in the mildewed bathroom. Slowly strolling reflectively down the hall, I noticed an opened door, Room L. I looked in, and there, sitting at his desk, was a young freshman slogging through summer school, who, to my fifty-year-old mind, looked no more than twelve! He glanced up from what he was doing and gave me a halfhearted wave. I lingered at his doorway and abruptly struck up a conversation, as old men are prone to do. I explained to him—whether he wanted to know or not—that this was once the room of Roger Sellers. One weekend, I rambled, Roger was back in Tennessee visiting his family. The rest of my dorm inmates gathered stacks of newspapers from all over town and, in round-the-clock, rotating teams, crumpled each individual newspaper page and tossed it into the room. By the time Roger returned to school, the room was completely filled. He opened his door only to hit a solid wall of stuffed, crumbled newspaper! To his credit, the kid had indulged me patiently but kept sneaking peeks at the unfinished term paper on his desk, so I moved on.

My constitutional and its concomitant reveries continued as I crossed the school parking lot, where I had once been caught fogging up my car with the daughter of a Christian celebrity, only to find the whole incident recorded in limerick form in the school newspaper, "The Antiochsidant" (healthy journalism in a field full of rags).

Still deep in thought, I sauntered off-campus and across another parking lot, this one for the patrons of the adjacent shopping center, which included a grocery and greeting-card store, along with a pizza parlor that had served as a superb homework hangout after a game of cheering on our championship basketball team—the Antioch Apostles—or a round of Frisbee golf in the park. It not being mealtime, I was not hungry, so I simply opened the door of the pizza parlor and stuck my head in to see if the place had changed. It hadn't! It was frozen in time with the same, redolent baking-grease smells wafting from the kitchen and the same chittering, trilling sounds radiating from the line of now-retro video games against the wall—Asteroids, Space Invaders, Mr. and Ms. Pac-Man, and Super Mario Bros.—the electronic cacophony sounding like so many crickets from Mars. The only thing missing was my thirty-year-younger self and my band of merry men pulling on triangular slices of pepperoni pizza from the extra-large, circular pan and laughingly stretching the strings of cheese from our mouths. I closed the front door with a grin, remembering fondly.

I walked over to the sprawling, neighboring public park that bordered the south side of the campus, and I sat on a high, picturesque knoll overlooking a large, oval-shaped duck pond. From this vantage point, I could see both clusters of buildings that made up the twin campuses of the Antioch Christian Academy and its companion School of Theology. I prayerfully looked at the undergraduate school and felt God pushing me. "Go!" He seemed to say. "This is not about your past." I turned my gaze to the seminary and felt God pulling me. "Come!" He seemed to say. "This is about your future." My decision was made. And, shortly thereafter, my application was accepted.

September 7, 2008

School started at the end of August. I was prepared. I was excited. I was nervous. And I was fifty! After hugs and well-wishing from my family, I drove down the freeway with a deep sense that this truly was the beginning of . . . something. The Antioch Christian Academy School of Theology was all abuzz on the first day of classes. So, I was bumping into people left and right who were thirty years my junior! I navigated the maze at the "Jot and Tittle" Bookstore and purchased the voluminous textbooks required for my three afternoon/evening classes. Then I had to find those classes. I was proud that I did not receive any tardy slips that day, if they were even given out to seminarians, even pre-Tribulationists!

Once I got used to the age disparity, the first class went well. The rather motherly teacher passed out the schedule of requirements for her class, better known in seminarian parlance as the "syllabus." I was shocked at all of the tests, quizzes, papers, projects and assignments that would be required of me for the next fifteen weeks. There truly was no time for breathing. But my first gasp from suffocation was only the beginning!

Class number two also had a "syllabus," with its own heavy load of tests, quizzes, papers, projects, and assignments that were also required of me for the next fifteen weeks!

By the time I received the "syllabus" for class number three, I was turning blue! During a much-needed break midway through my third class, I took a walk around the campus, sucking up lungfuls of essential, consoling oxygen. I ended up on the porch of the seminary's chapel, looking out over a vast, green lawn growing gold in the dusk of an outgoing sun. "I can't do this!" I said to no one in particular, although I am sure that God was listening, especially on a chapel porch at a Christian seminary. *There you go, Ian. Believing really bad theology on this, your very first day.* "I can't do this!" I said it again to convince myself—and won myself over. I came back into class determined that I could not handle this workload and all of the required scriptural lucubration. The difficulties of this day had all been a sign from God that He had other plans for my life. I thought of actually leaving the school at the class break and heading for home, but something enticed me to stay and hear the professor's introductory lecture on "Hermeneutics"—our previous Pastor Tony Meece's big, three-dollar word for the art and science of biblical interpretation. The professor was marvelous, and I was riveted. But I was quitting nonetheless. I drove home formulating a bevy of plausible excuses that buttressed my evacuation.

Maria listened attentively to all of them. She did not say a word. She didn't have to. She tried to suppress her disappointment, and she knew intuitively that this was not the time for another battle cry against Satan and his aspiration-assassinating demons throwing yet another roadblock at my whole graduate-school idea.

She let me argue once again with myself, with her merely eavesdropping. I knew that both of my daughters were saddened as well. But I promised them all that I would return to seminary for the Spring semester. Even my father-in-law, Paulo Ponticelli, showed signs of despondency when he heard the bad news.

September 8, 2008

I went to the Block Insurance office the next morning with the distinct feeling that I had let everyone down. But I was still convinced my pulling out of seminary at this time was the right thing to do. During breaks in my workday throughout the week, I completed a withdrawal form for the Antioch Christian Academy School of Theology to be ready for submission when I returned to school the following week. My newly purchased textbooks were boxed in the trunk of my Honda Civic, ready for the return line at the school's "Jot and Tittle" Bookstore.

The next few days also returned me to my meticulously repetitious routine. It was as if I had just been snatched by the skin of my teeth from some harebrained, midlife jungle safari or Amazon River-rafting trip down some ague-ridden River of Doubt and was anxious to get back to normal. But there was something that had been dislocated. Something that was off. Something that had been shoved into a desk drawer and was violently shaking it from the inside. I looked down at my own desk drawer in my office at the Block Insurance Agency and wondered. I then got up as if spoken to, walked down to my car, opened the trunk, and pulled out the textbook from my "Hermeneutics" class. Since it was slow this afternoon at the office, I might as well start reading and get a head start on the Spring semester, eighteen weeks away. So, I put my feet up on my desk and opened the ponderous, pricey tome to the Introduction.

> "... it can be daunting to face a voluminous Bible full of alien genealogies, barbaric practices, strange prophecies, and eccentric epistles."

My interest was piqued. I truly liked this kind of stuff.

> "We have to come to terms with the Bible as it is. And that is precisely what we intend to accomplish."

I stopped reading and looked around my office. It was then that I received a delayed divine answer to my desperate pronouncement last week on the porch of the Antioch Christian Academy School of Theology chapel: "You can do this, Ian!"

A line taken right out of Maria's playbook for dead car batteries. I closed the book, walked back out to the trunk of my car, and put it back in the box. By the time I returned to my office upstairs, I knew that there was one more thing I was supposed to do. I tore up the withdrawal form.

To say the least, Maria was elated. It was almost as if a bell had gone off in the boxing ring of her mind. The referee was counting down. Satan had been knocked down in the first round with a one-two punch. At least for now.

September 9, 2008

More hugs and well-wishing from my family as I boarded my Honda Civic for the second day in the second week of my second degree. I was still overwhelmed, but I had surrendered to a Higher Power that I could do this. Or, that He could do this through me! Maria was right. Round one was triumphant. But rounds two, and three, and four would be coming. Until then I was rolling down the freeway, heading once again toward the Antioch Christian Academy School of Theology, this time ready to receive an aptitude with an altitude and

"come to terms with the Bible as it is."

"Dude!"

"Who led them through the depths? Like a horse in open country, they did not stumble; like cattle that go down to the plain, they were given rest by the Spirit of the Lord. This is how you guided your people to make for yourself a glorious name."

—Isaiah 63:13-14

June 12, 2009

There you are, dear Diary! Or should I say, "Here I am!" I had no idea that the first semester of seminary was going to be such a journal killer. Or the second one for that matter. But your faded, feminine blue cover was replaced by other hardcover twin mistresses known as Greek, Hebrew, and a God-studying quartet named Theology I, II, III, IV. Now that "school's out for summer" (just like it was for Alice Cooper in 1972), I have had a chance to rediscover you, literally. You were not in a closet this time, but in a box buried under a stack of Old and New Testament Survey textbooks. What an ironic statement about my intellectual and personal life, recalling anew the insanity diagnosis governor Festus shouted at the apostle Paul in Acts, Chapter 26, concluding, "Too much study has made you crazy!"

When I extracted you out from under that mound of higher education, I felt like Hilkiah, the high priest some 2,600 years ago. King Josiah was in the throes of rebuilding the spiritual moorings in his capital city, Jerusalem, after the twin wrecking balls of his sinful father and grandfather had leveled the hallowed place. He emptied out every collection plate he could nab from the church ushers, in order to finance his temple-construction project. Once the contractors, builders, carpenters, and masons were in place, and the lumber and cement procured, the bulldozers arrived! Wearing a precautionary yellow hard hat at the site of the dig, Hilkiah stood atop a heap of rubble, carefully observing the progress of the first phase of excavating and ground-leveling. After quite a few uneventful days standing in Judah's hot, dusty sun, suddenly a tractor tire kicked up from underneath the protective mud flaps something shiny and gold! An ingot from Ophir? The sweating high priest recklessly ran in front of the bouncing earthmover, waving his arms for the driver to stop. When the engine was killed and the deafening diesel chug had ceased belching from the exhaust pipe, Hilkiah trudged behind the hulking shadow in order to investigate the parallel tread marks gouged in the scorched earth.

He spent quite a few minutes spreading, digging, and sifting the ancient, abused soil. At once, his eye caught a glint of straw-colored binding—like amber—protruding out from under the dirt clods. The high priest pulled at the solid object and extracted a book. Sensing spiritual significance, he carefully wiped off the pockmarked cover with the corner of his robe and discovered, after seventy-seven years, words to actually live by. As one can only imagine, King Josiah was thrilled! He immediately pulled out his card and checked out the precious Book of the Law before the church library was even rebuilt.

"Dude!"

I feel the same elation, dear Diary, that you have been similarly yanked from antiquity, just in time for me to update you on a few momentous occasions—the first of which would be the graduation from high school of our precious youngest daughter, Samantha! I remember our old missions pastor, Forrest Ripley, coming to visit Maria and me in the Maternity Ward at the Monument Hospital after the birth of Sharayah. He and I were standing in front of the traditional plate-glass window. On the other side were lined up, in multiple rows of bassinet formation, the latest newborns to come down the pike, the direct result of the pushing and screaming going on in the assembly line of rooms up and down the hospital corridor. We were staring at that beautiful baby in the second row, third from the left, coiled up in a pink blanket, with the plastic-encased badge hanging from the brim of the crib showcasing the black letters "Sharayah Block."

Neither of us broke our gaze from the dozing little girl, as if neither of us wanted to miss a second of her growth, even though she had been alive for only a matter of minutes. Forrest spoke to this when he placed his hand on my chest, as if to tamp down the Ecclesiastical eternity planted in the heart of every man, and said, "You blink, and they're walking. Blink again, and they're off to preschool. Blink again, and they're graduating. Blink again, and they're getting married. It goes so fast, Ian!" *Forrest should know*, I thought. After all, he had raised three quickly grown children of his own. What am I saying, Diary? *I* should know! You blink, and you're 50!

Samantha's graduation was a bittersweet event—full of the joy and potential that a proud parent should feel at this seminal moment in the life of his youngest daughter but also a pang of sadness at this photo finish of the race against time.

The family row of Samantha's cheerleaders on the Monument High School football field that day consisted of myself, Maria, Sharayah, "Papa" Paulo, "Ya-Ya" Ponticelli, and Samantha's old friend Ashley from church. Because Samantha's inclinations were more adept at the social aspects of high school rather than the academic, I secretly wanted her to hold onto her diploma for dear life once it was handed to her by the principal, lest it be taken away at a later date if and when her transcripts were pulled to re-crunch the numbers of her G.P.A.!

Because of those very same inclinations, our house was a fluttering lepidopterarium of social butterflies for the post-ceremony graduation party. They were flitting, cavorting, and giggling throughout every room of the house. I have never heard so many shares of gossip being traded under one roof! It was like the floor of the New York Stock Exchange, with the "tip" of the day starting with "Did you hear who has a crush on . . . ?" with very little to say about anyone's "futures." Because there was so much grist for the rumor mill, the party did not break up until the wee hours of the morning!

When I came down the stairs into the living room the next morning, I looked around at the devastation of paper cups still sporting the names of its previous owners, as staked out by a felt-tipped pen, crumpled napkins, grounded balloons now devoid of uplifting helium, and even Samantha's yearbook sitting on the coffee table—each page now autographed with illegible signatures accompanied by cute poems and promises to stay in touch. But it was the sound—or lack of it—that caught my ear. Silence. Soon, this would be the hearing-of-a-pin-drop future for Maria and myself. One day, following hard after Sharayah, Samantha would leave us to go out into the world, as they say. But that was just the point of the heartbreak for any empty-nesting parent. Not only do their children leave them, but they take their "worlds" with them.

The blessed chaos of phones ringing, music blaring, chick flicks screening, doors slamming, showers running, laughter erupting, blow-dryers blowing, car horns honking, an eighteen-year-old racket that had its beginnings with a colicky baby who could not sleep through the night. Open house, choir practice, competitions, football games, parent meetings, car washes, proms, homecoming, all came to an abrupt halt. And in its place, that often-longed-for-but-overrated peace and quiet. The worst part of an empty nest is the soundtrack; the chirping is gone. There is no need to go out and gather any worms or make a pizza run; the little mouths to feed have flown. But, before our house on Chestnut Street was rendered speechless, I had to first endure the eardrum-shattering roar of a jet engine!

September 20, 2009

I am getting this journal entry in quick before my next semester shifts into a higher gear that only the transmission of a Higher Power can sustain. Samantha enrolled at a junior college some forty minutes to the north of Monument, majoring in Equine/Horse Science, at which she was most proficient and needed only to whisper to her four-footed test cases. During this time, her social life began to tilt. Some of her old high-school friends, those who did not go off to college, still "hung around" the house on occasion. Her church friends diminished. And the void seemed to be increasingly filled with predatory boys with nothing between their ears, who only wanted to "make out" with Samantha—or worse. Maria and I were becoming more and more concerned about the questionable social circles into which Samantha was spinning. Having prayed Sharayah out of wrong crowds on two occasions, we saw this third time and its so-called charms coming a mile away. But we did not act upon it until it actually crawled into bed with us!

Samantha had come home late from yet another party. The ever-attentive Maria heard a clunky footfall coming up the stairs that sounded more like Quasimodo than a social butterfly. Instead of going into her room, Samantha mysteriously shuffled directly into the bathroom. No door, no matter how thick, could have successfully muffled the Special Report from Samantha's digestive tract that was being read on the late edition of the Evening News, as transmitted from the porcelain satellite dish. With a flush, the show was turned off, and one last, dull thud from the bathroom told the acute hearing of Mrs. Sherlock Block that Samantha had called it a night.

Maria slipped out of our bed and tiptoed down the hall, opening the bathroom door just far enough to see her youngest daughter beached on the tiled shore, passed out, the waves from the sea of firewater still lapping at her stomach lining and intestines. Maria offered no cold cloth on the forehead, no soothing words, no gentle escort down the hall to her room. Maria left her there, thinking that the bibulous Samantha had, in fact, made her own bed and should lie in it! But even in her drunken state, like a child after a bad dream, Samantha sought the comfort of her parents' room. No sooner had Maria returned to ours and slipped under the covers, lying in her usual position (on her side facing me), then there was more Quasimodo shuffling.

Our bedroom door opened, and, after a few more unsure feet, the covers parted to make room for a third party. Maria was hugged tightly from behind, and shoved over into my "space" in the bed. This intrusion woke me for a moment, just in time to see Maria's faced pressed next to mine and to hear groggy words coming from a stranger behind my wife's back, carried along by the distinct breath of alcohol. "Let's snuggle!" it said, in a sing-song, invitational sort of way. Even in the dark, Maria gave a look to the ceiling that only mothers can facially express, part "You've been drinking" exasperation and part satisfied "I told you so" smile.

When I awoke the next morning, we were back to a party of two. Evidently during the night, our little "snuggler" had been escorted back to her detox chamber. I sighed and rolled over, thinking of blameless Job and his burnt offerings to a Heavenly Father on behalf of his seven sons. A Monday morning smoke of God-appeasing aroma that choked out any potential sin, as it chased his boys and their rotating, all-night house parties every weekend, which routinely included Job's three curious—and innocent—daughters as well!

November 18, 2009

Coming up for air after a World of the Old Testament midterm, I was informed by Maria that she thought it might be a good idea if Samantha got out of Monument for a while. This, of course, after she had been severely grounded for taking off in coach on her flight of intoxication and then trying to snuggle in first class! The options were limited, however, when we assessed her overpowering social capabilities in a demanding academic setting. Samantha would love a life in a college-dorm experience until that first quiz arrived.

January 26, 2010

It became apparent after Christmas that Samantha's spiritual development had to be allowed to catch up with her already well-developed social life, and this, to our way of thinking, was best served at a camp experience, much akin to my summer at the Cheyenne Christian Conference Center, which was even discussed as a possibility. But the horse sense of Samantha's equestrian bent kept dangling in front of Maria like a carrot and became our biggest directional indicator.

March 10, 2010

After many weeks of prayer and contemplation on Samantha's behalf, Maria ran all of this by a trusted friend at Our Father's Evangelical Church. "What about a dude ranch?" was the response. Maria stated that we were looking specifically at a more Christian environment for our daughter.

"Why not a Christian dude ranch?" was her friend's reply.

"Is there such a thing?"

To which her friend smiled and answered, "Why not the Thousand Hills Cattle and Dude Ranch in Colorado? Our family has gone there for vacation nearly every summer, and it is fantastic. It's not advertised as a 'Christian' dude ranch, but I know that it is owned, completely run, and staffed by Christians!"

When Maria presented this intriguing idea to me as I took a break from a term paper on the hypostatic union of Jesus, I was intrigued by an idea that seemed perfectly suited for Samantha. We, in turn, presented this to our daughter, who was remarkably excited about the prospects as well. It seemed that she was actually growing tired of the stagnation represented by her post-high-school friends and wanted to get out of sleepy little Monument and have an adventure. We continued praying about this, until one night at dinner, Samantha confessed that she felt ever-so-strongly that she was being called to the Thousand Hills Cattle and Dude Ranch. I felt a fatherly shiver go down my spine, for the glimpse of spiritual maturity that my daughter's comments had revealed. Then a second shiver, from the distinct possibility that my little girl had actually heard God doing his best Horace Greeley imitation in calling Samantha from the opposite direction to "Go East, young lady!"—1,000 miles East, to be exact.

A third shiver.

May 12, 2010

Dear Diary: The pudding was proved when Samantha's application to the Thousand Hills Cattle and Dude Ranch was accepted. As decided, she will stop her junior-college equestrian studies in June and pack up for her calling to Colorado in August.

I, on the other hand, have no such academic agreement. So, back to the books!

August 31, 2010

After weeks of planning and all manner of preparations, in another blink of an eye (according to Forrest Ripley), I found myself pulling out of our driveway on Chestnut Street with Maria, Sharayah, and Samantha in tow, driving across Ridgeway Avenue to Valentino Avenue, turning left and heading downhill toward the freeway and the Burbank Airport.

We arrived early in order to make sure that all of Samantha's belongings were safely checked in and dutifully bound for Colorado. Then the four of us sat around, talking—not killing time, but cherishing it. Finally, it squirmed out of our grip, and it was time for Samantha to board her flight. I watched, as my little girl said a tearful goodbye to her older sister, a relationship with so many natural, sisterly ups-and-downs, but one that was also bonded by those very same ups-and-downs. When Samantha started crying on her mother's shoulders with her weeping sister looking on, I felt as if, after all these years, our cosseted little foursome was breaking up. I had very little time to rebuff God for this, His idea, as it was my turn to say goodbye to my youngest daughter. I remember exactly where we were standing on the carpet of the United Airlines terminal, holding each other against melting onto the floor. It took everything inside of me to let her go, and everything inside of Samantha to be let go. Into other Hands did I place her, those very same Hands that had gently pulled apart our embrace. I was admittedly reticent, terrified even, but knew deep down inside that it was the right thing to do. To do otherwise would have been disobedient, for both of us. We watched her go through security, hand the attendant her ticket, walk through the glass doors and out onto the tarmac, climb the exterior stairs placed up against the fuselage, duck her head under the aircraft's rounded entrance, and disappear from view. I could barely contain myself.

The three of us, for composure's sake, walked briskly out of the terminal and found an area by a chain-link fence that offered a clear view of the runway and Samantha's plane. We watched it taxi into position, knowing that, in one of the little windows dotting the side of the giant plane—like portholes on a submarine—was Samantha's tear-stained face, alone, and leaving us.

"Dude!"

The turbine engines began to roar, and the plane gained speed down the runway, finally becoming airborne right above our heads. I waved at the plane in case, miraculously, Samantha should catch a glimpse of us. With my feet firmly fastened onto the pavement, my craning neck feeling no ache, my eyes growing accustomed to the glaring sun reflecting off the flying object in the sky, I waited until the plane disappeared completely from view, lost in a crowd of low-flying clouds, whose job it was to gently erase the past. The three of us returned to our van and silently drove back to Monument and our home on Chestnut Street, with a grieving, heightened awareness of the empty fourth seat coming home with us.

> *"Like cold water to a weary soul is good news from a distant land."*
> —Proverbs 25:25

We sat in our living room, watching the clock and giving Samantha enough time to safely land in another time zone, gather all of her luggage, and find the unknown representative from the Thousand Hills Cattle and Dude Ranch, who was to shuttle her back to God knows where. When the phone finally rang, Maria jumped for it. Thankfully, Samantha was fine and in the car heading into the Rocky Mountains. As such, reception was sketchy, and the risk of a disconnection was imminent. Since all the vital signs were accounted for, with great difficulty we let her go to continue to get to know the cowgirl driver during their trip further and further into the interior. As she began to cut out and drown in static, I thought with great aggravation that she might as well have been using an old ham radio while she was skidding along on a rickety old dog sled, bound for some Ice Station Zebra in Antarctica! "We'd be better off with two tin cans and a string!" I snorted at the now-silent phone. It was the best word picture I could come up with in the height of my frustration.

But the signal was gone, and I got the signal from God, "Let her go! She's mine!" Even with practiced obedience to Him since my third-grade conversion, I went down kicking and screaming with this one. But trust was all I had at the moment. Trust and counting the days to Christmas, when Samantha would come back home to us. In the meantime, we stayed connected as best we could, what with the location of the Thousand Hills Cattle and Dude Ranch being a quest-less pinpoint on the map. In a fog of culture shock, Samantha was nonetheless adjusting to her new surroundings and getting to know some wonderfully committed Christian folks from all around the country. After all, this was a putative, highly rated dude ranch, an expensive vacation destination for many, and a sought-after employment opportunity for so many young Christians nationwide who wanted to hitch up their wagons and head for pastures greener than their currently plowed ruts. As time dragged on, it became quite apparent that I could trust Samantha's Heavenly Father. He was putting her through it, to be sure. But in so doing, He was drawing out of her strength, assurance, and fortitude—the likes of which I had never seen before—an extraction possible only in these unique circumstances. This revelation calmed her father down a notch or two.

But only briefly.

January 11, 2011

In spite of my counting the days to speed things along, the Ancient of Days was not pressured, nor was He rushed. Christmas arrived right on schedule. And what a reunion it was! The four

"Dude!"

of us in a big group hug at the very same airport at which we had suffered such loss four months before. Samantha did not stop relaying adventure after adventure on the drive back to Monument. And even so, she had barely scratched the surface by the time we turned into our Chestnut Street driveway.

The Thousand Hills Cattle and Dude Ranch was the pre-dinner conversation, the dinner conversation, and the after-dinner conversation. By the time Samantha had gone to bed in her perfectly preserved, time capsule of a bedroom, it was abundantly clear that God was working wonders in our little girl. She was working hard as a waitress in the dining hall, loved the dorm experience with the other female staff, and admitted that she had cast second glances at not a few of the "cute cowboys" who made up the male wrangling staff of the dude ranch.

For the next few days, to take the edge off another airport goodbye that was looming, the balance of Samantha's time with us was filled with Maria and me planning a road trip out to Colorado to visit her in February. But that edge was still successful in poking me right in the gut a few days later as we, once again, found ourselves saying "Goodbye" to our matured Samantha. At the very least, I was able to parry the emotional thrust with the promise of, "See you in a few weeks!" On this, our second, silent drive from the Burbank Airport back to Monument, I started counting days again—how soon it would be before her faithless father could come and rescue Samantha from that godforsaken wilderness.

March 30, 2011

Well in advance of our pre-dawn departure date, and much to the eye-rolling of my normally paced wife, I saw to it that our

Honda Odyssey was packed and ready, including a large cache of textbooks and homework. The Antioch Christian Academy School of Theology did not, apparently, care that I was going to visit my long-lost daughter after an absence of six months. Like time, seminary marches on.

We said goodbye to Sharayah, who was quite saddened by her not being able to make the trip, but nonetheless was charged with "holding down the fort" on Chestnut Street. Our past-prime van was not equipped with any GPS (Global Positioning System), so I had calculated beforehand that there were 19 hours and 20 minutes between our "Global Position" and Samantha's! And I purposed to beat the "System" and get there in 18 hours. Maria had to remind me that it was winter, and there was snow reported in Flagstaff, Arizona, rain in Albuquerque, New Mexico, more rain the next day in Santa Fe, New Mexico, and snow through the Raton Pass into Colorado. Flurries were predicted for the Front Range west of Denver, but none of these inclemencies were a match for a father missing his daughter. However, what I did not account for was how deeply the Thousand Hills Cattle and Dude Ranch was stowed away in the Rocky Mountain frontier.

"I can't believe any mountain range is this big!" I said in desperation to Maria, who was sitting maddeningly complacent in the passenger seat, 22 hours into our two-day road trip. It was getting on late in the afternoon and raining lightly.

"It's the Rockies, Honey! What did you expect?"

The wet road kept winding, and winding, and winding. A test, no doubt, to rid the highway of everyone save the most intrepid and foolhardy explorer!

"Turn here," said Maria, looking up from a map of Colorado.

"Where?" I slowed the van down.

"Here!"

Through the back-and-forth motion of the dueling windshield wipers, all I could make out was an obscure dirt road just right of the highway that opened up through the densely overgrown and overhung cottonwood trees that leaned into either side. By now, the rain had abated somewhat, which left long, dirty, water-filled trenches in the ruts as provided by the various trucks and cars that had used this road during the day. I turned onto it.

"I hope we can beat the darkness," I said gloomily, as we carefully off-roaded (in a vehicle that had no business doing so) our way in an unknown direction. We dodged potholes the size of hot tubs that surfaced with the regularity of Swiss cheese, protruding boulders making what was already barely one lane down to no wider than a trail. Low-hanging tree branches swiped the roof of our van with an eerie scraping sound, like some prehistoric car wash, and the serpentine twists and turns would have surely made the sight of any oncoming traffic our last! At least, that was what the insurance man in me thought, and often.

"Samantha drives this road?" I asked, somewhat panic-stricken. She had often mentioned that she occasionally was commissioned to go into "town" (wherever that was!) to get supplies and would use one of the Ranch's four-wheel-drive trucks to do so. Or, worse, all of her friends would pile into a conventional vehicle and careen down the dirt road just to go out for the night and navigate the return trip in the pitch blackness of some midnight hour!

"How much farther?" I said, like a little kid in the back seat after the first few minutes of a vacation in the family station wagon. Only this time *I* was driving!

"According to GPS, it's about twelve miles farther!" answered Maria, compliantly.

About halfway inside this haunt of jackals, there finally arose above us a great entry-gate arch made of gigantic logs. At the apex of the arch, hovering like a trail boss over the center of the dirt road, was bolted a large, metal replica of the Ranch's brand, a "TH" and a backwards "R."

"We're here!" I said. Relieved, with a capital "R."

"Six more miles," answered Maria flatly. I think there was a trace of a smile forming on her face.

I felt like I must have celebrated a few birthdays by the time we actually pulled into the Thousand Hills Cattle and Dude Ranch dirt parking lot. But the trauma of the last twelve miles of travel did not have much staying power as I cut the engine, opened the door, and scanned the Old West for my daughter!

"Daddy!" She had been waiting for us. I did not even bother to shut the van door. Like a scene from a movie, I ran across a rolling, grass field, heading toward what I would come to know as the "Milk 'n Honey" Dining Hall, with Samantha sprinting in her cowgirl outfit in my direction. We met in the middle, and there was no happier embrace! We clung to each other, spinning in circles from the momentum of our oncoming, individual runs, until we fell down in the grass, laughing hysterically and with great joy.

Maria called out, running up the knoll as well, and the whole scene was deliciously repeated with mother and daughter.

March 31, 2011

A very grown-up Samantha saw to it that Maria and I were properly checked in (introducing us to every fellow staff member who passed by, as if they were her best friend) and ensconced in one of the cute little western cabins that dotted the hillside, overlooking the swimming pool. Once we were settled in, she had to "skedaddle" because she was needed back at the "Milk 'n Honey" Dining Hall in order to prepare for dinner. She prompted us to listen for the dinner bell tower shortly—we couldn't miss it, as its ring reverberated throughout the entire canyon—and head on over to the Hall, where she would make sure we were seated at one of her tables.

The "Milk 'n Honey" Dining Hall was a massive, high-ceilinged room, burned with cattle brands all over the walls. Ten or twelve large round tables with red-and-white checkered tablecloths, each with a tall, kerosene lamp in the center, were placed about the expansive, square-dance polished wood floor. Around these, each of the many guests would gorge on heapin' helpings of sumptuous western hospitality while being stared down from above by stuffed buffalo, moose, elk, deer, antelope, bobcat, bighorn sheep, and even a jackalope named Obadiah.

The all-you-can-eat portions were so grand, the gravy so thick, the starches so sticky, the roast beast so heavy, the desserts so rich that digestive systems were waving white flags. I loosened my belt that was straining to hold onto the tightening circumference of my waistline. But Samantha kept the "vittles" coming like a real pro, stacking and balancing rows of plates that were teetering with additional mounds of savory food. Later, Maria and I euphorically belched and groaned our way back to the rustic cabin and slept the sleep of hibernating bears (to the hooting of an owl named Haggai, who apparently made the rafters above our cabin home, complaining all night long about having seen it in its former glory).

The next morning, after "breaking our fast" (which should have lasted for forty days) with bacon, eggs, biscuits, gravy, pancakes, waffles, grits, and mud coffee, Samantha took us on a tour of the Ranch. What an incredible facility! No wonder it had a quintuplet of stars after its name in all of the national tourism magazines. While it harkened me back to bygone days at the Cheyenne Christian Conference Center, my old camp was a dilapidated ghost town by comparison! 2,500 acres of the most pristine fields, forests, and purple-mountain majesty that I had ever seen. We walked for miles, soaking up both the local culture and scenery. Up and down mountains, around stockades filled with mooing cattle, we "moseyed" along the boardwalk of an old makeshift western town (complete with jail) that was propped up like a movie set and used for blazing nightly campfires, oversized-marshmallow roasting, and silly camp singalongs. We sat on a fence for the longest time, overlooking the stables (with jutting stalks of grain firmly wedged between our teeth), watching some of the wranglers not gittin' along very well with the little dogies, as they attempted to brand some of the calves—calves who did not relish the unfashionable idea of having "TH backwards R" scorched onto their hindquarters. Down the Old Chisholm Trail, we "hoofed" it around the large outdoor arena in which was held the Ranch's weekly "Wide and Narrow Road-eo," featuring everything from barrel-racin' to mutton-bustin'.

We even went over to the rifle range and tried our hand at skeet-shooting. The male staff working the range were all "duded" up in western attire. One of the staff saw only city-slicker green when he spied us coming up the road and sauntered over to us.

"Ya'll here to shoot?" he asked with an affable, laid-back friendliness.

"Yup!" I replied with my best Southern drawl. At which Maria and Samantha cringed with embarrassment, while the staff dude gave an indulgent smile, having heard this dialect

"Dude!"

from trying-too-hard tourists many times before. His name was "Shane." Yes, that was his real name. He was from Laramie, Wyoming. He gave us a quick verbal lesson on the art of skeet-shooting and then proceeded to show us how it was done. As he yelled "Pull!" the clay pigeons shot up into the clear, blue sky like they had been rustled out of the bushes by some rabid bird dog. With each ear-deafening explosion of his rifle, Shane blasted them into powder, like clay fireworks, with such ho-hum efficiency that he made it look plumb easy. Shane was the "real McCoy."

My shooting was for the birds that day, but Maria was a veritable Annie Oakley.

Walking around the ranch, I noticed that so many of the locations were "branded" with biblically referenced names, the quiet witness of a prestigious vacation destination. Along with the aforementioned "Milk 'n Honey" Dining Hall, the guys' dorm was called "Jacob's Gents" and the girls' dorm "Midian's Gals"—the former an apparent reference to Israel's dirty dozen and the latter the seven-headed harem from which Moses had plucked his wife Zipporah—"Floating Ax Head" Blacksmith, "Rise Up and Walk" Infirmary, and "Siloam Waterin' Hole" for the pool.

We arrived at the stables for a turn at horseback riding—the star attraction of the Thousand Hills Cattle and Dude Ranch. Not surprising, all of the horse's names were biblical ones: Issachar, Dan, Nimrod, Ishmael, Hezekiah, Jezebel, Jael, Zephaniah, Zebulun (not to mention a donkey named Zechariah—a colt, the foal of a donkey). This included three wild turkeys, who roamed the barns and haylofts, named Micah, Nahum, and Zerubbabel. The ranch hand in charge of the stables (Wyatt, from Austin, Texas), sized us all up, a necessary bulk evaluation for every guest at the ranch, considering the hefty amounts of artery-hardening food we were all consuming. After the visual head-to-toe once-over, Wyatt assigned me to a draft horse named "Nathan," Samantha to a beautiful brown-and-white paint called "Barnabas," and Maria, like a queen, on a dappled gray named "Sheba." With the exception of our highly trained and gifted Samantha, we three formed the tail end of a long line of novices on horseback as we said "Goodbye" to Ol' Paint and trudged straight up a trail-less mountainside, with wrangler Zane riding point in the lead, and Cash riding drag at the rear. The sensations were bracing, and the views were panoramic. By the time we reached the crest of the hill and could see for miles, I truly felt on top of the world, even without the aid of my fifteen-hands-tall "Nathan." In just shy of half an hour, Ian Block had morphed into Dan Blocker—Hoss Cartwright of *Bonanza* fame—with the T.V. show's theme music running through my head.

The lead wrangler reckoned that now would be a good time to pick up some speed. The horses were permitted to freely gallop across the gently undulating summit without too many irregularities in the ground condition. So, our little equestrian caravan "Hi-Ho Silver"ed our way across the warm, bare back of the Colorado foothills. For the inexperienced rider, the pounding, body-bouncing feeling of lost control can be terrifying. But a rookie rough rider must grab the horn of the saddle and yell "Giddy-up!" anyway. So we rode like the wind with much whooping and hollering until I heard a sound from Maria, who was bringing up the rollicking rear on "Sheba," just in front of Cash. The sound that Maria made was neither "whoop" nor "holler," but more like a "Ho!"—the only sound that her body could spontaneously express while flying from the ejection seat of her saddle. There was heard a dull thud and Cash yelling something in Western to Zane. The galloping line was halted. I turned in my saddle just in time to see Cash leap off his horse, "Laban," and squat down on the ground next to a heap of tourist, who I then realized was my wife. After a few moments of bent-to-the-ground conversation, Cash helped a limping, winded Maria to her feet. She had had the presence of mind to "tuck and roll" off of "Sheba" just as soon as she felt herself losing her grip, so the ground that broke her fall was at a much shorter distance by the time they abruptly met.

With Maria unable to ride, Zane trotted back to the drag, and Cash carefully lifted my stunned, groaning wife onto the back of Zane's horse, "Agrippa." Cash held the riderless "Sheba's" reins as our posse headed back to camp.

Maria was sore and convalesced in our little cabin for the remainder of the afternoon. She was doted upon with western hospitality by the dedicated staff of the Thousand Hills Cattle and Dude Ranch (who had all seen this kind of thing before, sometimes daily). Tanked up on aspirin and enveloped in heating pads, my determined wife made marvelous progress. She even got back on that horse, literally, for the next day's trail ride. Only this time, "Sheba" stayed home in Arabia, while Maria was safely given an old sorrel horse appropriately named "Methuselah," who could barely walk, let alone gallop! Maria's bruises were healing quickly, as quickly as the time was passing.

And, all too soon, it was time to pack up our van and actually "Go West!" We bid our daughter another blubbering "Goodbye." But between the sniffling, there was a satisfaction that we had been given a glimpse of her world and could confidently leave her there because we were assured it was right where God wanted her to be.

RAISED!

April 27, 2011

A few weeks after our road trip to the Thousand Hills Cattle and Dude Ranch, I received an unexpected guest at the Block Insurance Agency, my brother Owen. This was such a rare occasion that I suspected the worst. Once he was ushered into my office, and cordial, canned pleasantries were forcibly exchanged, I made sure that he was not there on the pretense of the Grim Reaper, or any terminal diseases in the family, at least not in the way that I perceived them. Owen sat in the brown leather chair opposite my desk, looking around my office for a moment, as if sizing it all up for the last time. He looked somewhat haggard—the bodily collision between middle age and a prolific, athletic youth. Not to mention two marriages and one nasty divorce. He then turned his gaze out the second-story window to the bustling midday traffic of Valentino Avenue below, and said rather brusquely,

"You know, Ian, your family is not even missed at the holidays. It's like you guys are dead to us."

While, after so many years, I would admit that our separated families had logged in quite a few Christmases without each other and made do, I thought Owen's assessment not only fatalistic but cruel and rude. I would admit, however, that his efforts in coming to my office after all this time, fighting traffic while motoring from Los Angeles to Monument, just to make such a pronouncement was a gutsy move, indeed. I had thought wishfully that Owen—like Joseph's scallawag brothers after daddy Jacob's burial—might at least try to put conciliatory words in our father's mouth as an excuse to begin a forgiveness conversation on both sides. But I posed neither the threat nor the desire. Although internally crestfallen, I gave him no response. He appeared to be unsure of how to proceed. But then an idea came to him that was surely culled somewhere from his experiences as a substitute science teacher—a conditional, trade-off job requirement for anyone wanting to coach in the state school system.

"You know—like animals are anthropologically attracted to their families." I raised my eyebrows. My brother mortician, who had just pronounced us dead, was now not only the avuncular father of one, but the informative host of some make-believe nature program. He tried again, "When a baby is separated from his mother, like in a herd of something, they can sense where they are, and locate each other by just smell or a call."

". . . of the wild?" I could not resist. I gave a hint at a smile, but it was not returned.

"That's what Julie and I are doing with Mom and Dad. We are gravitating anthropologically to them. Based on a natural desire and need. You know, instinct."

Something stunk all right. While I was not an experienced coach substituting as an expert science teacher, I presumed that a mother in the animal kingdom could pick out a whole bunch of calves, foals, cubs, chicks, ewes, bunnies, kittens, puppies, or guppies, from a litter, herd, pack, pod, flock, school, warren, swarm, or caravan, and not just one! But, to his point, Owen was now an only child in his claptrap animal kingdom! That being said, I had nothing to lose.

"We have a phrase for that in our family, Owen," I said. He looked at me quizzically. I gave him the answer, "You drank the Kool-Aid!" A not-so-kind, suicidal reference to the Reverend Jim Jones' drink of choice back in 1978 Guyana.

"We did not!" Owen protested, lamely. As lame as his anthropological analogy.

"Yes, you did. You have no idea about the other side of this equation. You have no idea what we have been through." Owen did not want to give me the opportunity to present another side and stood up to leave.

"Well, that's all I have to say," he stated as he headed for the door.

I gave him a hardened look, as much for self-protection as for making my point.

"Have a nice life," I said passive-aggressively (not exactly "You meant to harm me, but God meant it for good!"), while simultaneously offering my hand for a final shake. He took it limply for one so athletic, as if no longer caring, and turned to leave.

I sat down, taken aback at what had just happened so quickly on the heels of our return from the Thousand Hills Cattle and Dude Ranch in Colorado. It seems that the "anthropological" party for the prodigal son just goes on and on, while the obedient brother watches in turmoil. Or does he? While distant at first, it was becoming clearer from the proclamations of Owen's visit that there was the sound of "clip-clopping" in our future—an adventure right around the corner. I came home after work and relayed my conversation with my long-lost older brother to Maria and Sharayah over dinner. Whether as a defense mechanism, or simply because we could not help ourselves, the word "anthropological" became a running joke in our family.

The phone rang later this evening; it was Samantha! Through all of the now-expected phone static, I asked my daughter all of the crucial questions that were essential from any adoring, responsible father, and then handed the phone over to Maria. She and Samantha chatted for another half-hour while

"Dude!"

I watched T.V. in the living room. When they had hung up, Maria came and stood in the doorway, a known behavior that an announcement was pending. Obediently, I muted the sound on the T.V. and looked her way. She took a deep breath, and then cautiously smiled.

"Samantha has met a guy."

"Family of Choice"

April 29, 2011

I have just returned from an occasion that waxed very sentimental to me—the 25th anniversary of the first Sunday-school class that Maria and I started, the "Young and Married." Although many months after the quarter-century date in question, as better-late-than-never church planning goes, what an incredible celebration was held at the home of Lorne and Candice Carlson. It was a perfect, balmy Southern California evening, with more than seventy people milling around the Carlsons' backyard. Some charter members, others brand-new. Some no longer at O.F.E., others stalwart members. Some coming from far out of town, others coming from just down the street. All eternal friends who planned to grow old together. Later on, after a few congratulatory speeches, hilarious stories, and heartwarming testimonies, Maria and I cut into a large sheet cake proclaiming "Happy 25th Anniversary Not-So-Young and Married Class!" As the crowd of celebrants began to thin later in the evening, I found myself alone walking through the Carlson home. The beautiful painting of a placid English cottage and countryside above the fireplace caught my attention. I smiled to myself: this painting had been literally . . . caught! I basked in all of the wonderful memories that had taken place

"Family of Choice"

in this home, and in our deep and abiding friendship with not only the Carlsons but also with every one in our little flock, the "Young and Married Class." Maria and I were glowing on the short return trip back to Chestnut Street. Given the disaffection of my own genetic family, it was truly soul-stimulating to rub shoulders with our dear friends, devoted members of our beloved "Family of Choice."

"Car-Jacked"

April 30, 2011

"He has sent me to bind up the brokenhearted, to proclaim liberty to the captives, and the opening of the prison to those who are bound."

—Isaiah 61:1 (ESV)

During her bored convalescence from her car accident nearly four years before, Sharayah connected and reconnected with many of her friends from school and even church. One old friend in particular was actually a hybrid between the two. Jackson Osborne was a childhood friend of Sharayah's who had gone to not only the John Adams Elementary School with her, but also through the corresponding Sunday-school grades at Our Father's Evangelical Church. He and his family had moved down to the Orange County area once they had both entered junior high, but not before a lasting bond of childhood friendship had been formed between them.

Jackson was highly athletic, even surpassing the Olympian exploits of my Athenian older brother. From star of the football field (where he donned his black-and-gold jersey with the dreaded #5 emblazoned on the back), to rumored stud in the locker room; from life of the party, to king of the prom, Jackson discovered such a deep passion and astonishing prowess for all things sports that his childhood Sunday-school heroes, like Noah, David, Gideon and Samson, were quickly replaced with all-star quarterbacks, baseball pros, track stars, and Olympic gold-medalists. Consequently, he was easily swayed by the enticing sirens that can come with such attractive popularity, namely partying and promiscuity—a Babylon with bleachers that lurks beneath most grids, courts, fields, and diamonds—especially when the target is so proficient at them all. These sirens and their consequences Jackson offhandedly diminished from the underbelly of his young-adult landscape. But the very One who made Noah, David, Gideon, and Samson such household names—at least in the Hall of Faith—was not about to let His childhood convert Jackson Osborne settle for a simple Hall of Fame. By the time Jackson was a senior in high school and the notoriety was going to his head, God decided to get into it. But it appeared that the Holy Spirit's prompting was no match for a referee's whistle or a cheerleader's pompoms (Paraclete was out-scored by a pair of cleats). By the time Jackson was playing sports in college, he was spinning out of control, which was just about the time that God decided that his dark blue Chevrolet Silverado should do the same. He was well known for his ability to hold his liquor, but dipsomania was no match for narcolepsy! While speeding down a highway close to his home after a very long and late-night double feature of football game and victory party, the large palm tree in the median found him totally asleep at the wheel when it bifurcated the Chevrolet's hood clear up to the dashboard and wrapped the engine block around its trunk like a mink stole. Jackson was rendered unconscious upon impact and had fallen into a coma by the time firemen and paramedics had arrived. They precariously pulled Jackson out of what was left of the driver's side after the generator-powered teeth of the Jaws of Life were finished cutting, spreading, and pulling—crunching their upper and lower hydraulic incisors on deformed metal, frayed wires, and burnt rubber, all covered in a confetti of broken glass—allowing first responders to get a grip on their inert occupant. His parents rightfully feared for the very life in its jaws when they received that fateful phone call from a somber police sergeant in the wee hours of the morning. In a macabre twist, the scene of the accident was actually on the way to the hospital, so Jackson's father and mother gazed in horror at the nearly unrecognizable, crushed remains of the Silverado being hoisted onto a tow truck as they sped by, the visual of destruction adding mounting justification for them to fear that the dire twists of fate were adversely wringing out the balance of their son's fragile life.

"It truly is a miracle that he lived," said the white-robed surgeon, doctors, and nurses, many waiting-room hours later.

"A larger Hand of protection must have been on him." They all vaguely credited the inexplicable Higher Power that would so often providentially visit the halls of the hospital and at once turn their assorted medical degrees on their heads.

When Jackson came to, he also came to his senses. He was convinced that God was trying to get his attention, and that he may not survive the next attempt. For someone previously so active, Jackson's convalescence was a non-physical exercise in frustration with the prolonged confinement and immobility necessary for the complete repair of life and limb. If anything, it gave Jackson time to think, and to pray. It was obvious to Jackson (and to his relieved parents) that he had been given back his life, and the correct response to this was to re-dedicate it, scars and all. He was in just such a state when he checked his cell phone one day out of bored habit and found a text from a girl in Monument whom he had not seen or talked to for years. So that was how "Neck Brace" first contacted "Body Cast," to compare notes and competing stories on divine, car-crashing attention-grabbers, trying to make road kill out of independence and pride.

Jackson was a bigger guy, with even bigger ambitions—some driven by "as God is my witness" and others more "devil-may-care." Add to this his newfound lease on life, and he became a very attractive prospect for the correspondingly convalescent, and bored, Sharayah. When they both got back on their feet, they began to see each other. Their childhood friendship was aging rapidly. About the time I was finishing putting up my award-winning Halloween decorations in early October, they were officially dating. I liked Jackson. So much so that when they left our house on Chestnut Street to go on their first date, I shut the front door behind them, and muttered to myself after they both were well out of earshot, "Marry her!" This was, however, more the private wedding of my *own* impetuousness and overconfidence. Maria, however, was *not* out of earshot, and was staring at me from the kitchen with her standard folding-of-the-arms and knowing, corresponding look.

"What?" I said with a shrug, palms up, my inflections implying that I had only stated what I thought, at the moment, was the obvious.

Her smile back to me conveyed that she had given thought to the same thing.

It wasn't long before Jackson and Sharayah were, in fact, talking marriage. Even so, Sharayah would still come home from time to time frustrated after dates with Jackson and complain how "the blundering galoot was so clumsy and cagey at expressing himself." Whether about confessing a secret compartment of his (which he protected with an undercurrent of vagaries that kept him under the radar and out of any public or private scrutiny just as fast as possible—a shield he had polished to perfection for as long as he could remember), or simply giving a sincere compliment to her. On the occasions when I was included in these conversations about Jackson—which were predominantly just between Maria and Sharayah—I would wince at the gawkiness of some of Jackson's alleged attempts at communicating to my complicated and assured oldest daughter. I wanted to come alongside him and encourage him that he was not alone, at least in his feelings of emotional inadequacy. Not with history's long list of males who have tried to talk their way out of that same ineptitude, often with disastrous results already stacked against them!

No, no male is exempt, nor the marriages they enter!

JOURNAL "ISM": Even the wisest man in the world found he was just a "wise guy" when it came to girls. And it only got worse when he decided to break out in song! It was like he was trying to sort out some culturally confusing, Shakespearean romp, when Solomon's "Titillating Tune" turns her darling lily head to gaze at the ruddy prince singing on his purple-padded palanquin while rambling up the road, followed by sixty members of his palatial man-cave. Just then, a jealous shepherd-lover-boy creates his own private stag party by leaping around like a gazelle, and also heaping compliments her way in order to woo her away from a thorny, royal situation and regain her diverted attention.

"Hey, dove eyes! My little filly! I want to harness you and move your distracted, palm-tree body over here, so that I can look beyond your tower of a nose into those two swimming pools, and stroke the royal tapestry of your goat hair, and run my fingers over the bulging contours of the pomegranate sides of your face in your mountain-sized head. So that my horrible comparisons can make your ribbon-like red lips part into a simile smile that reveals a rack of lamb teeth unlike any other, oozing with milk-and-honey saliva like a bee's nest! And when you laugh, my wandering eyes cannot help themselves but to rapidly descend like King Kong down your ivory skyscraper neck—that is rattling all manner of chains, ornaments, and necklaces with mirthful convulsions—until they reach the quivering fruit clusters of your Bambi breasts! Then I spy your navel the size of a wine goblet, framed in a round waist like a bale of wheat held up by bejeweled legs of bling. When I breathe in the pungent smell of your apple breath and your garments fresh off the clothesline of a Lebanese flea market, I want to get punch-drunk, sweep you off your Shulammite, sandaled feet, thrust you under a garden fountain, and throw away the key!"

He could have saved himself a whole lot of trouble by just sighing while looking at her and quietly saying, "Flawless!"

May 1, 2011

As matrimony seemed right around the corner, our little family was endearing itself to the charming, future son-in-law, Jackson Osborne. Although no one in the family was exactly sports-minded (unless you count jump rope, hopscotch, cheerleading, and show choir), Jackson's mania for all things sports was a whole new world for us—and, at times, contagious. He was wild about baseball and a rabid fan of the Los Angeles Dodgers, "bleeding blue," as he claimed.

RAISED!

I remember actually borrowing Jackson's baseball uniform from his high-school days for a synopsis I performed for the retired and fun-loving, 70-something Crusader Class at Our Father's Evangelical Church. Given Jackson's brawny build, the uniform was understandably oversized to the point of being billowy. I looked more like Bozo the Clown than Don Drysdale. This assessment was also agreed upon by the pun-loving Crusader Class, who quipped that I actually *did* look the part of class clown. Nevertheless, there I was, standing in front of the cackling crowd, trying to look down from underneath the oversized baseball cap at the piece of paper taped to the palm of an ill-fitting catcher's mitt in my left hand, while simultaneously trying (for effect) to occasionally toss in the air a baseball in my right hand, as well as balance a heavy baseball bat that was wedged under my armpit—a feat worthy of any seasoned circus performer, for which I looked the part!

> *"It was the final inning. The playoff game of the camp baseball tournament was smartly favoring the Egyptians, who were ahead by three runs. But the Israelites were up to bat, and started with their famous pinch-hitter, Half-breed. Half-breed was known for his foul mouth. Through a wad of chewing gum, he would utter all sorts of blasphemous curses, especially when the Egyptian pitcher threw another strike with the stone ball. His Israelite mother, Shelomith, and grandmother, Dibri, were in the grandstands, trying to cheer Half-breed on, but all the while very embarrassed by his foul-ball mouth. A fight broke out between Half-breed and the Egyptian pitcher when he threw what looked like an intentional inside ball and hit Half-breed in the shin. Half-breed threw his bat into the stands and came running*

"Car-Jacked"

out to the pitcher's mound, swearing offensively. After they were pulled apart, Half-breed was confined to the Israelite dugout. The owner of the baseball team decided to punish Half-breed for his actions by letting the entire Israelite team throw balls at him while he stood helplessly on home plate. He could still be heard faintly cursing under a pile of rocks as the crowd emptied out of the stadium."

"Turn to Leviticus, Chapter 24."

RAISED!

May 3, 2011

I received an invitation from Jackson over the phone one afternoon at my office, during my semester break from seminary, after the award-winning Christmas decorations were, once again, warehoused in their pre-assigned Bethlehem manger doubling as my two-car garage. He wanted to take me out to a restaurant of my choice. This was simultaneously suspicious and exciting. First of all, it was suspicious because Jackson was apparently paying. It was also exciting because what could possibly be the only reason that Jackson was paying? The selection of the location did not take long. After all, I had had so many decisive exchanges under the eaves of this particular eatery, that it seemed only fitting that it should, once again, oversee this next conversation that I anticipated would also fall under the category of decisive. Henceforth, we were facing one another, ensconced in a booth at the Rush More Coffee House a week later. After the preparatory chitchat had run out of steam and silenced our booth, Jackson grew edgy. As such, I thought I could relieve his blatant tension by upsetting the balance of nature and asking him the question, myself! Only re-written from my perspective.

"So, Jackson, do you want to be my son-in-law?"

His fidgety body language and taut face instantly slackened, and he smiled from ear-to-ear at the relief of it all. "Yes!" he answered, enthusiastically. I still could not shirk my responsibilities, and, so, I put on my new father-in-law hat for a moment.

"Jackson, while Sharayah will be very busy over the next few months planning and preparing for your first wedding, you need to be busy for the rest of your life planning and preparing for your second wedding!" He looked at me with a combination of vexation and astonishment. I knew what he was thinking through all of the facial stupefaction, and I began to allay his befuddlement and put his fears to rest, but very slowly, so that the point would not be forgotten.

"At the next wedding, you need to present Sharayah 'radiant.'"

"*The next wedding?*" was all he could contribute and chomp nervous bites of hamburger at the same time.

"Yep," I replied. "The Apostle Paul tells all of the husbands at the church in Ephesus that they are to get off their major Asia Minor high horses and be more like Christ and His Church. The Head of the Church sets the one-and-only example for the 'head of the home.' Without that one-and-only example, the husband's 'home head' distinction becomes titular, wishful thinking at best. Mere job *title* rather than actual job *description*."

From the look in his big, brown eyes, I was possibly losing Jackson, or maybe he was subtly wrestling with the concept under *my* radar, so I got right to the point. "In other words, the groom does everything in his power to present his bride *radiant* from the first wedding day, right up to the second one, when Christ returns for His Bride, the Church. That's what the Greek word *endoxos* means, 'glorious,' 'splendid,' 'honorable'—in a word, 'radiant!'"

Perhaps a bit too much seminary over lunch, but I couldn't help myself. This had just been inserted into my theological brain and was at the top of the homework heap, readily extractable.

"If Sharayah, over the years, becomes tired and worn out, haggard, defeated, then you're not doing your job . . . biblically. This tiredness is not necessarily physical, but in her spirit, her outlook, her demeanor. In all ways, she needs to be fed and cared for. At least, that's what Paul says."

"I agree!" affirmed Jackson with alacrity, warming up to the concept almost too immediately. Regardless, he seemed genuinely excited to get things started, no matter how formidable the potential obstacles.

"Another thing," I continued, deflating Jackson somewhat. "Earn the right to be submitted to." I let this one simmer for a minute. "Paul also tells the wives at the church in Ephesus that they are to submit to their husbands. Why?"

Jackson was about to attempt an answer, but he caught that my question was meant to be rhetorical, and so advisedly took another bite of his hamburger while I elucidated.

"Because the servant leadership of Jesus is in view here. But it puts wives in a dicey position if the husband is not living up to his end of the bargain. They just want to bark orders and make all of the decisions, thinking they have been charged by God to do so. On the contrary, they should have their noses in Scripture and their knees on the ground. Then, and only then, can a husband inspire confidence and assurance in his wife. Only then can his judgment be trusted." Jackson nodded. He seemed very receptive to this unintentional mini-sermon on all things husbandry coming from the future father-of-the-bride. At least my advice was a far cry from that of Memucan, who, with the insubordinate queen Vashti in his crosshairs, took up a good chunk of Esther, Chapter One, by railing against the entire race of women in general, right in front of a tipsy King Xerxes, in order to protect the paper-thin respect and precarious control of all Persian couch potatoes with remote controls under their right thumbs and their kept women under their left.

"One final thought. Sharayah has had her share of abandonment issues. So I am handing you damaged goods in a sense. But aren't we all?"

A nod of understanding from Jackson, again with a mouthful of food. When they had swapped colorful, car-rallying testimonies early on in their dating, among other things, he had heard Sharayah's story about her ordeal with my parents.

"So I would make one request of you, Jackson."

Jackson's look to me was anxious to comply.

"Never just tell my daughter that you love her." I paused. An unexpected, deeper emotion was trying to bubble to the surface and constrict my throat, water my eyes. "Tell her that you love her and that you're not going anywhere!"

A light bulb switched on in Jackson's head, and he gave me another nod of agreement, along with his famously winsome, reassuring smile.

I nodded back, transparently.

"That's what Maria now has to tell me."

June 24, 2011

Hello, Journal! Now that I have a summer break from seminary, I can relate the events of Jackson and Sharayah's wedding, after his proposal to her, right on the front porch of our Chestnut Street home! It was planned for June, and it was upon us in another one of Forrest Ripley's "blinks." Jackson and Sharayah had always loved the beach and so decided that the Osborne-Block wedding would take place on a stretch of beach in front of the historic Hotel Del Coronado in San Diego. The small, intimate wedding would include only immediate family (with five from the Block side missing, of course). Samantha flew in (or arrived by covered wagon—I am not sure how she arranged overland transportation with the Thousand Hills Cattle and Dude Ranch). A larger reception was to be held the following week in the gymnasium of Our Father's Evangelical Church. So, there we were, the groom and groomsmen all dressed in black tuxedos like so many barefoot penguins out for a day at the beach (except for one old-fashioned penguin, "Papa" Ponticelli, who could not possibly parade around in bare feet—webbed or otherwise. Sandy beach or not, this particular penguin insisted on wearing shiny black wingtips fresh out of a shoebox tucked in his closet expressly reserved for weddings and funerals). The bride and bridesmaids looking "radiant" in a barefoot, fairy-tale ball sort of way, completely incongruous to the flightless, aquatic male birds waddling 'round about them. In the center of it all was the Reverend Reginald Osborne, Jackson's octogenarian grandfather, who came out of retirement one last time to expressly officiate the wedding of his grandson. It was a beautiful wedding, unfolding to the gentle soundtrack of ocean waves and calls of seagulls floating overhead, a soundtrack that had been heard by the nearby hotel guests since 1888. A cozy, intimate gathering of bride, groom, and family members. It was also intimate between father and daughter, who were about to enter into a new, adult relationship with one another, as initiated by my over-rehearsed line that I spoke expressively while facing the peaceable witness of the blue Pacific Ocean,

"Her mother and I!"

June 25, 2011

A church gymnasium oftentimes does not get enough credit for the many memories that it fosters. That is usually reserved for other, more obvious venues like church sanctuaries, family rooms and kitchens of your childhood home, classrooms and hallways of your old high school, and frequented hotels at vacation destinations. But a church gymnasium is not limited to just athletic events—a memorable experience as well—but also has the distinct advantage of being able to be transformed by its occupants to fit any necessary occasion: a ladies luncheon, hoe-down square dance, missions fair, craft bazaar, birthday "gala," AWANA awards ceremony, haunted house, and, yes, a wedding reception. For me, to walk into the gymnasium at Our Father's Evangelical Church was just such a walk back in time. The more the years "blinked" by, the more these padded walls could talk, the more the varnished, hardwood floor gave up story after story, the more we gave thanks for the memories.

Another one was on the way as our music minister, Caspar Goodnight, acting as resident D.J., put on the traditional wedding march over the portable P.A. system and "Neck Brace" and "Body Cast" emerged from their plaster testimonies and entered the O.F.E. gymnasium all cleaned up, once again in wedding dress and tuxedo, after a week-long honeymoon in San Diego.

Associate Pastor Grayson Pomeroy presided over the proceedings, after which all of the usual components of a wedding reception commenced: giving introductions, offering congratulations, proposing toasts, eating cake, throwing bouquets, all within a bona fide fairyland of twinkling white lights, white lace, and elegant table centerpieces, compliments of our dear and dedicated friends at Our Father's Evangelical Church.

Another memory to be piled on for me in the O.F.E. gymnasium was the father-daughter dance. Sharayah and I swayed to the title song from Disney's "Beauty and the Beast." Both a little scared, neither one prepared, we held each other close, a loving, substantial, sentimental hug that capped off more than two decades of living together—bittersweet and strange, finding you can change, learning you were wrong. We whispered, laughed, and cried, the only two in the gymnasium, or the world for that matter, for those 2 minutes and 29 seconds. When the song concluded, and applause broke out from all quarters of the gym, Sharayah and I embraced again, knowing that even though we were about to enter a new phase in our relationship, we would always and forever be the best of "Buds," as certain as the sun, rising in the East.

June 26, 2011

The next day, the immediate family gathered together once again, this time at our home on Chestnut Street for the opening of Sharayah's and Jackson's wedding presents. When it was all said and done, we loaded up their car and bade the new husband and wife "Goodbye," as they drove away to their new apartment—located just down Valentino Avenue past the Rush More Coffee House, on the corner of Garbo Way at Chaplin Circle, north of Max Stellar Blvd., a block east of the Museum—in other words, right here in Monument.

"Adopt-Shun"

July 6, 2011

I returned to my office late yesterday afternoon to find the usual arc of sticky notes forming a half-moon curvature around the central desk pad. One particular sticky note at the apex of the bow caught my eye. It read "Seth Block," with the corresponding phone number, as dictated, underscoring the name. But my secretary, Jill, not knowing the gravity of what just such a phone message from the owner of our business might portend, and harkening back to the many discussions we have had together about the rubber-stamping banality of Christian bumper stickers, tried to be funny by adding a quote of her own below the number, "Your father is coming. Look busy!" I smiled at the note and Jill's playful intentions, in spite of another chill doing a hundred-yard dash up my spine.

I made the return phone call with great trepidation, sensing . . . something. My father, somehow knowing it would be me on the other end of the line, answered crisply. He got right to his needle-sharp point, requesting an audience with me. Then, quite demandingly, he set the exact time—for tomorrow afternoon. His tone over the past years was now becoming predictable and bothersome, a stiff combination of bluster and bully. I wondered with not a little presentment at both his initiative and his exactitude. With what felt like the scraping of the bottom of the barrel of a son's obeisance, I cleared my calendar, and he hung up.

When I arrived back at the office after cutting short my lunch with Tristan Holbert today, Jill informed me with nonverbal expressions perfected over the years (not only in business, but from her insightful observations about life, family, and their rough edges, as gleaned from her occasional abrasions from being tightly sandwiched between two immovable Blocks, and she being the only person at times who prevented them from scuffing one another, with the foregone conclusion that they would surely rub each other the wrong away) that my father was already sitting in my office, waiting. But the look on her face—usually as clear to me as skywriting—was trying to tell me something more, and there seemed to be no clear-but-discreet facial expression for "Ambush!" The intended smoke signal had dissipated in a whiff caused by the opening of my office door.

I found to my surprise that he was not alone. He had brought, by way of backup, his attorney and "wingman," Bergen Stevens. (The ambush was textbook Sanballat, Tobiah, and Geshem, the Three Stooges of Nehemiah, Chapter Six, and masters of the slapstick, comedic art of opposition to God. The trio wanted so badly to perform their intimidation act on the plain of Ono, which—for those in the know—should be pronounced, "Oh, no!") I had met Bergen occasionally over the years when my father ran the Block Insurance business, and Bergen would "pop on over" with his father from their high-rise, lawyerly perch in Los Angeles, to discuss some pressing legal business. Still snakelike, he nonetheless sensed my look of recoiling surprise and stood up to greet me with the congeniality of Benedict or Brutus, depending on your preferred century. His attempt at small talk, under the silent, impatient eye of my father was so convivially oily as to feel like last rites from a not-so-compassionate priest obviously anxious to get on with it and see one quickly ushered into the hereafter. At a rather ostentatious position shift from my father in his chair, accompanied by the classic, clarion call of throat-clearing, Bergen got the message, and any further, hollow cordialities were abruptly halted.

My father leaned back and said matter-of-factly, "I am selling the business." Period.

This throw, out of left field, hit its mark.

"What?" I said, gobsmacked. Surprise and heat rising to my face by a rush of blood, the result of a swift prediction of an incoming onslaught to my central nervous system. Like bellows in a blacksmith's smelter, my heart increased its pulsating to the cadence of inner-space demands screaming from every corner of circulation, as all sensorial systems went to DEFCON 1, bracing for impact.

Seth Block, owner of the Block Insurance Agency, a family business that he had purchased from his founding father, Colby Block, in the mid-1970s, let the third and final generation know that it was the end of the line. He had been in secret negotiations with another insurance agency in nearby Pasadena for the past three months, that was very interested in snatching up the Block Insurance empire. The papers had been drawn up, and the deal had been done (I remember as a kid walking backward while clam-digging in the frigid, waist-high ocean at Pismo Beach and being stung in the back of my bare leg by a jellyfish. At the moment, that bygone feeling of searing pain had less surprise and venom than this meeting).

According to my father, our chummy quorum was merely a "courtesy call," with Bergen merely listening in, who was presently nodding . . . courteously.

"When?" I weakly squeaked out.

"July 25." Nineteen days!

"I wouldn't buy a television that quickly!" I was gaining my footing on a swelling ocean floor, which was saying something, as I did not even notice the brief earth tremor that shook the office and vibrated my desk at that moment.

"You will be well taken care of at the new agency, Ian." It was Bergen, ambulance chaser becoming ambulance driver. "They are willing to hire you, Jill, and the staff in order to work the files from the sale of your dad's business, for the sake of client retention, you know," he explained rather nervously.

I didn't like the way he had turned this phrase. While my father might still own the business, the files were, in fact, *my* clients. My father's clients had been leaving precipitously over the years, especially since he and my mother had moved to Ventura. The bulk of the business was now clients that I had written, a goodly sum of which were members of Our Father's Evangelical Church. It was these faces that paraded before my eyes, as I pictured Seth Block pulling the plug on the family business, like some newly emboldened Assyrian army from the north, coming down to claim land already promised to another, of which I was now just a "retainer."

"You can't do this!"

"It's already done, Ian," answered Bergen sibilantly.

And then the final blow from Block to chip. "I have leased the office to the new agency, as they want to establish a second branch in Monument, so they will be coming by next week to look things over, and to meet with you about hiring agreements

"Adopt-Shun"

for you and the staff. You will be working for them on July 25." He looked over at Bergen and nodded—their cue. They both stood up to go, with Bergen smoothly sliding an employment proposal from the new agency onto my desk. Glancing down upon it, I looked no further than the logo and letterhead of the new agency triumphantly bedecking the top.

"No!" I said to both of their backs.

My father turned around. "You have no choice, Ian." The insouciant formality in his voice was so uncharacteristically calm and confident as to be chilling. How had my father and mother hatched this scheme, all closed-up in their Ventura condo? As they say, "An airless room produces bad decisions." Or, could it be the very breath of God, who means for good what first looks like a whole lot of harm?

If so, I still sat there in my office, stultified by a wave of guilt and shame that *I* had somehow caused all of this, not by any deficiency in business sensibilities, but by sheer upbringing or just plain existence. (In an unfair comparison from which I am more than paled, I think about Jesus, on donkey-back, hearing the hooves crunch the rows of fronds strewn out in front of him, the sound barely audible over the "Crown Him King" screeching of the crowd—a crowd that would screech "Crown Him King" again, one short week later, for completely different reasons, with completely different consequences. The Son of God—the only accurate palm reader in history—knew how to read these enormous tea leaves all too well as his burro plodded along.)

There was something about Ian Block that had become so unlovable from the perspective of his family that he was no longer worth fighting for. Or, perhaps I was simply a painful reflection of my father's own shortcomings and imperfections. Regardless, he had delivered a heavy boxful of unanswered questions that day, finally relieving himself of the burden, as he dropped the weighted package in my lap, the label on the return address reading "Sins of the Father."

JOURNAL "ISM": Like father, like son? I remember now. It was in the Bereans class around October. I had darkened the door of a migratory Halloween costume shop that had temporarily occupied a vacant warehouse on Max Stellar Boulevard down by the freeway for more visibility. It was a macabre experience that seemed to require triplicate sixes on the right hand or forehead for entry, and one that I did not relish, in spite of my affection for this time of year. The reminiscent smell of ghoulish, rubber masks was distinct, as were the recorded blood-curdling screams coming from highly advanced, mechanical decorations. Large, hairy spiders suspended from the ceiling and giant eyeballs right out of First Corinthians 12:17 staring up at you from round, black bins. I stayed motivated and undeterred by my noble cause and picked up a light-purple, paper-and-glitter unicorn's horn that attached to my forehead with the aid of a rubber band. Careful not to mess up my overly sprayed blond hair, I stretched the rubber band around my head the following Sunday morning, as I stood in front of the class and read about God's fiery difference between "incense" and "incensed."

> *"Being a crooked mayor kept Amaziah very busy covering his tracks, so he was never home for dinner. Consequently, his bored wife, Jecoliah, started her own business, the 'Scents of Salem' perfume shop. Her son, Uzziah, used to help in the store until he, too, became mayor after his father's untimely death. One Sunday at church, his mother caught crooked Uzziah sitting in the pews, with bottles of perfume stolen*

"Adopt-Shun"

from her shop hidden in his jacket. While running back down the aisle, with his mother in hot pursuit, Uzziah tripped and fell on his face as one the bottles of stolen perfume broke on his forehead. The shards of glass and spilled scented oil so disfigured and stained Uzziah's now-bulbous forehead, that he was forced to live alone in disgrace, with a sign painted above his front door, 'Mayor Unicorn.'"

"Turn to 2nd Chronicles, Chapter 26."

July 10, 2011

This game-playing of hot potato with father-son blunders is far more than scapegoat identity crises. Far more confusing than knowing the difference between Milton and Bradley. It renders the strained recipients both stained and shamed. As the tossing back and forth of the now-sizzling spud of sin between my father and me accelerated, I did not have time to wash my hands properly between rounds. Finally, I was left in a constant state of grime for my crimes, in desperate need of an entire bloodbath. The little plastic communion cups at Our Father's Evangelical Church sometimes feel too miniaturized to do the trick. Sanctification by shot glass. The task at hand is so complex that oftentimes I am inclined to pour the contents on top of my head in an effort to cover all of the bases.

After all, it is what symbols do best. A fingerpost pointing to the real thing from that very first, last supper (on which night Jesus was "delivered over," not "betrayed"—that word sounds more like an anthropopathism—giving a surprised emotion to an omniscient God. The element of surprise would only come from our human perspectives being caught off-guard and not understanding what was really going on. During the whole ordeal, Jesus was about the business of voluntarily giving Himself up—nothing Prefect or Priest could do would catch Him by surprise). A few hours later, the real stuff would flow from the real body of the One whom we have pierced, and the cleansing for all humanity would begin. The temptation to avoid the excruciating pain afoot was, I'm sure, a real teaser for the human half of the God-man. But He submitted to the earth-shattering cup-drinking nonetheless. All of this the direct result of a much more functional Father-Son relationship.

"Adopt-Shun"

As such, the Lord's Table is a good place to dive under during blitzes of incoming taters!

July 27, 2011

The employment proposal from the Pasadena agency was out of the question. The cut in salary alone made our life as we now knew it unsustainable. It was decided that I should make a plea bargain to Bergen Stevens to see if he might entice my embittered father to come to his senses.

That night, I thought empathetically of poor Yamani from another synopsis that I had given to the Lifetime class at O.F.E. during a "Return to Sender" series on the prophet Isaiah:

> *"In 714 B.C., Yamani was the newly appointed operator of the strategically located Ashdod drawbridge for a large corporation, the Southern E & E Company. One day, rival Tartan Industries, owned by an even-larger corporation, Northern Sargon Enterprises, told Yamani to lower the drawbridge so that their huge cargo ships carrying military transports could pass through; he refused. Security from Tartan Industries stormed the tollbooth, threw Yamani into the river, and declared martial law, creating a corporate monopoly for Northern Sargon Enterprises and seizing control over all of the Ashdod assets. Fearing for his life and career, Yamani escaped back to the Southern E & E Company, only to find that it had rebranded itself as a nudist colony!"*
>
> *"Turn to Isaiah, Chapter 20."*

That Monday, Bergen Stevens said that he would try, more out of pity than reality. In the end, his appeal only made my father all the more hardened. "I'm sorry, Ian," said Bergen over the phone. "It appears you still have no choice."

After I hung up the phone, I leaned back in my desk chair and stared up at the ceiling. That was the second time in as many days that I had been told that I had no choice. But was that really the case? It was then that I remembered an old "Option to Buy" agreement that my father had lovingly drawn up with Bergen Stevens for his younger son years ago during better, halcyon days between us, that gave me just that—an "option to buy" the agency at half price! Perhaps my father had thought that I had forgotten the binding agreement after all these years since I was so involved in church ministry and worked the insurance business only to pay the bills. But crises make one remember things . . . quickly. I opened a lower drawer in my desk and found an old, battered Manila envelope, whose edges looked like they had been a teething toy. Upon breaking the seal, I let my fingers do the walking through the yellowed pages, and there it was, the "Option to Buy" agreement. At the bottom of the second page of legalese were the signatures of my father, myself, and the eel-like scrawl of a young Bergen Stevens, consummating the deal.

In spite of the widespread pastoral advice to the contrary, I still felt like I was flying in the face of the Chapter Six counsel from Saint Paul's first letter to that lawsuit-happy, dysfunctional family of God hiding under the increasing shadow of the rock-hard Acrocorinth, and who were morally straddling their Corinthian feet as wide as the nearby Isthmus. Even so, I asked for legal counsel from a member of Our Father's Evangelical Church, the large, stout, impeccably dressed and undeniably

"Adopt-Shun"

brilliant Tiberius Vaughan, who would represent me against my father and his Latter-Day Saint, Bergen Stevens.

A few days later, I received a copy of a document with the letterhead of the Los Angeles law firm of "Vaughan, Fisk, and Sternberg." The document stated the firm's new representation of one Ian Block and the action demanding the exercising of the Block Insurance "Option to Buy" Agreement. This letter of the law and all that was behind it was no match for the small-town (by comparison), father-son corporation of "Stevens and Stevens." With little to no pushback, the half-price sale of the business was rapidly moving through the levels of legality to reality. There was a "We'll take it from here" attitude from Tiberius Vaughan and his flock of legal eagles, and it was not a small price to pay for the service. For a sizeable chunk of change pulled out of our savings, they were handling all of the back-and-forth communications between "Vaughan, Fisk, and Sternberg" and "Stevens and Stevens." I was taken out of the loop, and my input was rarely required.

The only time I heard from "Ti" was a personal email sent to me during the final portions of the settlement agreements. All it said was, "You were right about your father." Implying, I suppose, that my initial descriptions of my father when first retaining Tiberius Vaughan were being proven correct. It was rumored that this assessment had been advanced by my father, who did not want to give a penny more of financial aid to me than what had already been stipulated in the agreement. Or, in Vaughan vernacular, my father wanted to "reap his field right up to its edge," using Leviticus, Chapter 19 as his Exhibit A.

JOURNAL "ISM": I remember, during his all-too-brief tenure at O.F.E., Dr. Banning's oft-repeated invitation artfully interspersed throughout his earlier, eloquent sermons, that, either by force or natural causes, all of us should get up off the pews and "join the dance!" I remember feeling quite intimidated by this "join the dance!" entreaty for some reason, and, after a few weeks, I wrote a letter to square-dance-caller Pastor Banning stating as much. Not sure what God thought of me during this time of suing, dishonoring, and its parental upheaval, I wrote that I was not too keen at the notion of looking God in the eye right about now, and quite content to sit safely against the wall of the gymnasium—like pre-king Saul skulking among the baggage—silently nursing a harmless glass of punch, misanthropically watching others triumphantly two-step with Jesus, while I gently patted the pocket of my sport coat that secured my blank dance card in unmarked secrecy. I was not surprised that the very busy, heavily scheduled, world-traveling Dr. Banning did not respond to my letter in kind. However, the next time I saw him, he marched right over to me and gave me a tight, prolonged, knowing hug. Nothing was said. It didn't need to be. That's what fathers do with their sons.

The downside to this particular "dance with Jesus" is that I not only had to leave my seat, I had to sell it!

July 28, 2011

After putting my "John Hancock" on a stack of legal-sized documents requiring the signature of Ian Block in order to close the case, it became clear that, in order to pay for even half the value of the Block Insurance Agency (and mounting legal fees), there was no alternative but to sell our Chestnut Street house. This was something I thought I would never have to do again since

"Adopt-Shun"

Owen and I dismantled our childhood home on Vista Street when my parents first moved up north.

Trying to process all of this was an enormous emotional undertaking. It was offset only by a good dose of Psalm 25, twenty-two verses from brooding King David, who likely had no idea that his plea would help not only himself in his current predicament but also millions and millions of other people down through the ages in and on trial, including me.

"Ian, it's time to downsize." That was how Maria had courageously summarized our plight, which both of our emotional daughters had also summarized as "selling their memories." While the cause for this uprooting seemed cruel and unusual, it did make sense at some level. We both held on to this tenuous perspective, as we began the arduous task of packaging a quarter century of life from under one roof into transportable samplings to be exported to another, unknown shelter. This undertaking would take months. While the wheels of justice slowly turned in Los Angeles at "Vaughan, Fisk and Sternberg," and our frenzied realtor scoured the Monument listings for a new house for Maria and me, I could feel a burdensome self-wavering as I walked from task to task. Not from an earthquake this time but from psychological underpinnings upon which I had always relied, being knocked out from underneath me by a Messianic mallet, held by the very One who had a stone for a pillow! With my good ear, I could hear the tearing of roots from unforgiving earth. Embedded vines of recollection and undergrowth of routines were being severed as I was being pulled from non-giving soil. Little did I realize how entangled I had become, until I was slowly, tortuously disentangled. At least all of these adjustments—hard as they were—were still within the seemingly unchangeable embrace of my beloved hometown of Monument.

I could handle anything, provided it happened within my city limits!

Still ringing in my ear was Commandment Number Five, made at 7,500 feet above sea level to those squabbling families down below that had been pulled out of their comfort zones, ready to turn on God and each other, "Honor your father and mother, so that you may live long . . ." I thought sardonically that the reason you needed to live long is because it would take you that long to recover from the honoring!

July 29, 2011

The realtor called with yet another prospective house in our beleaguered quest for new lodging. But this time, it was a keeper. A beautiful little, one-story, scaled-down yellow cottage about a mile east of our current home that had just come up for sale in the Hollywood Heights subdivision, with not only a great view of the right side of Rudolph Valentino's head to our left but also a panoramic view to the southwest of the declension of the valley sloping all the way down to the freeway. I thought that I would feel like the gang with poor priest Ezra, who started bawling their heads off as soon as they clapped their eyes on the Temple sequel all shrink-wrapped and growth-stunted. But Maria and I fell in love with the little home at once, and we pounced. In spite of all our preparations over the months, the move was still an enormous undertaking and could not have been survived were it not for the "family of choice" at Our Father's Evangelical Church lending a hand and breaking a back on our behalf.

Once we were settled in, Maria and I were happier than we had ever thought possible. While beloved, our old house had become too large, too unwieldy, too expensive to adequately maintain. Our new cottage, nestled in Hollywood Heights, had simplified things significantly, to the point that we did not even give much thought to our previous life on Chestnut Street, a memory morphine for which we thanked God, Who always likes to shake things up a bit, all the while knowing that His children are often not too keen on the idea! He had even said to His troubadour David that He much preferred traveling in tent-flapping tabernacles rather than being tied down in stuffy old temples, even with torn curtains. It's as if the Unchangeable One thrived on . . . change! At least for our sake.

September 9, 2011

Tonight, I am sitting in a wingback chair with a book in my lap in front of a roaring fire, surrounded by all of our surviving "stuff" that had made the cut from Chestnut Street to Hollywood Heights. I am also now the sole owner of the Block Insurance Agency, and, dear Diary, still slugging it out in seminary! But I can see the light at the end of the tunnel.

At the Antioch Christian Academy School of Theology, Spiritual Formation classes are foundational, and required. This is driven by the fact that the school can ably teach you Hermeneutics, Greek, and Hebrew, to memorize Scripture and recall spiritual insights like the back of your pencil-cramped hand. But all that comes to nothing if you are later caught as a church leader in some moral indiscretion or scandal, all the while wearing an A.C.A. sweatshirt as a testimony to your supposedly "higher" education. Bible learnin'—at any academic level—is, at times, no match for the opposing ground troops of background, upbringing, personality bents and traits, along with the air strikes of psychological tendencies. It is this delving into the forces of one's "spiritual formation" that lifelines are stretched, examined, connected, and reconnected. A good preacher must know his audience, but a great preacher must first know himself as well.

To that end, I was enrolled in a whole host of Spiritual Formation classes, each tackling some area contributing to the makeup of Ian Block. But, given the fact that I was now in my 50s and frequently finding myself 30 years older than my classmates, I had, unfairly, more work to do! More dirt to unearth, more skeletons in my closet, more drama in my family, more pages in my diary, more scars on my testimony.

One such class required us to undergo a complimentary therapy session conducted by a licensed counselor from the A.C.A. Psychology Department. The session was to last the standard hour, but that was for 29-year-old lifespans! Mine lasted much longer, as I unpacked more than fifty years of testimonial information—the ins and outs, highs and lows, ups and downs, backs and forths—to a very interested, nodding young female therapist. When I had finished, breathless, she looked at me with a satisfied smile and, "out of the mouth of babes," confidently drew a conclusion to my life story thus far with one simple sentence:

"It looks like God is becoming your father."

"Shotgun Wedding"

November 16, 2011

Colton James was lying on his dorm-room bed at the University of Northern Colorado in Greeley, staring at a poster of the Denver Broncos. His roommate, Trey Hart, had just left to go to class, but not before giving Colton a piece of his college-educated mind. Colton was in a "place," and Trey knew it. Not from any particular insight or clairvoyance on Trey's part, Colton had simply unpacked his personal history in conversational bits and pieces to Trey over the past Spring semester. At the behest of Colton's parents, who valued a good education over breathing (as he put it), Colton had spent a couple of semesters right out of high school at the Pikes Peak Community College in Colorado Springs (or "The Springs," as he called it) and then, for reasons no longer clear to him, ended up in the agricultural backwaters of Greeley, trying, ever so diligently, to finally finish his sluggish and circuitous college degree. During his formative years, his family was highly involved at the Christian Chapel in Chisholm, Colorado—originally a small town that was now growing like a weed, just west of Black Forest, and just north of "The Springs."

When Colton was in middle school, there was an overheated turnover within the leadership at their church and an abrupt ouster of accused perpetrators as well. One was an elder, excommunicated not because of immorality or embezzlement; he had simply questioned the efficacy of some old, institutional traditions that were held so near and dear at the church. He was shown the door—a large, distressed oak door that, incidentally, was original with the building of the church a quarter of a century earlier. Through that door went the "sinfully progressive" elder, his wife, and their son—who just happened to be Colton's very best friend from early childhood. At fifteen years old, he was not able to control any of the playing-at-power that goes on in church boardrooms, often with scant regard for its trickle-down effect. Colton just bore the consequences of missing his good buddy, who had disappeared—gone from his life, almost instantly. Understandably, this implanted in young Colton the seed of resentment toward churches in general, church elders in particular, and, more specifically, toward a God who allowed these kinds of things to happen in the first place. In short, the Christian Chapel in Chisholm, Colorado, had wantonly stolen his best friend. Who needs a God who plays so fast and loose with young and innocent hearts? So, Colton began to flounder, his passions deflating like a tire, forcing his sense of direction to falter. So, he sought the usual array of activities to fill the vacuum created by the removal of trust, and in increasingly complex fashion as he got older.

After much oat-sowing, job-bouncing, and school-hopping, he had ended up here, on his dorm-room bed, staring up at John Elway making the same "Hail Mary" pass that he was thinking for his own life, as he seemed to be going nowhere. These thoughts had been the direct result of his recent conversation with roommate Trey Hart, who, after living under the same roof with Colton, had offered a solution to his malaise. Trey had had

"Shotgun Wedding"

his own bumps in the road of life—some so high as to be above the tree line—but he was now quite grounded, or re-grounded, in his faith. Much of this turnaround he attributed to his time as a wrangler at the Thousand Hills Cattle and Dude Ranch. It was this testimonial encouragement from Trey—so convincingly framed—that it was high time his roommate get off his mule-headed behind and get back in the saddle with God, which had caused Colton to fall horizontally on his bed, and eventually to look vertically.

His parents were hesitant at his proposal to leave the University of Northern Colorado at the end of the Spring semester to join up with some spin-off of Buffalo Bill Cody's Wild West show. They had always put supreme importance on getting an education, especially the finishing of one's college degree over and against almost any other competing aspiration. So, this request from their son was, at first, perceived as ridiculous, even a bit seditious. But their years of church involvement at the Christian Chapel in Chisholm carried the day, and they warily agreed that such a brash and daring adventure might be just the thing for their wayward and despondent son. If anything, God would certainly have the good sense to shut the barn door quickly if the whole scheme turned out to be some cock and bull story.

And, to everyone's surprise, Colton's application to the Thousand Hills Cattle and Dude Ranch was accepted, even though Colton, ever the gun enthusiast, still had no horse, or cattle, or dude-ranch experience—breaking, branding, bridling, roping, shoeing, corralling. Unless, of course—his parents quipped—you could count the rocking, mechanical-horse riding he experienced as a child in front of the Walmart in Colorado Springs for just a quarter! At the end of the Spring semester, Colton said "Goodbye" not only to the University of Northern

Colorado in Greeley but also to his Medicine Man of a roommate, Trey Hart. He packed up his meager belongings and drove his questionably drivable Toyota Camry from the sprawling farmlands and rolling hills of Greeley, Colorado, to the jagged peaks encircling the hinterlands of the Rocky Mountains into which was embedded somewhere on the map, the Thousand Hills Cattle and Dude Ranch.

Colton's first summer season at the Ranch saw a stellar rise in his potential and vast expansions of his experiences. He became quite adept in all aspects of his job as a wrangler, and he rose rapidly within those ranks. He was a lead in a matter of weeks. After years of disillusioned encrustation, he regained his winsomely funny, social magnet of a personality to become one of the most popular rodeo clowns of all at Thousand Hills. As such, the summer flew by, and a very different Colton James emerged as a result. A gallant young man, whose full attention God now had. Not wanting in any way to go backwards or impede this spiritual trajectory, Colton didn't hesitate for a minute to remain on staff by signing up for the Fall season at the Ranch Office on a warm summer night in late August.

He left the office and was joined by his best buddy Remington and a herd of fellow wranglers, who had also saddled up for another go-round, and they all decided to celebrate at the "Milk 'n Honey" Dining Hall. No sooner had they grabbed the gold-plated rope handles, and opened the large wooden doors to enter the National Park-size lobby of the Main Lodge, when their posse was greeted by another stampede coming from the opposite direction, this one all lady-like! One, in particular, caught Colton's eye, and turned him on his heels as if he'd been lassoed. She was still gazing up at the massive, twisted elk-horn chandelier hanging in the lobby, while trying to deflect the glass-eyed stares from the hordes of stuffed wildlife that looked as if they had apparently shoved their assorted animal heads into the sloping ceiling from outside, sticking their necks out to sample the warmth from the crackling fireplace below. The girl nearly crashed into a fellow female initiate in front of her as their tour of the Ranch was abruptly halted by the oncoming cattle drive of ruddy wranglers. Colton grabbed the cowgirl tour guide, who was lagging behind, and who also was one of his many female friends and admirers, and asked the name of the new girl. She followed his eye and the tilt of his head, matched the impression with the list on her clipboard and answered,

"Samantha. Samantha Block."

As they say in the West, right then and there: "The horse had bolted!" No one on staff was allowed to date at the Ranch, except for going steady with God. So Colton and Samantha became experts at subtleties. From deft glance-stealing between trail rides from across the horse corral, to playing booted footsies under one of the pond-sized mahogany tables during staff meals. Colton soon made his intentions known that he was "retiring!" He would step down from lead wrangler and leave the Thousand Hills Cattle and Dude Ranch staff at the end of the Fall season for the express purpose of becoming non-staff and thus permitted to date—in particular an on-staff waitress—one Samantha Block.

With backfiring phone connections like an old, neglected, big green tractor, Samantha was lobbing hints over the ensuing months to her exhaust-breathing mother during their routinely hissing and disconnected telephone conversations. But she finally decided to come clean to both of us one Spring evening and confess that she and Colton James were, in fact, an "item." Samantha endured more grilling from her family about this cowboy from Colorado when she arrived at home for her brief, second Christmas break between the Fall and Winter seasons at the Ranch, as well as playfully deflecting every Western stereotype we could throw at her with a confident smile on her face. It was early the following January that Samantha had arranged some time off from the Ranch (due to the slower, less-populated Winter season), so that she and Colton could fly to Los Angeles, and he could meet her wacky California family in Monument. I took the phone from Maria, after Samantha's travel plans were made known. This was getting quite serious and required a father's intervention.

"Samantha?"

"Hey, Daddy!"

"So you're bringing this fellow Colton to the house to meet us?"

"Yes!"

It was time to do a little masculine posturing, seasoned with a bit of fatherly coercion.

"So do you want me to be waiting for him on our front porch when you arrive? Sitting in my rocking chair with my .22 across my lap?" I gave the phone a tough, satisfied look at my he-man blandishments, complete with the universal language of masculinity . . . weaponry!

Samantha chuckled, "Dad, he builds guns!"

I could feel the bullets being ejected one by one from the cartridge of my paternity without me firing a single shot. I was just going to have to try a new approach that did not involve the NRA. "I guess I will just have to intimidate him with my words!" I salvaged. Samantha snickered again over the phone. It was so good to hear her laugh, even if over the subject of her obviously getting very serious with this spawn of Wyatt Earp. So serious that it now required a formal introduction.

And I was unarmed!

"Shotgun Wedding"

January 12, 2012

The cow-couple arrived the first week of January. We took a liking to Colton James immediately. While shorter in height than expected, he still retained a healthy dose of the other two courting essentials—dark and handsome. Colton was polite, charming, and hilariously funny in a playful, distracted, attention-deficit sort of way, which was all communicated with the country drawl, mannerisms, pace, and assurances of the old West—where character mattered. We could see why our younger daughter had been smitten so quickly. They stayed for a week, and we gave Colton a crash course in all things Southern California: famous landmarks, amusement parks, movie studios, favorite restaurants, and star sightings. When we said a tearful "Goodbye" at the airport, Maria and I knew that we had not seen the last of this boy from Chisholm, Colorado. Indeed, we both had a gut feeling then and there that we had, this past week, rather said "Hello" to a future addition to our family. Over the ensuing months, I had a chance to get to know Colton better—both by crackling phone conversations and now by breaking-up Skype chats (a program added to our home computer just to make it seem like Samantha was closer to that same home)—in order to observe his testimony, and to hear his heart. Above all—in my estimation—Colton James had already proven his mettle to me by his courageous navigating of that dreadful, death-defying, twelve-mile dirt road to-and-from the Thousand Hills Cattle and Dude Ranch just to date my daughter! And not in a John Deere, but a Toyota Camry.

March 10, 2012

A few days ago, Colton requested a private Skype conversation with me at my earliest convenience. It was arranged for tonight, and we chatted electronically—a parley of pixels—for more than two hours. My suspicions were confirmed. Colton asked for permission to ask Samantha to marry him, and I heartily agreed.

I did, however, take the screen-to-screen opportunity to give Colton my passionate, "Earn the right to be submitted to" speech, while trying my best to hold any scriptural atomization from my seminary training at bay. It was somewhat "new and improved" since my first daughter giveaway, but the fatherly heart and soul behind it had remained unchanged. Colton, a man raised with a refreshing sense of duty, and the flag-carrying, jingoistic concepts of honor, guts, and glory, all bound together by your word being your bond, took to my little speech immediately. He took to it like a duck takes to water, or like a deer to a forest, a bear to a cave, a buffalo to a prairie, a pheasant to a bush, a pig to mud, a chicken to a coop, a bee to honey, a dog to a hearth. Fortunately for Colton, before I could bury him in nature's cliched idioms, our Skype conversation was disconnected. But not until he, too, had promised to always tell Samantha that he "loved her and was not going anywhere."

April 4, 2012

News was ticking down the telegraph wires and waking up the roosting buzzards by early spring that Samantha Block of Monument, California, was betrothed, and getting hitched to Colton James of Chisholm, Colorado, with a wedding planned for June at our family's favorite vacation destination, Estes Park—the gateway to the Rocky Mountains. To tie the knot, Colton had reserved "Aquila" and "Priscilla" from the stables, two of the Ranch's best horses for mountain trail riding—ones that would not get too spooked by the strong winds that can suddenly come up on the plateaus of the high country—and a picnic lunch courtesy of the "Milk 'n Honey" Dining Hall. He led Samantha up to the round knoll that marked the top of Mustard Seed Mountain—the highest summit on the Ranch's 2,500 acres—got down on one knee, and proposed.

The minute Samantha said "Yes," it seemed that Maria had her hands full as mother-of-the-bride, trying to plan and coordinate a wedding from 1,000 miles away. But plan and coordinate she did, determined to pull off what would surely be a spectacular event. During a rare lull in all of the emotionally combustible hustle and bustle, it suddenly dawned on me that Samantha was not coming back to California! She was about to plant roots in foreign soil, made more so by the long geographic distance between herself and her father. Fortunately, I did not have ample time to digest this fact of finality, as I was abruptly requested by Maria to see to some wedding detail.

June 27, 2012

As you can see, dear Diary, those very same "wedding details" have caused you and me to become estranged. As a matter of fact, I have only a few minutes before I have to rush off to my next task, something to do with cute, western centerpieces made out of horse shoes. But all of it—so I was assured—pertaining to, and crucial for, the matrimonial bliss of the soon-to-be very happy couple! It turns out that the wedding of Colton and Samantha will be a "destination" for many of our friends from Monument; Malcolm and Daniella Davis, and Lorne and Candice Carlson are each going to fly in for the occasion. Dennis and Patty O'Connor are now going to include Estes Park on the itinerary of their long-planned, summer road trip that just happens to occur around the wedding date! Of course, arrangements also had to be made to get Sharayah and Jackson, the elderly Papa and "Ya-Ya" Ponticelli, along with Maria's sister Angela all across state lines and to the chapel on time!

July 17, 2012

The next 48 hours were a whirlwind of activity, with our local hotel suite being turned into Command Central and my wife posing as Joan of Arc, all ironically overlooking the serene waters of Lake Estes, and not France. Errands to everywhere were run on fifteen-minute intervals, usually with the father-of-the-bride at the wheel.

The weather miraculously "held" during the afternoon ceremony, which is how one has to describe atmospheric conditions in Colorado, because if it is not "held" by a greater Hand, it runs amok, like a moody teenager. The ceremony took place at our hotel, under a gazebo on the lawn in front of the lake. The ranks of pre-set folding chairs forming the bride's side represented a flattering showing of dear friends making the long trip from the Golden State. The other side of the aisle, on the groom's side, was filled with what looked like the gun-totin' cast from *Lonesome Dove*, the 1989 television mini-series.

The wedding came off without a hitch in its git-a-long. It was officiated with a drawl by Cab Elliott, the current, bow-legged, ex-rodeo rider turned pastor at the Christian Chapel in

Chisolm. I felt a lump in my throat as I uttered for the second time that life-changing line of permission—first proclaimed four years earlier over the resonant pounding of crashing waves from the Pacific Ocean, and now to a bunch of "fourteeners" poking their pointy heads up from the Rocky Mountain range to see what all the commotion was about,

"Her mother and I!"

The reception was held in the grand ballroom of the hotel and was a splendid affair. Samantha and I danced to the song "You've Got a Friend in Me" from Disney's *Toy Story*. Our dancing embrace had the same emotional tug as had our first goodbye back in August 2010. Only this time we were swaying, and this time my little girl was not coming back! I whispered as much loving sentiment into her ear as our combined composures could handle, all to Randy Newman's promise over the loud speakers,

> *"When the road looks rough ahead*
> *And you're miles and miles from your nice, warm bed*
> *You just remember what your old pal said . . ."*

Before Colton and Samantha departed for their honeymoon in Jackson Hole, Wyoming, another father-daughter hug was required, only this one without an end game. I was so happy for Samantha and the life she had chosen for herself here in Colorado. Colton had already rented a nice apartment for them in Centennial. He had secured a job as a restaurant server while he finished school at the University of Colorado in Denver. Samantha's equestrian talent was spotted a mile away, and she had no trouble obtaining work giving horseback-riding lessons at a nearby stable. We stayed clinging to each other for as long as possible, knowing that, once again, when we let go, there would be 1,000 miles between us.

> *"There isn't anything I wouldn't do for you.*
> *We stick together and can see it through."*

July 18, 2012

Over the next few weeks, Maria and I put our lives back together again in our little cottage in Hollywood Heights, after that matrimonial monsoon known as wedding planning. It was nice to be back home in Monument again, with Sharayah and Jackson just down the street, and Maria's parents right across town, even though we deeply missed Colton and Samantha. But all of this was felt with that facial tingle of Sinai sunburn—supreme gratitude for the incredible blessings that that Trail Boss in the Sky had lavished upon us all. I could parrot an overwhelmed and appreciative King David, who said when the blood on his hands caused God to pass him over and give the general-contractor job of temple-building to his artsy son, Solomon,

> *"Who am I, and what is my family*
> *that you have brought us this far?"*

Still basking in all of God's good fortune as specifically represented by the recent wedding of Colton and Samantha, I wore a rented tuxedo to the Crossroads Class at Our Father's Evangelical Church the next Sunday. Maria actually joined me on this day during my brief series on the book of Esther, "Playing Hangman," wearing her beautiful, sparkling wedding dress (into which she could still fit). We stood at attention in front of

"Shotgun Wedding"

the class like a wedding-cake topper, a statuesque Maria firmly holding a bouquet of silk flowers to her beaded bosom as I read,

> *"It cost a king's ransom to use 'C&H Royal Wedding Planners,' but then daddy's little girl was sure to get hitched! The male proprietors were anything but. However, Hegai and Shaashgaz ran the rigorous "C&H" (Concubines and Harems) one-year program like two effeminate drill sergeants from Susa! A veritable virgin bootcamp of training in oils, cosmetics, perfume, and low-calorie food. 'To Mede out the best in a Median, and Perge out the worst in a Persian!' they dramatically promised their slogan with a flamboyant flair. They were right! 'X' marked the spot where so many were chosen to be Queen for a Day. Rare was the reject upon whom Hegai and Shaashgaz could not work their matrimonial magic, and who ended up on the Vashti trash heap of spinsterhood."*

"Turn to Esther, Chapter Two."

After my lesson, Maria and I walked back to our Honda Odyssey in the parking lot still in costume. We silently held hands as we strolled, looking at each other. Maria was as radiant as the day we first were married. I could only hope that she thought I was as accurate a flashback in the handsome department. She squeezed my hand. Apparently, she did! I squeezed her hand right back.

> *"And as the years go by*
> *Our friendship will never die*
> *You're gonna see it's our destiny*
> *You've got a friend in me."*

"Cell Block"

August 2, 2012

Presently, I do not own a cell phone. I don't tweet, I talk (occasionally, I "post" on Facebook, which is an oxymoron—it's neither). This is not necessarily by way of atavistic protest; I just find the newfangled, walkie-talkie contraptions impersonal, alien, and an individual, beck-and-phone-call preoccupation and distraction so magnetic as to render the entire civilized world a silent, thoughtless society of automatons.

There! I said it!

After all, what exactly is the I.Q. of a phone called "smart"?

I am not about to be one of those millions of adults caught in a virtual tractor beam with their heads down, electronically sleepwalking addicts running into either one another or into some inanimate object blocking the path—obsessed with checking messages—while in a deep brain-freeze to the inevitability of more embarrassing collisions. They don't even register any such abrupt course corrections to their trek, as befitting shuffling, technological zombies: chin on chest, starry-eyed, gazing at their tricorder. If I ever become one of these millennial mutants, then I have three words for my succumbing to this enterprise: "Beam me up!"

What could possibly be the use for that little handheld pocketful of tears?

"Cell Block"

Driving directions, perhaps. Or, on the off-chance that some accident, emergency, or catastrophe required its use to initiate a rescue or check on the well-being of a loved one. In such cases it might be worth its light-weight in gold. But, until then, we are just a sorry bunch of lonely game pieces going about our separate businesses, like isolated penitents each bowing down to our cellular gods, waiting for some event big enough to shake us into keeping our chins up . . .

"Razed"

February 16, 2013

The first fissure formed tens of thousands of years ago, from a chance series of primeval raindrops that eventually cut not one but two gravity-induced, precipitous, downhill pathways perfectly outlining the proud contours of "The Sheik." They were hairline fractures at first, but, like a festering wound, had gained significant, cavernous depth over time, which laid open wider and wider the lips of the surface edges, making the gaping maw an invitation for more drilling down by the weather's elements.

Three converging conditions made this a combination of explosive proportions:

One. The more observable results of nature's handiwork in perfectly tracing around the face of Rudolph Valentino were, in fact, not. They had been obscured, over time, by protective foliage not afraid of heights, that had originally dipped their root systems into the once-shallow fissures trickling with a consistent water supply, thus resulting in a splendid array of tenacious flora and fauna that had masterfully spread its leafy wings to cover the tracks. This verdant fanfare of nature was in concert with the more subtle ebb and flow of topsoil erosion, which filled in any lingering lightning-bolt cracks, completely camouflaging the relentless, gnawing excavation going on underneath. No human—professional geologist, soil specialist, energetic hiker, or touristy spectator—had the slightest idea what Mother Nature was up to.

Two. All of the elements took the path of least resistance. Like insidious, geological brain surgeons, both rivulets of water and tangles of root instinctively sought to skirt the impenetrable granite of the 100-foot carving, wending their way around and behind the sculpture, as provided by the far more permissive, sedimentary rock that held the face to the cliff. Over time, they had accomplished an impressively intricate, complicated network; a complex system of clinging vines, twisted tendrils, and calculating crevasses—from small pencil lines of calligraphy drawing themselves in the sand, to larger, menacing, jagged, grinning mouths like jack-o-lanterns—all suffering from separation anxiety and screaming under the rock-solid pressure to constantly push the envelope outward, one soiled millimeter at a time.

All of this was compounded by a seemingly reckless decision, made some ninety years earlier, when Max Stellar, fueled by an innate and fierce competition with Mount Rushmore—more than 1,300 miles to the northeast—decided to enhance the side-view special effects of "The Sheik" by giving Rudolph Valentino a more dynamic, realistic presentation in the round. This would be achieved by more aggressive dynamite blasting and jackhammer boring into the rock that formed the parenthetical mountainsides on both the left and right profiles of the 100-foot face, and pushing back the natural, securing plant barriers into a curvature (like shaping cuticles on a fingernail) on the exposed cliff that now traversed behind the famous head for a spectacular three-quarter headdress view, all for the pleasure of the transfixed, camera-laden, neck-craning movie buff shambling around in the semicircle viewing area below.

This process of "stretching," as it was impulsively called by Stellar (who seemed to be born with a silver screen in his mind), was deemed feasible not only by the original, barrier-breaking sculptors of the 1920s but also to a new generation of artisans, architects, landscapers, demolition experts, and "granite grafters" at the turn of the twenty-first century, who took it upon themselves to consummate the eighty-year-old dream and "call forth" the non-chiseled right side of Rudolph from its monolithic morgue, to present a fully three-dimensional, complete and uncut head of the silent cinema star. However unknowingly, the increased, load-bearing weight of the entire bust of "The Sheik" was shifted forward as the two, vertical retaining walls of conglomerate shale, slate, and shrubbery that remained on either side were commensurately "stretched" and charged with an impossible task of holding the massive granite head securely in its clutches, a grip which was severely weakening over time.

Three. February 10, 5:48 a.m. My stage-three REM sleep sub-consciously detected the foreign, incoming sensation by splashing an image of me on the dream screen of my somnambulant mind, tottering on the trembling sidewalk of an unrecognizable street in an equally unrecognizable town. The scene was abruptly interrupted by my being violently shaken in real life from the comfort of my own bed. My mind caught the panicky scent of invading reality as the cobwebs of nightmare instantly faded away. I realized the mattress on my actual bed in our actual bedroom was convulsing underneath me like some Serta bucking bronco, and Maria was yelling something at me or to me that was completely drowned out by the tremendous roaring of our entire house, our entire city, that was coming unhinged.

"Razed"

"IAN!" Maria screamed, "WHAT IS IT?"

Even though I knew this to be one of those "birth pang" harbingers of the apocryphal end, there was no time to answer her shrill entreaty, as we were both plunged onto the floor by the combatant force of bouncing box springs. Shrouded in binding sheets and blankets that had crept around our limbs during the night, we drunkenly gained tenuous footing and groggily staggered to the doorway of our bedroom that was spinning like some sadistic aerospace simulator, while we were hailed upon by the deadly combination of jagged glass projectiles and carpet bombs of every book and knickknack that we had accumulated over the past decade.

At 5:52 a.m., when the seismic shifting and deafening rumble had somewhat abated, we looked at each other for the first time. Both breathless and white-complected, with tears streaming down Maria's face. I held her tighter and then opened my mouth to say some calming, "head of the home" reassurances that may or may not be true, when my potential, non-emitted words received a tongue-tied burial as I heard the explosion. Embraced, we both locked eyes on each other. Barefoot, we safely positioned ourselves for a sightline out our bedroom window. We could now clearly see the flashes of light popping systematically down the distant valley below, like military signal fires creating a glowing, "connect-the-dots" aspect, contrasted against the blackness of the alluvial swath of civilization before us. And then it dawned on me. "Electrical transformers at the power plant." Just then, another hot white blast of incarcerated lightning, but this time the escaping flash was more distant, accompanied by a second explosion.

"Burbank or Glendale," I abbreviately explained to Maria. I was trying to mollify her with matter-of-fact intonation—as if stating the commonplace—while, ticking off like cruel clockwork, power plants in the surrounding areas were erupting in a shower of electrical sparks from earthquake-induced surges and bursting into flames.

When the explosions subsided, Maria and I actually caught our breath, and began to move about the bedroom to assess the damage and determine what to do next. I absently bent down to pick up a shattered picture of myself, Maria, Sharayah, and Samantha all smiling at the camera while sitting on a log at the Cheyenne Christian Conference Center—a photo that was now succumbing to more sepia tinges with age. My taut senses first became aware of a new auditory intruder to the darkness, a distant cracking sound, like a two-by-four being viciously kicked by a boot heel. Only this sound grew more akin to a two-hundred-by-four-hundred-foot plank of stubborn wood being high-kicked by the cleats of God.

This was followed by sequential, tectonic belches and moaning that, too, seemed distant, but were guttural, subterranean, with grinding ruptures that seemed to reverberate many miles beneath the Earth's surface. Something gargantuan was protesting. Something monstrous was giving way. Something immense was breaking loose. And then, at 5:57 a.m., a second dawning was upon me, only this time I would not know it until much later. I thought glacier calving took place only in Alaska, but now, a mile away from our cozy yellow cottage nestled in the Hollywood Heights subdivision of the sleepy town of Monument, the unthinkable was happening. The front-loaded, stony visage of Rudolph Valentino was tearing away from its cliff-clutching moorings and back-sliding down the mountainside.

Like an unexpected launching of an aircraft carrier, the granite ship pushed free from the removed blocks and rapidly increased the starting knots of its inexorable march to the sea, gaining avalanche speed as it rolled down the prescribed track of destruction. As Rudolph first slipped downward, he vacated an immense enclave as he fell away from the mountain, an odd indentation that kept a blackened, recognizable representation of the back of his head. The Sheik, still in a vertical position, slammed, chin-first, into the unprotected base of the mountain, just north of the intersection of Valentino and Ridgeway Avenues. Rapidly sliding with an unearthly groan into a horizontal position, the granite face, now looking upward, was drop-kicked and bounced relentlessly down the street. As it did, the gaining momentum spewed granite projectiles from the most delicate facial features of the carving—that were breaking apart in all shapes and sizes and shooting out like supersonic meteors—ruthlessly pummeling and demolishing unsuspecting targets in an ever-widening circumference with gashes and craters. The atomic force of the careening cranium pushed up a rising tidal wave of lighter municipal body parts and civic detritus that were hurled ahead and burst as warning shots all over the freeway far below.

What remained of the disfigured Valentino gave chase to the debris and roared down the length of his namesake Avenue, carving up the pavement and gouging out all of the frontage property, be it commercial or residential. The racing head chewed its way down the slope until it finally crash-landed into the freeway overpass at the intersection of Valentino Avenue and Max Stellar Boulevard, snapping misnamed guardrails like twigs and knocking out the freeway supports underneath. But not before the remnant of Rudolph mowed down the Union 76 gas station at the bottom of the hill, raking off the caps of the subterranean gasoline storage tanks, which exploded upon impact from the electrical fire already well underway from a severed power line that was caused by precariously swaying telephone poles from the earthquake just minutes before. The blast knocked out a half-moon of the southbound freeway, leaving a jagged edge of concrete and brandishing claws of exposed rebar. The impact from the gas explosion also blew out the entire front of the Monument Hospital (already scraped clean beyond recognition by the sawtooth ridges of granite as the head thundered by), causing pandemonium among on-call doctors, night-shift nurses, and bedridden patients.

"Hear that?" I whispered to Maria. I thought it was another power-plant explosion, but this one not only sounded different, it was closer. Too close for any power plant known to me.

It was the Union 76 station going up in smoke. After which it got strangely quiet.

Maria and I held our breath, agog as we once again embraced, now in the bedroom doorway, trembling from the sensory overload.

The intermittent silence was ominous. It did not herald peace. It seemed to wait for the right, vulnerable moment. A spirit of fear brooded over the waters of untold wreckage.

Wait for it.

Wait for it.

Then we heard it.

First the sound like a mighty rushing wind, followed by the auditory tricks of a thunderous, military cadence marching in the tops of poplar trees from the Valley of Rephaim, exponentially increasing in ear-splitting decibels and ferocity with every second. By the time the congealing, cumulonimbus cloud of airborne old earth reached our home, it had become a monstrous brown fist that slammed into our cottage with what seemed to be the force of an F5 tornado, engulfing us in a swirling, dirty vortex that broke additional windows and sent both Maria and me coughing, sputtering, and sprawling onto the debris-cluttered floor. (I was only able to write this six days later, when I found my journal on that same debris-cluttered floor, wedged under a bookcase—the final resting place of involuntary flight from the runway of my bedside table, a room away. It was unrecognizably caked in a thick layer of dust and grime.)

When the supersized sandstorm finally subsided, Maria and I cautiously brushed off the stratum of soil, litter of paper, and fragments of glass and wood. We pushed aside piles of books flung from the bookcase, including a heavy Bible commentary set that would have been deadly airborne. I mechanically rescued a first-edition, signed copy of Milton Derringer's first novel, *Founding Fathers*, whose dust cover had sadly been torn away. We grabbed pillows from off the bed, surviving vases bereft of flowers and articles of clothing sucked out of the opened closet, and unfolded ourselves into rickety standing positions. We were shaking and pale from shock, although our complexions were completely encased in a foundation of makeup from the good earth. Striving after the wind, we made our way to the bathroom, assessing and addressing with gauze and poultices the multitude of bloody cuts and scrapes that we had received during the ordeal that needed immediate first aid.

I knew somewhere in my head that there was a checklist that the "man of the house" must investigate: gas mains, water supply, electricity, any and all compromises in the foundation and construction of our little home. But the abnormality of this event made sheer curiosity the driving force.

This was no ordinary, run-of-the-mill California earthquake! There was something else going on here. And, if it was nuclear,

I wanted to know sooner rather than later. I instantly checked myself. If it was nuclear, there *wouldn't be* a "sooner" or "later." So, what was it? I held Maria close to me as we made our way across the irregular waves of bowed strips that now characterized our undulating, buckled hardwood floor, a rippled surface that now creaked more frequently than usual, and into the living room, equally as decimated. I gently put a stertorous Maria in one of the two wingback chairs, miraculously upright, placed in front of a fireplace that had vomited its soot all over the room. I then crept into our dining room, frequently looking back to make sure a dazed, insecure, and confused Maria could keep me in clear view.

I hunched over to look out through the few transparent splotches on an otherwise dust-caked, dishwater-brown windowpane in our dining room. All I could see was our front lawn, which looked like a horizontal version of the windowpane—a bronze surface plowed under with decrepit, ancient soil, and then raked over into rolling, zig-zagging furrows. The once-grass rectangle was also disfigured by the occasional boulder outcropping or mesozoic dirt clod. Frustrated with the limited views, I skittishly opened the front door. With dawn now brightening, I could still keep Maria in sight in the fleeting shadows of the house through the opened front door. I then crept to the sidewalk like a soldier cautious of land mines. This afforded me a better view, but not necessarily clearer. The dust clouds were still rolling wherever the soft sea breezes dictated. To my right and left, the rows of Hollywood Heights homes sat quietly as if they were doll houses in an attic that had been ignored for a millennium. Oddly, not a soul was outside. The fields were white, the laborers few. Perhaps this paucity of neighbors was because they had their own life-and-limb issues going on inside.

I returned to Maria, who had regained her mother-hen resolve to make sure her older little chick and her husband were safe in their vulnerable house of straw just a short distance away, down on Max Stellar Blvd. She was not receiving local cell-phone service and so would continue to route communication (as part of our pre-discussed earthquake plan) through her younger chick and her husband in their nest in Colorado. While she had her cell phone to her ear, I pantomimed that I was going back outside. She nodded distractedly, as she continued telling Samantha and Colton (on speaker phone) our story, asking them to please call Sharayah and Jackson to assure them that we were O.K. and to please relay back to us that they were the same.

Not at all conscious of the mile-or-so distance, I tentatively headed west down the few blocks toward Our Father's Evangelical Church. The old Holbert family home, situated as it was right next to the church, looked as if it had been gored by bull, a massive shard from the Rudolph Valentino headdress had broken away, and the razor-sharp, serrated edge skewered the house in one long swipe across its midriff, the result of some mammoth Middle Eastern scimitar. Some years before, the church had purchased the property from the Holberts to use as a parsonage for missionaries. Fortunately, it was unoccupied at the time.

I veered to my left and found myself tottering on the edge of a cliff forming the circumference of what looked like a planetary crater! I steadied myself. It was then that I realized that the cleaving of our cityscape had had its beginnings right here, on the property that used to be the invincible, gothic edifice of Our Father's Evangelical Church. What remained was now a ragged, bowl-shaped hole where the movie star's jutting chin had smashed into the first horizontal ground to offer any resistance.

At the south end of this Martian lakebed, there was a wide breach interrupting the cliff's curvature that opened up onto what looked to be a large canal, or canyon, that stretched all the way down to the freeway—a landing strip for Gog of Magog. I stepped back from the precipice and turned my head away from what could not be fully comprehended at present. And I thought that the church kitchen fire at O.F.E. so many years ago had seemed like such a mess!

I arrived back home in time to help Maria make contact with other concerned friends in and out of state, once confirmation was received that our Southern California brood of Sharayah and Jackson, Papa and "Ya-Ya" were all shaken and stirred, but otherwise in one piece. We both breathed that well-known exhalation of stabilizing calm; the sigh of relief. Just then the blaring sound of police cars, fire trucks, and ambulance sirens could be heard increasing from every direction in the distance. To this soundtrack, Maria and I went to work on sweeping the ocean of cleanup in our home that had been dust-free and spotless just three hours before. We also went outside, connecting with and consoling our neighbors, who were now milling about and comparing war stories, many of whom were still dumbfounded and weeping. Some were themselves bleeding from various injuries. We reassured one another—loving neighbors as ourselves—especially during aftershocks, providing the necessary help and giving succor, as it was needed for each other throughout the coming days.

That night, Maria and I slept on a blowup air mattress next to the front door—for a quick escape. Still raw and jittery, Maria did not want to be caught dead in that deathtrap of a bedroom, even for so much as a sonic boom! Sirens continued howling intermittently throughout the night, automated coyotes speeding toward their latest injury or fatality.

"Razed"

February 17, 2013

As near as I can remember, the next day, the sun came up in glorious fashion, unseasonal for February even by Southern California standards, suffusing a sapphire-blue sky in the ether with intermittent sparkle and even a shimmer or two. It was as if all of the working parts of sunrise had complete amnesia of the tragic goings-on underneath just 24 hours before, as it proudly presented the dawn of a new day on the warming carcass that was once the town of Monument.

After cold cereal for breakfast (the electricity was miraculously back on after our candle-lit evening with limited movement supported by flashlight, so the milk had somehow survived in the lukewarm refrigerator), I walked outside our house and, by routine now, turned down the sidewalk to the right. I stopped at the first decent, detailed view that afforded me some level of perspective and panorama from which to rationally and calmly assess my findings. I am not sure "What a difference a day makes!" I was still not prepared for the vast devastation that had piled up at the corners of Valentino and Ridgeway Avenues and beyond. The sight confirmed that both Orson and H.G. Wells might have been right all along. Yes, the surviving portion of Rudolph had, in fact, slid down to the freeway and was just sitting there, looking upward. As if a granite head of Lemuel Gulliver had come up for air while doing the backstroke up Valentino Avenue, and hundreds of scurrying Lilliputians with shovels, trucks, and bulldozers had bitten off pieces of his impassive face, like so many reflecting orange piranhas in hard hats.

As confirmed from the previous day, Rudolph's cleft chin—when it first hit the ground at the back of the church—drilled into the upper crust of surface ground cover with a hundred feet of granite stone under force of gravity, coupled with the terminal air velocity of a fifty-foot head start. It bored a hole some twenty feet deep. The sheer force of the multiple tonnage had plowed a trench the width of a football field.

The imagined result of some Greek god scooping out a colossal riverbed. Or, for a tall-tale western analogy, a thirsty Pecos Bill getting a stick and digging the Rio Grande. Or, for folk-legend aficionados, rough-housing Paul Bunyan playing tug-o-war with his blue ox, Babe, and pushing up the Grand Tetons. Or, for Bible fans, "Behemoth" and "Leviathan" doing twelve rounds on the main street of our town.

The granite bust gouged not a mere indentation but tore out a sizable canyon all the way down the hill, erasing any trace of Valentino Avenue, and cutting Max Stellar Boulevard in half—like the future Mount of Olives—with an impassable gulf by the freeway below.

Broken pipes—once underneath the street—now stuck out from the canyon walls, spewing out questionable water in all directions, disgorging and drenching the remains on the canyon floor, and causing puddles of oozing mud and slime in our very own Slough of Despond. Tree tops looked the victims of a crazed Mother Nature buzz cut or were mowed down altogether—the aftermath of all four, chomping species of Joel's prophetic locust.

I had never seen such devastation! Buildings had been leveled, one after another, into misshapen mounds of masonry. Streets and sidewalks had curled up indiscriminately, as if by rough, horizontal strokes of a cosmic carpenter's planetary planer. Sheared off or broken gas pipes had ignited, and conflagrations had broken out all over the area. Firefighters throughout the Southland had come to lend a hand to the over-taxed Monument

Fire Department at putting them out. All across the valley, there was dust rising, as it caught the offshore breezes that are so indicative of this region. As such, the moving air, completely unaware of the vast topographic changes now underfoot, gently sent ribbons of powder, silt, sand, and ash twirling up into the air, making the sloping, denuded landscape of Monument spotted with what looked to be hellish specters of steam rising from the Yellowstone caldera.

Caution tape had to be strung along both sides of the eerie canal because the drop into the bottom was so precipitous. Add to that the hazards of all manner of rubbish, from barbecues to birdcages (one looked exactly like the home of Midge, the yellow pet parakeet kept by my Grandpa Colby and Grandma Melba), wheelbarrows to washing machines, ping-pong tables to tricycles, as they were strewn about in the morning's wake and lit up under the fresh spotlight of that same morning's sun.

All that was left of one house down by the freeway was a large, brass four-poster bed covered in dirt, now teetering precariously on the ledge above the tremendous declivity. This was apparently all that remained of the owner's earthly possessions. How sad! The rest of their home and its belongings had exploded upon impact and been taken down the current, forever lost and destroyed. The bed was just balancing there, pillows askew, with the comforter dangling from the railing at the foot into the gulf below. It reminded me of the last remaining memory of old Og, the *fee-fi-fo-fum* tall king of Bashan. His whole region of Argob was plundered by the Israelites, but his captured thirteen-foot-long, six-foot-wide iron bed was such an oddity that they had the good sense to put it on display in the Rabbah museum so that, for years to come, little Ammonite children could gawk at its elongated immensity.

I walked back over to the O.F.E. property and the edge of the newly formed bowl. Only now my progress was impeded by an endless strip of yellow caution tape running the entire width of the property, staked out every ten yards or so. I followed the yellow ribbon to my left and found that the tape was literally lining both sides of what used to be Valentino Avenue. It even fanned out and traced the outlines where houses and businesses once stood—contiguous squares, rectangles, and parallelograms where a vanished Rush More Coffee House, Victorian City Hall, and the Monument Museum once stood—all a sobering grid against trespassing, a yellow-streaked blueprint of the "totality of the circumstances," in what had once been the main artery of our city.

Within days, there were quite a few officials, workers, and law enforcement now milling about, investigating the immediate area around the barren property of Our Father's Evangelical Church. They were combing the grounds, bending over shovels and picks, sweeping the area with metal detectors, on their knees with trowels. K-9 Officers from the City Department strained with police dogs on leashes. I walked up to a bearded man in plainclothes suit and tie whom I had never seen before, and who seemed to be as in charge as anyone had reason to be. His hands were nonchalantly shoved into his front pants pockets, the angle of his elbows parting the flaps of his coat like a curtain to reveal a shiny, gold badge attached to his belt that read "T. Flagg," I came to find out that he was part of a Special Investigations Unit recruited from Los Angeles.

Rescue efforts all over the Southland had been spread quite thin as a result of the widespread earthquake. The U.S. Geological Survey office in Pasadena had, of late, confirmed that the epicenter was under the mountain community of Frazier Park, some seventy miles from Monument and right on the dreaded San Andreas Fault. The initial Richter scale magnitude was between 6.7 and 7.0. The subsequent aftershocks, while slowly abating in intensity, were coming with alarming frequency, as if poking the already terrified population in the psychological ribs with the idea that all of this destruction was just a preamble to the predicted "Big One!" But, as the problems in Monument represented a unique set of complications, first responders and fire and rescue teams were dispatched as soon as they became available.

I told "T. Flagg" who I was and asked if I could stoop under the caution tape and help in the search. He balked only for a moment, as his reconnoitering resources were already tapped, and one more set of exploring eyes in an able-bodied volunteer like myself couldn't hurt (also, I could discern from where I was standing, a large group of other commissioned searchers who were obvious "civilians" now spread out about the property). He pointed to a truck bed with a rack of hard hats as my required first stop and said to check in at the Command Post. He then raised the caution tape for me to pass under. Actually, I was not much help. I was ordered to search an obscure area at the back of the property, where the "King's Kids" play yard used to be. This was probably due to safety factors, because, here, there was less instability and wreckage. The bulk of the structures, beginning with our church, were pushed directly down the hill, only spilling out to either side, as the crushed buildings started rolling up on top of one another like an enlarging snowball, and, with the harrowing speed, began to break off in different directions on the descent. Consequently, so thought "T. Flagg" wryly, I was likely to find only plastic bottles and crayons.

In what was left of the "King's Kids" playground, there were still some jungle-gym remnants. The brown plastic slide had been extensively mangled and wrenched from its structure, now laying half buried to one side of the sectioned-off area. I tripped over numerous bricks; I found an offering plate with a jagged gash down the middle, reminding me of some superhero shield from a Marvel comic; a ripped "Members Only" jacket, marked with a tag from our church's "Lost and Found," that must have been hanging in a church closet for decades; intestines of ferromagnetic brown tape spewing from the plastic fragmented remains of what was once an all-the-rage, state-of-the-art, dual cassette player with built-in speakers. I also turned up one or two colorful rings, obviously part of a larger outdoor set with the others lost forever; a couple of metal folding chairs bent into submission, and a plastic sandbox toy that now had acres of space for its use. I looked skyward at the sudden sound of helicopters that were aiding and abetting, with their bird's-eye view, the Search and Rescue teams that were combing the hillside. I could also see the uniforms and equipment of the combined forces of the Monument and Burbank Fire Departments, as they scurried like so many picketing ants, carrying shovels and other tools all over the mountainside, looking to throw suffocating dirt on any spot fires caused by sparks from existing ones currently burning down the hill, and carried along by the shifting air currents. Even members of the U.S. Forest Service and the Forestry Division of the Los Angeles County Fire Department were inspecting the base of the foothills, looking for potentially dangerous areas that would necessitate protective netting and barriers topped off with an anticlimactic warning sign, "Watch for Falling Rocks."

After an hour or so, I turned in my meager findings to "T. Flagg" and headed back home, where I could be more useful. It was quite apparent that the real "treasures" were covered under thicker layers of earth movement, and could be discovered only by machinery specifically designed for this sort of thing.

February 18, 2013

By day three, I had noticed that there was already a fully functioning "Incident Command Post" set up at the Monument High School that was monitoring all manner of needs and cleanup within our community. The Red Cross had set up a treatment area in a large warehouse next to a newly formed dirt lot down by the freeway. This, for folks triaged as "yellow" for non-life-threatening injuries—in order to prevent local hospitals from being overwhelmed—and folks with "red" markings were dispatched immediately to those very same local hospitals. There was also a homeless shelter filled with rows of cots for the many new conscripts without roofs over their heads that was now fully operational in the converted, smaller gymnasium of Monument Junior High School, as well as an annex in the "cafetorium" of the non-damaged portion of the John Adams Elementary School.

Since the frontage of the Monument Hospital had been first sheared off by the granite movie star, and then blasted by the gas explosion from the Union 76 station across the street, most of its current patients and new injuries were transported to either Verdugo Hills Hospital, the Adventist Hospital in nearby Glendale, or to Saint Joseph's Hospital in Burbank, all of which were already near capacity with their own injured citizens. As the freeway was closed for a mile and a half due to severe damage and structural compromises that presented extreme hazards in both east and westbound directions, as well as to its on- and off-ramps, some of the more critical patients had to be air-lifted by rescue helicopters the short distance to the adjacent, cooperating hospitals. I had also heard on the news that the federal government had declared the entire affected area in Southern California to be an official disaster area—which seemed to me like stating the obvious. However, the Federal Emergency Management Agency could now be mobilized, and financial aid could start pouring, or trickling, in, as the case may be.

As all of the perpendicular roads on both sides leading to the plowed-up Valentino Avenue were now blocked and guarded by law enforcement, the alternative, circuitous routes to work added quite a few minutes to my previous stone's-throw commute. Fortunately for a goodly portion of the population of Monument, the small-business building—particularly the structurally more-fragile second story housing Block Insurance—had been miraculously spared of any significant, dysfunctional damage so as to allow the occupying employees to be "open for business" and to sort through the mound of work to be done! In our agency's storied history, we had never been so deluged with claims of all kinds. Even Maria came in (when she could be spared from overseeing the bevy of contractors and repairmen frequenting our own home in Hollywood Heights, when *they* could be spared from other, more-pressing emergencies) to handle all of the insurance needs of our war-torn Mayberry. As a coping mechanism for all of the pressing phone calls and paperwork facing my enervated staff every waking minute at the office, we started cynically calling ourselves "Rubble Indemnity." A few times, Jill, in overworked weariness, mistakenly answered the phone that way!

On my fifth 14-hour day, I carved out a minute to read the *Daily Granite's* (a name no longer relevant) front headline from three days before. It took up the full page and read:

"EARTHQUAKE! HEADS ROLL!"

(Even during one of our city's darkest hours, my grandfather's pithy sense of justice still carried weight.) Below the caption was an eerie aerial photograph taking up the rest of the page of our very own "Tornado Alley," a trough that stretched half a mile down the dark-shadowed void of Valentino Avenue, showing, in living color, a wake of loss and destruction.

March 10, 2013

Dear Diary, so sorry it has been so long. But, one month later, we are still climbing out of the worst disaster in our city's history and entering into a post-Valentino era. There has simply been no time to write for the past nine days—or breathe, for that matter—even if the air was actually not polluted! Regardless of the air quality, however, time marches on. Tonight, our doorbell rang unexpectedly after dinner. To our pleasant surprise, it was Sherman Moody (who was anything but. In fact, in the course of his daily personality, any mood at all rarely made a cameo appearance on the scene of his face), a member of our church's Elder Board. Maria and I ushered him into our living room, which, for the most part, looked like nothing had ever happened—thanks to Maria, the sanity-keeping, cleaning machine! He sat down tentatively, like he did not intend to stay long. His hands remained in his jacket pocket (an outer garment he did not shake off, even when Maria had offered to take it), but I did notice that one side of his coat bulged much larger than what would normally be caused by the shape of his smallish hands. He got right to the point.

"Ted asked me to give this to you. It was given to him by someone in Search and Rescue. He thought you should have it, but he didn't feel well enough to make the trip over here."

Ted had been looking more and more exhausted every time I saw him. Maria and I were both worried about him.

Sherman answered the question of the lopsided bulge in his jacket pocket by pulling out a large zip-lock plastic bag. He leaned forward and handed it to me. I held the bag up to the light and looked at the contents. The plastic had seen better days of transparency; it was smudged with dirt and misshapen from a deep crease or two. Consequently, I poured out the contents onto our coffee table. There was a faint jingle as an old, silver "W.V.W.W." bracelet spilled out onto the surface and lodged next to a coaster.

"Weaker Vessel: Wanna Wrestle!" I pronounced with a nostalgic smile, delicately picking it up, dangling it between my thumb and forefinger, a "precious thing" indeed. (I felt like weepy prophet Jeremiah, when God nudged him in the ribs, assuring him that the Almighty kept tabs on His sacred stuff—even after it's been misplaced for seventy years. At the proper time, He "recalls" it. Literally.) I found myself thinking back instantly, like it was yesterday, when the anti-misogyny womenfolk at Our Father's Evangelical Church tried to wear the pants in the family, which nearly unseated Pastor Tony Meece!

"Oh, those Proverbs 31 women!" I exclaimed over the gentle tinkling of the bombshell bangle.

"A chapter written by a *man*—a king no less—whose mommy had to teach him what to write!" Maria chimed in, with a mischievous smirk.

"You had to get that one in, didn't you?" I chuckled, with mock exasperation.

Then, to my surprise, out slid two or three charred ballots from the rigged Wesley Zimmerman election at the

"Razed"

First Christian Church. "How on earth did you get these?" I asked Sherman. With both hands back in his coat pockets, he shrugged.

"I don't know. Ted said there was tons of stuff found buried at the church property and even carried down the street. It took the officials quite a while to sort it all through and get what could be salvaged to the right people. And they're not done yet. Ted only gave me these because he thought you, especially, would be interested in them."

Their existence after all this time was inexplicable. But my attention was diverted to the little book that was the final item in the spillage. It was an old, dog-eared New Testament. I dexterously opened the brittle cover, thumbing to the "Presented To:" page, just before the "Marriages," "Births," and "Deaths" sections, to see a faded, but legible name written in confident penmanship, "Richard Albright."

"This must be from the '20s!" I said. "But why give it to me?" I asked again.

"Maybe Ted thinks you're kind of like a church historian or something. Or maybe because of your grandfather," responded Sherman, again with another coat shrug.

For nearly a decade, the mantle of self-appointed church historian had never been ceremonially passed, apparently until now. But I never got the memo! I did confess to Ted one day about my private journal—and my grandfather's—but that was quite a while ago. Perhaps he thought these would help, with an entry or two—of course, after they were properly catalogued in some church archives, or somewhere!

Sherman left as quickly as he had come, leaving us to ponder the contents of the plastic time capsule.

JOURNAL "ISM": Thanks to the Internet and a few genealogy data bases, Maria and I were able to track down and contact Richard's son, Cody Albright, living in a retirement home in Hutchinson, Minnesota. He was now between 85 and 90 years old, and was surprisingly spunky and high-spirited on the phone. He volunteered without explanation or clarification that he still kept in touch with the Stellars, specifically Max's nieces and nephews on his sister's side (as if we would, of course, know who he was talking about).

Then he added with great enthusiasm, "And you'll be happy to know that all of them are Christians!"

March 12, 2013

Once again, I walked through the vacant lot that used to be our church (I never quite got over this shock, having logged so many years on this strangely tilled soil); the peculiar quiet made me keenly aware that the investigators had all been called away; the local searches were now officially over. After days of delicate sifting, bulldozers had come to remove the larger debris, and now the property was being graded.

I spied Ted McGowan, slowly sauntering up to me through the dirt rivulets and gullies, but with obvious intentionality. He had a somber look on his face.

"I received a call from either the Monument Police Department or L.A. County Sheriff's Department this morning, Ian. I can't remember which. A Sergeant Perry, I think it was . . ." His eyes looked skyward as his mind wandered, as if it was a comfort to follow any tangent other than the subject at hand. "He wanted to advise me as Chairman of the Board of the fatalities connected with our church."

"Fatalities?" I said, with a bit too much harsh surprise. "No one was at the church during the . . . accident!" for lack of a better word.

"Apparently there were two," replied Ted, with a sigh of regret.

He suddenly swayed and then righted himself. These days this was due either to a diminishing aftershock or a light breeze, given Ted's frail frame. He repositioned his stance to face me from another direction, get the sun out of his eyes, and to be more comfortable. He could not stand too long in the same position without some internal pain flaring up. *Honestly*, I thought, *he really should be using a cane.* "Grady Storm and Emilio Paas. Apparently, they were walking through the upper classrooms and gymnasium discussing paint colors for our upcoming facelift. Maybe it was also the bathrooms and library, or was it the kitchen?" He was trailing off again, harkening back to an earlier elder-meeting discussion that had inadvertently turned from spiritual to practical.

"It was the only time they could meet . . ."

I was in shock from this news that our sleeping church had actually lost people, when, I thought again, since the "accident," it had been reported that no one was on the property at the time.

Ted had to talk louder. A large dump truck was lumbering along Ridgeway Avenue, its air brakes wheezing and the diesel-exhaust pipe rattling, disturbing the eerie stillness as it inched its way across the base of the mountain to a landfill. The deafening decibels sounded as if it were producing a much greater truck speed than the slowly crawling, giant mechanical June bug that was drowning us out.

". . . and both families had reported Grady and Emilio missing right after that morning."

I was heartbroken. I loved those two men! Emilio, before becoming an elder, had been the church custodian for just about as long as I could remember, and the fortissimo prayers of Grady Storm kept the Throne Room busy on behalf of Our Father's Evangelical Church. I thought, as I broke eye contact with Ted and looked around me to gain some composure, that the church would not need a custodian for quite some time, but we sure could still use the appeals to almighty God from Elder Storm!

"Do their families know?" I asked, returning like a lighthouse to full gaze upon the Chairman of the Board.

"Yes. The authorities told them first and then called us afterwards. We need to plan some sort of memorial service. I just don't know where . . ." He was drifting again. He was thinking of how to properly pay our respects without a church building in which to do so. Our church's two interments would obviously take place at the Monument Memorial Park and Gardens, which, relatively unharmed due to its secluded location, was doing a brisk business these days.

While Ted was mentally and physically rolling with the tide, he suddenly came to and watched me as I processed all of this. His look grew penetrating. His fixation betrayed the fact that he was no longer wandering elsewhere for distractions. He also seemed to be shedding his years while I stared back. A youthful vigor was returning to his whole countenance. A divine switch had been flipped. With the sun's rays behind him, he leaned into me, completely violating my personal space, as his face was inches from my own. Unblinking, he said to me in a gruff whisper of intensity that sounded more like an ancient prophet from Midian than a retired C.P.A. from L.A., "We need to rebuild. Without delay."

"Razed"

That said, his wan, frail body made an impressively military about-face, and he walked away. All that was missing were the sandals, camel-hair robe, and staff.

"Raised"

April 10, 2013

"We are hard pressed on every side, but not crushed; perplexed, but not in despair; persecuted, but not abandoned; struck down, but not destroyed."

—2 Corinthians 4:8-9

"We are the only church in town, and we don't have a roof over our heads! Where are we going to put all these people? We can't 'forsake the gathering'!"

Obviously, the dust had literally settled in the aftermath of having much of our city leveled to the ground, and other pressing matters not thought of in weeks began to call attention to themselves. One of these, Elder Townsend Stevens (no relation—spiritual or otherwise—to that gavel-headed shark that my father had retained), brought to the fore while the entire elder board was standing in the middle of O.F.E.'s dirt field, right where the worship service used to be held, and ought to be again. He had raised the age-old, cautionary warning to those among the Hebrews who might opt for Bedside Baptist with Reverend Sheets and the Pillow Case choir (a description of what some are in the habit of doing that I first heard with great glee during my summer working at the church's "Fun in the Son" Summer Day Camp). With no place to lay their heads, Our Father's Evangelical Church had been displaced, its people dispersed—a present-day diaspora. And now, here we were, the entire elder board standing in a huddle, on a bright Sunday morning in a vacant lot—shepherds with pocket watches—counting sheep and wondering how to *get them to the church on time*. Of all people, it was a clear-thinking, moodless Sherman who came up with the tent-meeting idea, and there was an instant revival among the brethren that nearly generated a group hug.

It took a lot of phone calls, mailers—both "e" and snail—and countless personal contacts to get the word out that, in one week, Our Father's Evangelical Church was going to hold its first service in nearly two months! But that's not all, folks! The other, traditional, ancillary ministries like the choir, nursery, child care, youth programs, "Alpha-Omega" college group, and, yes, Adult Christian Education, would also be springing up like wells! It was quite the tax-deductible investment that was made at the sporting goods store in nearby Glendale just days after the elders' Little League team formed an unbroken circle, pledged themselves on a stack of dedicated hands, gave three rousing cheers, and left the sandlot. We were all pleasantly surprised as to how many technological and practical advances the art of tent-making had received since the trio of Paul, Aquila, and Priscilla first took needles and thread to animal hide. There were plastic windows, sidings with extensions and add-ons, screen doors, and even awnings making a porch. Everything that could pop up and pop out was on the market, with dimensions ranging from dog house to convention center. I looked for one with a second story and fold-out spiral staircase just out of curiosity but found none. At best, you could stand your kid on your shoulders inside the tent's vaulted canvas ceiling! To the clerk at the sporting-goods store ringing us up, I am sure we looked like those responsible for providing shelter for refugees during a crisis.

In many ways, I suppose we were.

April 17, 2013

The following Sunday, with the limpid, spring weather turning in our favor, there were so many makeshift, colorful tents on the O.F.E. property of so many shapes and sizes, that it looked like the children of Israel, allotted tribe by tribe, camped out at the base of a now faceless Sinai.

In the main Adult Christian Education blue tent, I was stunned to have filled all of the teaching posts for ten Sunday School classes (I think having the rug pulled out from underneath you aids in volunteering to serve under canvas pitched above you), spread out in state-of-the-art pup tents around the larger command post. The only teacher vacancy left was for the "Young and Married" class. It was then that I decided to volunteer myself and try a much-longer series with a class so near and dear to my heart. And the visual aids were all around us.

Everywhere you turned, like giant Erector Sets, Monument was abuzz with reconstruction activity: scaffolding, cement mixers, cranes, girders, pipes, noisy trucks stacked with drywall, lumber, or Sheetrock. All of this a positive, visible, audible, tactile conclusion to paperwork victories going on behind closed doors. The squabbling with city planning commissions, design-review boards, and building-permit offices was kept to a minimum by the media-driven event that was Monument's unique disaster—which greased the processing wheels—as city officials sought to save face at every turn and get this town rebuilt, pronto! And, as they say, *you can't stop progress.* Even with many insurance claims still "open" at the Block Insurance Agency from the granite shadow that had passed over us last February, sunlight was now moving back up the slope—from freeway to mountain base—bathing our little hamlet in a whole new day.

And so, with uplifting construction all around us, I began a new series called "Real Estate" in the yellow-and-green-striped "Young and Married" class tent. This originated as a seminary nugget discovered in the Housing Department of two of the gospels. In both Matthew and Luke, Jesus argues for a specific, rock-hard foundation as essential in weatherproofing a home. And when the tax collector used the Greek word *tethemelioto* when taking down the Messianic dictation, there was nothing more to report—the home stood because "its foundation was on the rock." However, the doctor's prescription from the parable takes into account something more than location, location, location. In his often illegible, prescription handwriting, he uses the Greek word *oikodomesthai,* which gives at least partial credit for the home successfully withstanding the element—not just because of its stone floor, but also "because it was well built."

With the growing reappearance of the Rush More Coffee House, the Monument Museum, Hospital, and our Victorian City Hall, along with all manner of residential-building revivification and repairs, the wise men and women in the "Young and Married" class were now going to get a crash course on quality of construction. The ground covered would be every biblical comparison with the foundation, framing, drywall and plaster, roof, plumbing, wiring, heating and air-conditioning, colors of paint, and choices of furniture, all with a determination to build well *here*, even as an eternal moving day approaches.

May 19, 2013

Sunday after Sunday, we in the "Young and Married" class would ask ourselves, "How's the construction going?" while our little cluster of colorful tents were moved closer and closer to the outside perimeter of the property as, center stage, construction was beginning to take shape on the new-and-improved Our Father's Evangelical Church's main sanctuary.

At Block Insurance, I had been handling the total loss claim for the church buildings in all its gory details. I even recommended from my copious connections a company who specialized in the building, or rebuilding, of churches, "Many Mansions Construction," who, by God's divine calendar-clearing, actually had time in their busy schedule to pencil us in.

May 25, 2013

Our ground-breaking ceremony was quite a celebration, indeed, as it was also a granite-burying ceremony! With special permission obtained by a stalwart church member who just happened to be the Assistant City Manager, a massive chunk of Rudolph Valentino was pried off what survived of the white skull down under the freeway by a team of trained "special forces" armed with pneumatic drills, chisels, and crowbars. Not unlike cables undergirding a ship's hull, heavy metal straps were pulled under the granite mass and secured by chains to a large crane. With the residents of Monument looking skyward, the arm of the crane carried the huge remnant of Rudolph over the forming, new creation of the former Valentino Avenue, to an equally huge subterranean hole prepared right in the middle of the O.F.E.

property, compliments of a swarm of bulldozers and backhoes. The crane lowered its burden into its perfectly fitted sepulcher with a ponderous thud. The crowd cheered. A brand-new House of God would still be built on its Chief Cornerstone, but the actual stumbling block embedded underneath would forever be in a state of having its head crushed from the weight above.

Our church had finally had its last laugh over the heel-bruising movie industry!

With that, decorative shovels were shoved into the dirt by similarly decorative dignitaries as an on-the-spot hired brass quartet played "The Church's One Foundation," accompanying a full-throated choir of returned exiles.

Our reconstruction had officially begun!

This was all in front of a backdrop of an increasingly substantiated rumor. Having allowed enough time to pass for sensitivity and sentimentalism, and in consideration of the many city businesses that were just now starting up again or starting from scratch, the city officials submitted a formal request to the State of California, now circulating through the Capital somewhere in the approval stages, to change the name of the town from headless Monument back to the more Spanish, California-sounding "Vista Pacifica." I thought this name change a bit shortsighted. I know the carving is now associated at some level with wanton demolition, but, for crying out loud, there is so much about this town and its many names throughout that tip hats to Hollywood's heyday!

September 30, 2013

So sorry, Diary! In order to graduate by December, I had to take a few summer online classes offered by the Antioch School of

Theology. To say the least, they have kept me busy. Too busy, in fact, for me to provide a play-by-play commentary on the rising from the ashes—behind a cloak of scrim and scaffolding—of Our Father's Evangelical Church. But rise it has! The gothic main sanctuary, with its brand-new steeple and bell tower, is larger and more beautiful than ever (with a pew-filled worship center now capable of handling even larger crowds). The new fired-clay bricks are perfectly aligned in their finely smoothed mortar—while still preserving an Old World feel—imbued the place with a clean, fresh feeling of both newness and stability. With upper-story classrooms now available, many of the Adult Christian Education tents were stricken from the pitched camp all around the growing structure.

A new Educational Christianity building, complete with more Sunday-school classrooms, fellowship hall, and gymnasium, was finished shortly thereafter. Before their completion, construction for both buildings had continued as simultaneously as possible, while bobbing and weaving around constantly repositioned tent villages. The Educational Christianity building, whose utilitarian, architectural ancestor was contemporary for its day—with only a brick veneer to match the main sanctuary—was now conflated and built entirely to specs of the same bricks, giving the two buildings a cohesive, gothic uniformity that they previously did not share. This was all frontage for a brand-new, state-of-the-art "King's Kids" play area, complete with so many new slides and tubes that it resembled an arid water park.

October 7, 2013

Today, Diary, we lost a very good man, a humble man. Theodore "Ted" McGowan has finally laid down his sword after a long

"Raised"

battle over the years with many complicated health issues. While no one is in complete shock—this was somewhat expected—the void he leaves is another kind of body blow altogether.

He will truly be forever missed. In spite of his widespread popularity in both "Church" and "World," the family has requested a very private ceremony at the Monument Memorial Park and Gardens, with any donations to be made on Ted's behalf to "Our Father's Evangelical Church Reconstruction Fund." The weak and enfeebled old prophet had wanted to see this thing through, even after death. Ten days later, through benedictory binoculars, he got his wish.

November 12, 2013

Just days before our Grand Opening, troupes of landscape artists were still seen working around the clock under both daylight and floodlight, frantically finishing the shrubbery and flower beds on the newly planted grounds around the campus, while the cement was still drying on the stairs and walkways leading up to the large oak doors of the main sanctuary and the bank of glass doors of the Educational Christianity building. The marquee on the new brick sign on the corners of Valentino and Ridgeway Avenues appropriately read:

"Inauguration Service! Associate Pastor Grayson Pomeroy to officiate!"

November 20, 2013

It was a cloudy, chilly Sunday I will never forget. In spite of the nippy weather, there was actually a line of people snaking down the pathway, spilling out in both directions of the sidewalk at the traffic-congested intersection, waiting to get in, all under the clangorously hymned bell tower tolling happily. To the sweet sound of applause and cheers, Pastor Pomeroy and acting Elder Chairman Townsend Stevens at once opened the double doors as the flood of attendees was greeted by two crisp rows of the business-suited elder board, who stood all prim and proper in formation in the entry hall to heartily welcome both church members and newcomers alike once again to O.F.E.!

I noticed, when I finally gained entry, that a new glass case—custom built for the entry hall—ran the entire length of the right side of the room. But where the "Joyful Noose" had once hung, strangling its millstone over an ominous Bible passage, there was now a large oak panel upon which gold plates had been fastened that were engraved with the names of every senior pastor who had been under-shepherds over the O.F.E. flock:

Wesley Zimmerman	*Nelson Finch*	*Tony Meece*
Preston Hale	*Sheldon Abbott*	*Roland Jeffries*
Angus Ritchie	*Milton Derringer*	*Clint Banning*

(I was to later find out that the specific dates of office had been omitted in order to discourage comparing and contrasting terms of service—whether they were short or long. Each and every one of these names were dedicated servants, genuinely called by God for such a time as that).

"Cannon," I said in a feigned, concealed cough, with my fist to my mouth, not breaking my stare into the glass case, while standing in the crowd next to Maria, Sharayah, and Jackson, who all turned my way.

"Raised"

"They forgot Phineous Cannon, the 'wee little man'!" I whispered. Perhaps this was some clerical error of omission by Susan, our overworked Senior Church Secretary. Or, she simply did not have the time to check her facts with any self-appointed church historian. Oh, wait! That was, apparently, *me*! I let a moment or two go by before I offhandedly pointed out to my older daughter that her great-grandfather would have thought that the late Pastor Sheldon Abbott's morality was as "crooked as a dog's hind leg!" which got a snicker from her and a head-shaking, wide-eyed frown from the wife of my youth.

At the top of the glass case was written in large, gold-embossed letters, the familiar words of Psalm 145:4

"One generation will commend your works to another."

Of this, I can bet at the moment that Maria did not think I was doing a very good job! But, all throughout the orations and anthems of our splashy Grand Opening ceremony going on in the new sanctuary, my mind kept remembering back to 1997, reminiscing about the old Deacon Board and the indomitable Chairman Samuel Caldwell, during the notorious Sheldon Abbott extramarital affair. I thought back to his impassioned speech to the Elder Board, when—in the heat of the moment—he had gone all "nursery rhyme" on us, and called our defrocked Senior Pastor "Humpty Dumpty!"

It was too bad that Sheldon Abbott couldn't have stayed on that Wall of Fame in the glass case of my mind.

Speaking of "Humpty Dumpty" and walls, in a one-time effort to move from prosaic "Synopsis" Sid to a more poetic, "Iambic Pentameter" Ian, I was reminded of King Hezekiah's two "watchmen" from the 700s B.C., who had very different opinions on the stewardship of God's vision for themselves and for their nation. It amounted to an allegiance to either Mother Goose, who was cooked, or to Father God, who was compensated.

> *"Shebna, Shebna sat on a wall,*
> *Shebna, Shebna, prime minister of all.*
> *In spite of your tomb*
> *With its lofty price tag,*
> *Almighty God will wad you up like a rag!*
>
> *Eliakim, Eliakim sat on a wall,*
> *Eliakim, Eliakim, the servant of all.*
> *In spite of your kingdom keys*
> *Hung on a peg,*
> *Without trust in God*
> *Judah's on her last leg!"*

"Raised"

Then I told the "Young and Married" class to turn to Isaiah, Chapter 22:15-25.

To their great relief, the never-ending "Real Estate" series was almost over!

"Papa"

December 20, 2013

I received a very sweet Facebook post this morning from my older daughter:

> *"Ian Block it is your graduation day from the Antioch School of Theology!!!! I could not possibly be more proud of you!!!! And I am insanely excited to see what God has in store for you!!!! So lucky to be your daughter and to get to celebrate this big achievement with you!*
> *Love you!!!!!! xoxo"*

My watery eyes and cracked smile matched the little, round yellow emoji at the bottom of the post. Yes, it was finally here. . . . graduation day from seminary, even after having to take an early withdrawal from classes because of the earthquake and Arab avalanche. If I do say so myself, this was no small feat, considering the frequent clash between the school of thought and the school of life! Since the ceremony—held in the gymnasium of the undergraduate Antioch Christian Academy—was in December, this afforded the unique opportunity for the large space to be tastefully (as befitting academics) decorated for Christmas. There were groups of trees in each corner twinkling with white lights, oversized red bows around the walls (artfully covering up collapsed basketball backboards), connected by swagged strings of colored lights. The stage was a red carpet of poinsettias, with a pathway cut through the plastic pots for the parade of graduates soon to be walking the stage to receive their diplomas, and one of them would be me!

Along with Maria, Sharayah and Jackson, Samantha and Colton (who flew in for the occasion), Lorne and Candice Carlson came down to show their support, as did Dennis and Patty O'Connor (making quite the statement, as their appearance involved a much longer road trip). Malcolm Davis (Daniella, regretfully had taken ill—a popular consequence to the around-the-clock hustle and bustle of the Christmas season) returned to his old haunts to cheer on his former roommate. Even Papa and "Ya-Ya" Ponticelli braved the hard, wooden seats of the gymnasium to congratulate their beloved son-in-law. The ceremony was beautiful, as it was interspersed with glorious Christmas hymns and choruses, giving the proceedings a reverent joy for the momentous occasion of this day, as well as anticipatory celebration for the One to come in just four days. All too soon, I was standing in the wings on the stage, listening intently as the dean of the school announced into the microphone the next set of graduates, of which, on account of my last name, I was the first.

"This is the degree Master of Arts,
Theology concentration—Ian Block."

Although imperiously frowned upon on such an austere, highbrow, scholastic occasion, I could still hear, in the darkened gymnasium, a distant uprising of clapping, yelling, and whistling from a cadre of cheerleaders cloistered high up on the bleachers against the wall on the left-hand side—my wonderful, incredibly devoted family, and family of choice!

We had a delicious celebration dinner at a nearby Italian restaurant (yet another college-day haunt for Malcolm and myself), capping off what was, dear Diary, a day I will never forget. Little did I realize that the *next day* would be given the same description!

December 22, 2013

The next evening, with all of the family still in town and gathered in the living room of our newly refurbished little cottage in Hollywood Heights, Sharayah and Jackson announced that they were pregnant! As they explained, they had received confirmation from their doctor at the newly renovated Monument Hospital the previous day but did not want any "bun in the oven" baby talk to rain on my graduation-processional parade. Amidst all of the congratulatory kisses, hugs, and happy tears, I was thinking that much of my "second degree" would now be spent on my hands and knees, playing with my grandchild!

June 10, 2014

Sorry Diary, but, as they say, "a baby changes everything!" Speaking of, I don't even know where last Christmas went, or my birthday, or even Easter (just like the crack-of-dawn, embalming team of Mary and Mary, by the time our family got to the tomb, it was already empty!). I am not holding out much hope for Independence Day either; the famous letter to King George will have to wait. There is so much to do—showers to plan, supplies to buy, nurseries to decorate—that there

"Papa"

is hardly time to think about anything else. Sharayah is doing wonderfully; her doctor checkups are all very positive. Both she and Jackson agreed that they were not interested in heightening any more suspense and wanted to know the sex of the baby as much beforehand as possible. When it was confirmed, they made a personal appearance at our home to announce the name of their coming baby boy, Josiah Adam (middle-named for his great-great-great grandfather) Osborne!

August 3, 2014

No more apologies, Diary! I just became a grandpa! The birth turned out to be an all-nighter, so our temporary domicile for the past 24 hours has been the Maternity Ward waiting room of the Monument Hospital, perfectly patched and mended just in time to receive the fourth generation from the Block family! An exhausted Jackson, on the brink of becoming a brand-new father himself, had the wearisome role of playing town crier to the two sets of soon-to-be grandparents squirming and pacing in the waiting room. When his routine visits curiously stopped some time before the fourth watch, we knew it was soon. Exhaustion had been replaced by elation when Jackson finally burst open the waiting-room door and announced, "He's here!"

Our joyous ride had begun . . .

October 2, 2014

Call me "Papa"—to borrow, once again, from the opening of Herman Melville's *Moby Dick*. Maria is sticking with the traditional "Grandma" (for fear that she might become another "Ya-Ya" or worse). "Papa!" I like the sound of that. As it turns out, it became a name that was whispered below all other names by Josiah, just as soon as he began to form words. I became more and more aware as to why his little mind would single me out in such an under-your-breath manner. It wasn't as much reverential as it was special. A name-calling testament to a very unique and bonded grandfather-grandson relationship that I never saw coming, for I had neither the experience nor the preparation for nurturing boys.

It started with him sleeping on my chest, followed by reading stories at night out of plastic-paged books that he stared at with attentive fascination well beyond his years or months. And then the marathon stroller-walks during babysitting days at our little cottage in Hollywood Heights. We would be gone for hours, in any direction! But our most frequent destination was Aqaba Park, a beautifully landscaped outdoor facility ensconced in a five-acre plot of land tucked into the top of the foothills, which used to be flanked to the west by the Middle Eastern rolls of the completed Sheik's cascading headdress. The highly desirable, available land ascending toward the mountain base was snatched up in 1996 by a farsighted city council and instantly designated for a park and playground in honor of the seventy-fifth anniversary of the famous silent movie. The playground equipment situated next to the Gulf of Aqaba kiddie pool was a cement facsimile of Scheherazade's palace from *The Arabian Nights*, complete with arches, mosaics, minarets, and a sultan slide, looking like it had all stepped right out of a Hope-Crosby "Road to Morocco" movie. Probably quite politically incorrect at many levels, but the general public knew that the Parks and Recreation Division of the City of Monument was only innocently interested in a creative way of keeping with the theme of the half-head of Rudolph Valentino above. Now, with the entire head missing from the mountain as a whole, what was left of the park's original intention and theme had only a distinct Arabian affect bereft of any movie tie-in whatsoever. Since Josiah was completely unaware of any of this colorful history, he simply played prematurely but joyfully with his plastic shovel and pail, without a care or a clue, in the designated rectangular box known as "Sandsibar."

As I would stare down into the stroller to see the happy face of this beautiful, innocent baby boy, I would renew my hopes for a timely, Pre-Tribulation rapture, one that would spare not only my grown children but my grandchildren as well. But, as the stroller bounced along on the sidewalk heading back toward Hollywood Heights, and Josiah, with his lighthearted squealing and fondling of the educational pile of pine cones, flower petals, and leaves that I had thrown into his stroller, I also longed for the day when Josiah would confidently cry out, "Abba, Father," just so history would not repeat itself! And that he would know sooner rather than later that, in this case, adoption papers are worth their weight in gold! Perhaps he might even start a junior journal of his own—long before I did—without the pain of getting there.

But my reveries and wishful thinking were cut short with our arrival back to the little yellow cottage, with an aproned "Grandma" Maria standing on the front porch smiling with her hands on her hips and asking in a mock tongue-lashing, "Now where have you two been?" as I laughingly parted the gate of the white picket fence to push the stroller through.

DECEMBER 4, 2014

Watching Sharayah and Jackson interact with their baby boy gave me such a thrill. Again, I "blinked," and my oldest girl was now a grown mother! For Maria and me, it has been a great run raising two daughters. The bedtime stories, baths, building forts, hikes, birthday parties, homework help, trick-or-treating, and yes, even the "Great Santa Claus Caper!"

For the sake of infusing their imaginations (and perhaps a subconscious potshot at my bubble-bursting older brother), I sought to make sure that my two daughters believed in Santa Claus until an unnaturally late age! To augment the verbal myth, on Christmas morning, I would make our fireplace on Chestnut Street look exactly as if the "chubby and plump, right jolly old elf" had actually popped out from our chimney to spread gifts throughout the living room. After the children were "nestled all snug in the beds," and while Maria was placing gifts, their dad would go to work on deception creation by spilling over all of the fireplace utensils, and then sweeping ash and soot out of the fireplace and onto the brick porch of the hearth. Then couch pillows would be thrown pell-mell around the room. I would even go so far as to not only consume the milk and decorated cookies my children had left for Santa on his annual designated plate, but would personally nibble the carrots left for Rudolph in an old typewriter fashion so as to perfectly replicate (so I supposed) the marks of reindeer teeth. Each year, very late on Christmas Eve, so late that it was often the starting moments of Christmas Day, I would step back to admire my handiwork. The fireplace and living room looked just like it would if the stories were true. *It doesn't get any better than this,* I would sigh.

Many years later, a tango with suspicion was replacing the "visions of sugarplums" previously dancing in my daughters' heads, questions now promenading about the existence, or non-existence, of Santa Claus. This was often brought upon by an enlightened, skeptical playmate at school. Not wanting to lie to them, I would remind Sharayah and Samantha of the ransacked disarray the North Pole Night Stalker made of our living room each and every Christmas morning, and simply ask an obfuscating question right back with an obvious, logical answer, "Would I do that?"

For the time being, the argument was tabled.

Each year I provided some fortification for preserving their belief system. One year I crammed an old black boot up into the flue, pulling it out at just the right time on Christmas morning exclaiming, "Look what I found!"

Another year, when our roof was being replaced, I leaned a broken plank of wood framing into the fireplace with a piece of torn red-velvet material hanging on a protruding rusty nail. "The roof construction must have been a real mess for Santa!" I explained. "Look! He's ripped his pants!"

Or the year we found misplaced reindeer reins coiled up in our driveway. To which I lamented, "I hope Rudolph's team got Santa's sleigh home O.K.!"

Speaking of Rudolph, there's that red-blinking light atop the radio tower on the mountain behind our house—as seen through our daughters' bedroom windows—that doubles for Rudolph's nose on foggy Christmas Eves.

In one of the last years the belief system held, Maria and I had bought a family computer for our den. We took the computer and all of its accessories out of their boxes and placed the gift, with a red bow on top, in clear view, on the couch for the children to see when they reached the bottom of the stairs. On Christmas morning, I asked out loud, as if thinking to myself, "Now why would Santa take the computer out of the box? Could our chimney flue be too small?" As if following clues, I went out the front door, followed by my contagiously curious daughters.

Upon reaching the middle of our front lawn, I turned around and looked up, as did my children. There, scattered about on top of the roof around the chimney were opened computer-shaped boxes, packing paper and styrofoam. Sharayah and Samantha stared in disbelief (as did our neighbors), or . . . belief! Had they only known, I had bought not only the computer—I had bought more time!

And now, it's Sharayah's and Jackson's turn . . . if they can only keep a secret!

January 29, 2015

Speaking of Christmas, I am sure it was fueled by the first Christmas with their only great-grandson, but the first "Papa," Paulo Ponticelli, made an abrupt announcement while sitting in the wingback chair by the fireplace in our living room one night when the three families were together for a spontaneous dinner. From his cache of stored-up retirement money, courtesy of his successful contracting days, Paulo Ponticelli wanted to give a large financial gift to the penurious Jackson, Sharayah, and Josiah. (We were all taken aback by this, as the close-fisted daily stipend known as the post-Depression Ponticelli budget would not ever betray the trove of rainy-day dollars he had been siphoning off and submerging under mattresses.)

"I want you out of that dingy apartment off Stellar Boulevard!" was how he put it. For an old-school work ethic like Paulo's, rent money, in all of its contexts, was just like "throwin' money out the window!" was how he put it, again.

Consequently, he wanted to provide a down payment for a starter house, with no obligation for reciprocity. Everyone was pleasantly shocked at the supreme generosity from this patriarch of our brood. I would even argue that little Josiah, as I glanced his way, uttered a coo unlike any other of his infant sounds, surely expressing his "Rock 'n Play" level of appreciation.

March 3, 2015

Good news, Diary! Sharayah and Jackson have bought a house! And, by great good fortune, it is just down the street in our Hollywood Heights subdivision. This is an added convenience what with all of the babysitting taking place at our cottage, and the driving back and forth with a car-seated Josiah in tow. The house is a perfect size for their family, just starting out. Every time they saw him, they could not thank "Papa" Ponticelli enough for launching them in this way—for all those years "making rocket fuel in his basement" for another generation.

April 6, 2015

Along with the rest of us, "Papa" and "Ya-Ya" were also aging. This meant listening at your own risk to that which proceedeth from the mouths of grandparents. It was their impulsive turns of phrases that were becoming an entertaining rotisserie. Phrases like the "pot calling the kettle black" was orally gerrymandered into "the pot calling the kettle back." "Stop whining" became "stop winding." A cool "headband" was now a "Band-Aid." In the heat of anger, matronymic "S.O.B." became "S.U.B." And for Samantha and her horseback-riding skills, "tightening the reins" was now re-branded "tightening the range." I can't fathom (or, as they would say, "I can't phantom") how this has happened, but these "word salads" continue to be tossed out, at any time, to anyone!

RAISED!

And then, this Easter, Maria, Sharayah, Jackson, Josiah, and I took one for the team (or, "took lunch to the team"). Our Father's Evangelical Church treated the Easter Sunday services as a family affair, so *everyone* was invited into the sanctuary. Men, women, children, even babies. Ever-organized Sharayah had packed an arsenal of occupational distractions for Josiah in order to avoid the hazard of hearing him scream. We were all sitting in the pew before the service began when Josiah started flailing in his Rock 'n Play, a sure-fire precursor to some vocal protestation. While Sharayah rifled though her baby-supply bag for the next toy assigned to stall for time, Grandma "Ya-Ya," seated right next to her, took it upon herself to occupy and console the confined Josiah. Looking down, she said in what might be called a very loud whisper, clearly audible to everyone crowded in the pews in front and behind us,

"There! There! Don't cry Josiah! It's Easter! You know, we're here to celebrate the Erection!"

From either side of our long pew row, we were, at first, jolted by this disturbance in the force. But, quickly, we all burst out laughing. Heads were turning from every direction, and we all knew why. Of course, "Ya-Ya" had meant to say "Resurrection," but in her prurient mind had replaced it with another shortened version that understandably sounded similar, but was worlds apart. It was irretrievable, as well. There was no rolling a stone over this gaping gaffe. The grammatical tomb was empty. The "gardener" told Mary, Mary told Peter, Peter told John. There was no telling how quickly all of the disciples would know . . .

"Gift Exchange"

April 16, 2015

"Dear Member,

The Search Committee of Our Father's Evangelical Church is pleased to announce that our own Associate Pastor Grayson Pomeroy has respectfully asked your Elder Board for him to be officially considered for the position of Senior Pastor of Our Father's Evangelical Church. Pastor Pomeroy is an honors graduate with a master's degree from Harrington Scholastic Temple in Virginia. He is also working on his doctorate through Vision University in Diamond Bar, California, under the advisement and counsel of our former Senior Pastor, Dr. Clint Banning. We know that all of you love and appreciate the excellent pastoral care that Pastor Pomeroy has brought to our church. He is truly a servant of God. We also know you will join us in prayer, especially for wisdom for the Search Committee, as they seek out God's man for this important calling, and if Pastor Pomeroy is him.

For the Cause of Christ,
Townsend Stevens, Acting Chairman of the Elder Board and Search Committee Spokesperson"

Very straightforward Christianese so characteristic of Elder Stevens. Maria and I had just returned from a week-long vacation in Colorado, visiting Colton and Samantha. We had a wonderful time. They both are so perfectly suited for life out there! Candice Carlson picked us up at the Burbank Airport and drove us back to Hollywood Heights. After throwing our luggage on the bed, I went to the kitchen table to sort through the stack of mail that Sharayah had graciously brought inside on her daily strolls with Josiah. Once the bulk of the mail was pronounced junk and returned via air mail to the circular file, I spied the official-looking letter from Our Father's Evangelical Church and wasted no time in discovering its intent while still standing.

"Well, he's done it!" I said after folding the letter back in thirds. "It took him long enough, but he's thrown his hat into the ring!"

"What are you talking about?" yelled Maria from the bedroom. She came out with our heavy winter coats draped over her arm, which were still quite necessary in Colorado, even with Spring in the air. Both were now bound for the unused majority of the year in our hall closet in California. I handed her the letter, which she read slowly.

"Hmmmmm," was all she could muster to fill the airspace, as she weighed the appropriateness of verbalizing what she really was thinking.

"I don't have a good feeling about this," was apparently appropriate. She threw the coats over a kitchen-table chair and sat down. I sat down opposite her, giving her the look of an inquiring mind. "He's just not that good of a preacher, Ian. I don't think he's gifted." She had read my mind. "I agree," I said. We rifled through the rest of the mail in silence, giving the other bills and notices only glazed looks, as a preoccupation with the giving and receiving of the Lord's gifts was provoking our thoughts.

April 18, 2015

However, both the Search Committee and the Elder Board had a very good feeling about it. As a member of the board, I expressed the fact that, while I understood this was turning out to be, by far, the longest pastoral search in our history—going on a decade—I was concerned that we were throwing in the towel too soon. Maybe even settling. Since he was acting Senior Pastor at the time, Grayson was present, as usual, at the elder meeting and heard my concerns. He flagged me down on the sidewalk afterwards, friend to friend.

"Would you keep the preaching rotation?" I asked, friend to friend.

"Why?" he queried. He seemed suspicious. Since I had been asked to preach in this rotation on occasion, more now that I was out of school, I thought it a legitimate question.

"Yes!" he answered, almost consolingly. "I think the preaching rotation is a great idea, Ian! It has been a real help during this overlong transition. And your contribution has been invaluable." While I appreciated the pat on the back, it seemed a distraction just then to the real issue at hand.

"Do you feel you're up to it?"

"Up to what? Preaching? Sure! I may not be called to preach, Ian, but I am definitely called to lead!" I thought this an odd, if not convenient shift in focus, like taking the prerequisite out of the course requirement.

"But what about all that stuff you told me when you first moved out here? About how being an Associate Pastor 'made you tick'? You want to be 'out with the folks,' as you said, and not 'cooped up' in an office preparing sermons? You're a wingman!" My inflections unintentionally gave this last, presumed personality trait of Grayson additional force, making sure he knew the seating assignments in the airplane cockpit.

"Now, I believe God may be calling me to be a lead pilot! Look, Ian—over the past many months—years—I have fallen more in love with the people at, what do you call it? O.F.E.! And now I want to take the next step and shepherd them as permanent Senior Pastor and, yes, even from the pulpit."

I decided to come right out and vent Maria's concern: "Do you think you're gifted?"

He seemed slightly affronted at this. "As much as anybody!" I was not sure what that was supposed to mean; this wasn't a competition, so I pressed him:

"I mean have you looked over the spiritual gifts in the Bible with maybe one or two elders to have them validate where your passions may lie?"

"The passages on spiritual gifts are pretty messy, Ian!"

"Romans, First Corinthians, Ephesians, and First Peter," I interjected while nodding. I wanted Grayson to know that I was not picking on him but, having done my homework, was only trying to accurately pick apart the Bible instead.

"There is no way to properly compile one correct or complete list," Grayson continued. "They may be only suggestive. It is hard to specifically apply them without falling into the danger of just another personality test."

I rephrased my question. "But have you met with any elders to specifically discuss whether or not you have the spiritual gift of preaching, as it is described in the Bible?"

He paused, as if cornered, "No."

"Gift Exchange"

"From him the whole body, fitted and knit together by every supporting ligament, promotes the growth of the body for building itself up in love by the proper working of each individual part."

—Ephesians 4:16 (CSB)

May 24, 2015

At the Congregational Meeting tonight to vet the new candidate (while all of the other contenders had been moved to second- and third-round dust-caked stacks of resumes over the years), the members of O.F.E. voiced the same "preaching concerns" about Pastor Pomeroy. To a person, they thought that the universally likable Grayson was one of the best pastors the church had ever known, but not necessarily a preacher. There was some soft-shoe salesmanship going on in the Elder Board presentation, allaying the fears of the congregation by always returning to the "preacher rotation" model, which had been met with such high approval and would, of course, remain. This placated any perishable thoughts of a Pastor Pomeroy perpetually preaching, and, once again, shifted the discussion focus from "pulpit fill" to "bedside manner." Finally, Grayson, Caroline, and their four kids were asked to leave the sanctuary as the congregation took a vote. The O.F.E. members, by the beckoning of an Elder Board now nearly ten years older and ten years more exhausted, went down a convenient path of least resistance, going for a well-known commodity, rather than an unknown—and unfound—one. As such, Grayson Pomeroy was called to the position with an 87% "yea" and 13% "nay" vote. I was one of the "yeas," primarily on the basis of the preacher-rotation preservation, and secondarily because Grayson was my friend. As it turned out, these two motivations were behind most all of the "yea" votes church-wide.

"Why didn't you run for the office, Ian?" This, from Galen Holmes, from the "Canes and Able" class, during the old-fashioned ice-cream social after the meeting. True, it was the Elder Board at O.F.E. who had first set the idea of my obtaining a Master's degree in motion. But, finally arriving home from my scholastic journey with the coveted prize, I felt oddly re-directed from the position. Perhaps this, too, was a matter of correctly fitted, spiritual gifting.

July 21, 2015

This was my final elder meeting tonight, as my extended term is up. Something inside me decided not to opt for yet another term, of which I was by-law eligible. At last week's congregational meeting, Patrick Hamilton and newcomers Griffin Collins and Ross Henderson were voted onto the board.

Trying to preserve the union with a new Senior Pastor on the horizon, I came to church all dressed up in western attire—cowboy hat, scarf, vest, chaps, boots, and spurs. I clinked my way into the Becomers' classroom, pulled out an old piece of brown paper burnt around the edges from a leather Pony Express mail bag and read,

> "The town of Faith was peaceable indeed. Not a commotion, never! Sheriff Tim saw to that fer sure! All of the townsfolk was appreciative of ol' Sheriff Tim's efforts to keep the peace. Even the local 'Sin Saloon' was closed by dusk. After that, the only movement was the trail of a tumbleweed, the only sound was the caw of a crow, the only action was the scurryin'

"Gift Exchange"

of a varmint. Until the 'Shipwreck Gang' come a-barrelin' into town from their hideout in Satan's Camp! Hymenaeus, Alexander, and Philetus—the three most notorious gunmen ever to ride the plains of Asia Minor!

They was itchin' to do some serious harm to Faith. But what they didn't bank on was Sheriff Tim! Tim fought those three outlaws hard with the good fight, lickin' them within an inch of their sorry lives. He sent them hoofin' right outta town, back to where they came from . . . forked tails between their bow-legs!"

"Turn to First Timothy, Chapter One."

This was to be my last synopsis at Our Father's Evangelical Church.

My old friend Patrick Hamilton has not only been voted back onto the board but also has had the oversight of Adult Christian Education unanimously bestowed upon him by the elders, in my place. He returned to the post with energy and vision, along with a whole slate of newfangled ideas for Adult Christian Education. As a result, there were no new teaching opportunities for me. I began to feel like Sheriff Tim: "This town ain't big enough for the two of us," meaning Maria and me.

Add to this, once Pastor Pomeroy was firmly in place, the Elder Board took financial stewardship and opacity to a whole new level. After beating their breastplates and rolling the Urim and Thummin, they came up with a gem—concluding that since Pastor Grayson "Grape" Pomeroy was receiving a generous, full-time salary with health benefits, as well as a house in Monument partially financed by the church, the church should, in return, be receiving its due of 52 sermons a year from said pastor. In a word, they wanted more Bible bang for their buck, so the preaching-rotation model was quietly disbanded.

As was expected, this sent a ripple effect throughout the church body, once everyone had noticed that Pastor Pomeroy was filling the pulpit week, after week, after week. "Maybe he'll get better" was the hopeful resignation. He didn't. Nor could the people just resign themselves and get used to it. Spiritual gifts don't work that way. They aren't graded on a curve. More and more of the congregants approached the leadership to make their opinions known and to ask for an explanation about the broken promise. This was all met with a dismissive, deflective, and defensive posture from every man on the Elder Board. Pastor Pomeroy's warm personality and friendship had captured the hearts of the church leadership—a cognoscenti that had decided to prioritize camaraderie over calling. In other words, an insular Elder Board had circled the wagons . . . around a "Grape"!

With our ministries drying up, and with this unsettled feeling continuing to fester in both Maria and me, I decided to divert my mind elsewhere. I pulled down my three-speed, banana-seated, Schwinn Stingray bicycle from the rafters of our garage—the very one I used to ride to the John Adams Elementary School when I was in the fifth and sixth grade. It was a rusty, faded old mess by now, but I wanted to have it restored. It was an expensive labor of love that took quite a few weeks of dismantling, having parts sent out for re-chroming, a new matching banana seat from eBay, custom painting by local professionals perfectly replicating the original, metal-flecked color, new brakes, gears, spokes, chains, tires, and then re-assembly. Finally, it was completed, looking like it had just rolled out of a bicycle-shop showroom of the 1960s! I sat on the curved seat and leaned back against the spoiler. I felt just like Frank Holbert, on Travis Yoder's "Flash" way back when, flying down the "Funicular Fang" in the middle of town, with my teenage father cheering him on. Standing there, at the end of the deliciously diverting restoration of my beloved Stingray, straddling the bike with my toes touching the pavement, leaning against the support of the kickstand, another thought occurred to me: *Still not being able to shake the feeling that there was no longer any place for us at O.F.E. is like a kid on a bike, who is now capable of riding on his own, so the two training wheels—namely Maria and myself—are removed. And the bike wobbles off in a completely new and different direction, steadying as she goes.*

August 18, 2015

At one of my last lunches with Grayson Pomeroy at the remodeled and enlarged Rush More Coffee House (whose once-clever name now made no sense), which were growing more and more tense, the awkward subject of the diminishing crowds at O.F.E. came up. I mentioned Grayson's preaching as probable cause.

"You know," Grayson said, "at the church I attended back in Virginia, I was a celebrity. Whenever I preached, the place was packed."

I didn't have the heart to tell him that he was no longer in the "Old Dominion State" but the "Entertainment Capital of the World" and that gifts can get lost in the translation.

"O.F.E. is out of alignment, Grayson. Which is always the case when people are not put in the right slots. Your gifts have been shuffled around in such a way as to perhaps hinder the Holy Spirit. 'Round peg' does not always fit into 'square hole'! And that's what's happening in my view. There is no harm in you going back to your Associate Pastor position; it is where you soared! The organic church is not a business. There are no vertical ladders in church hierarchy, or shouldn't be, but only horizontal. It would not be considered a demotion—at least not in God's economy—but rather a lateral move that would free everything up to work as the Body should."

There! I'd said it. But he apparently wasn't listening.

"Perhaps you can't hear me anymore, Ian." Grayson sighed, ruefully.

Perhaps I couldn't.

But there was Someone else who Maria and I heard loud and clear.

"Gift Exchange"

August 21, 2015

Maria was getting very confused. She did not want to simply leave the church, nor could she abide by the notion that we were being kicked out. Even though it looked like we were supposed to go, it seemed that we were still desperately trying to hold on to the pant leg of the church leadership, begging them to give us a ministry, while they, at a command from on high, were gently trying to shake us off.

I came home tonight to find Maria on the phone in our bedroom, talking long distance to Patty O'Connor. Maria could always count on her wisdom, insight, and perspective, and all with the added objectivity of distance. After what seemed like hours, Maria returned to the den, with a combined look of relief and confidence on her face. Since I could guess what their conversation had been about, all that she said to me was the mutually agreed-upon conclusion. In a word,

"We're being released."

"New Vistas"

October 4, 2015

"Annabelle Maria Osborne"

Josiah and I were having the time of our lives playing trains, banging on the piano, hunting insects, having water fights during bath time and tickle wars before bedtime, when out came the name of his new sister and our new granddaughter! The pregnancy announcement was made three months after Josiah's first birthday party. And, once the sex of the new baby was confirmed two months later, the name was in lights. Maria was elated to have an Italian middle namesake from the Ponticelli lineage. But this was not the only surprise. The other shoe was yet to drop, and it was not a baby bootie! After the birth, the four of them would be moving to Colorado. With Sharayah a stay-at-home mom, and now with four mouths to feed, the cost of living could not sufficiently make ends meet in Southern California. The generosity of Paulo Ponticelli had placed them into a new home, its skyrocketing real-estate value now able to launch them anywhere. So, if they had to move, thought Sharayah, she wanted to be close to family, namely, her younger sister, Samantha.

"New Vistas"

October 20, 2015

Maria and I were back at it, seated at the kitchen table, wondering what to do next. It seemed as if God were, in rapid-fire fashion, opening and closing doors as fast as those on the "Joke Wall" of Rowan & Martin's old *Laugh-In* show. After many endless discussions about this, looking at our situation from every angle, and dousing the whole thing in prayer with a supplicating fire hose, Maria and I reached our conclusions. With the inevitable approaching and our two daughters soon to be living with their families in Colorado, on our next visit to the Rocky Mountain State, Maria and I purchased a log cabin—like Solomon's House of the Forest of Lebanon—perched on five acres just southwest of the *other* Monument right off a fully-immersed Baptist Road, about a forty-five-minute drive from Colton and Samantha in nearby Centennial. The house was perfect for us, and even came with a furnished basement for the imminent migration of the aging Paulo and "Ya-Ya."

I stood on the porch overlooking our property, and the acres and acres of forest beyond that would exhilarate any tree-hugging dendrophile. After another visual sweep for the umpteenth time, I exclaimed inside my head, *Five acres! Wow! That's a lot of land.* I felt like praying Jabez and his enlarged territory. But I quickly realized that this all came at a price—and not a monetary one. It was the prophet Isaiah who gave the set-location name-change to Zion. The land would be called "Beulah" and would, from now on, be married to God.

"Beulah!" I pronounced out loud to myself with appreciative satisfaction, holding fast to the log railing as if it were the bulwark of a ship, just before Maria called me back inside to discuss the down payment with the realtor.

November 4, 2015

It seems all we do is sign papers these days. Both for the sale of the house and for the sale of Gideon's family altar, the Block Insurance business. The perfect insurance-agency buyer came my way right on the heels of our new-home purchase in Colorado. A smoother business deal was never made! In no time at all, I was saying a heartfelt goodbye to Jill and my dedicated staff and closing the upstairs door on the family business just shy of its 90th birthday.

November 18, 2015

Before we knew it, Annabelle was born, and plans were taking off for the Osbornes to move out of state. They purchased a little country farmhouse in Larkspur, close enough to Jackson's newfound job in Castle Rock. After much packing—wrapping, boxing, taping, and loading—they were ready to go.

It was a tearful farewell as we said "Goodbye" to Sharayah, Jackson, Josiah, and Annabelle when they got into their car to race the moving van to Colorado. But we were giving thanks that we would all be reunited again soon. Before plopping into the driver's seat, Jackson looked at me and said, "See you on the other side," referring to that three minutes of silence from an Apollo spacecraft before communication is once again established upon re-entry into the Earth's atmosphere.

"New Vistas"

December 9, 2015

After more packing—wrapping, boxing, taping, and loading—of our own earthly possessions, it was time for Maria and me to finally pull out of our driveway in Hollywood Heights.

We had just heard the news from a farewell-bidding neighbor that it was official: Monument was now "Vista Pacifica!"

But even with a new name, the many memories from this town—with its noble people and church—would remain the same, standing still in time. And even though its city limits would forever embrace it all, I would take all of it with me. Monument was me, as it represented multiple generations of the Block family.

But it was time to wrench myself from these thoughts if we were to ever make it to Colorado by Christmastime. My foot shook the brooding reminiscences out of my head, as it pressed down and put the pedal to the metal. We are a convoy! Maria would be driving our Honda Odyssey van, and I would be running blocker for her in my dented and scraped Honda Civic for the next thousand miles! With a fertile, teetotaling imagination, I pretended that my sorry excuse for a car was the black Trans Am from "Smokey and the Bandit," as I turned on Jerry Reed's signature song, "East Bound and Down!" on the CD player. All that was missing were CB radio handles, as "Block Party" and "Italian Grams" sped down the highway! Under the cover of darkness, the music was a welcome distraction, as the lights of "Vista Pacifica" faded into the distance. But between Jerry Reed's verses—now blaring through the car speakers—I could not help getting chills—sudden moments of disbelief and terror, at what was really happening. We were actually leaving my hometown and moving away!

"We're gonna do what they say can't be done!"

"Monumental Move"

December 28, 2015

"It's a deer!" Maria was right. We were walking along the gravel road of our new neighborhood, crunching upon a dusting of new-fallen snow. The pine trees gave off their pungent Christmas smell, making the whole world seem fresh and remade. The only foreign scent that did intrude was the occasional whiff of Colorado garbage. It was trash day, so in front of each house were a cluster of barrels, boxes, and all manner of containers—some lidded, some not. We were coming up on the next grouping of last week's waste when I noticed an odd shape sticking out of one of the barrels. Like Houdini with horns, it was stuffed into an open trash can with its four legs sticking out, hoofs upward. I looked down into the circular space, where, from its scrunched, petrified position of putrefaction, was a canned deer. It did not seem to be intact, which would account for it successfully being shoved into such a limited space. Even so, glassy, lifeless eyes were staring right back at me.

Colorado's version of "the snare of the fowler."

"Monumental Move"

January 5, 2016

Once we arrived at our log cabin, we had immediately begun decorating it with the requisite, touristy bear toothbrush holders, moose toilet-paper dispensers, and pine-cone salt and pepper shakers, all to complement the many elk-horn lamps and chandeliers already enhancing the place. We even purchased two rocking chairs for the porch outside to watch the sunsets. It was fun but also hard work making the place our own. After a while, Maria and I were exhausted, and declared for ourselves a "snow day"—which is what the locals do when there is actually a sufficient amount of the stuff falling down to warrant such a proclamation. But our "snow days" were not dependent upon the weather but on "whether" or not Maria and I felt like working on the house at all, or anything else, for that matter. Sometimes, just watching an old, classic, black-and-white movie on television is the perfect pastime in "Colorful Colorado."

It was one of our first spontaneous family gatherings at our house. Once again, the ever-generous "Papa" Paulo announced that he was giving an equal sum of money now to impecunious Samantha and Colton so that they could purchase the forty-acre spread they had dreamed of for their new horse business. They found just what they wanted on the rolling plains of Kiowa. Once purchased, they had a riding arena constructed and purchased six horses, all named after a half-dozen disciples: Thaddaeus, Alphaeus, Bartholmew, Simon, Philip, and Peter (in keeping with the equine Bible names at their old stompin' grounds, the Thousand Hills Cattle and Dude Ranch). They were now ready to inaugurate the "Goose Bar Ranch," whose title is derived from the book *My Friend Flicka,* by Mary O'Hara. When Samantha was a child, we read all three books in the trilogy together before bedtime, which continues with "Thunderhead" and "Green Grass of Wyoming." I noticed in Samantha's bookcase, when we were over at their apartment in Centennial a while back, that same trio of books prominently displayed. I got a lump in my throat, as I realized that the books were actually coming true for her. She is living the dream she has had since she was a little girl, right here in the green grass of Colorado!

January 23, 2016

Maria and I had started going to a church in Monument called "Purple Mountain Chapel: Proclaiming His Majesty on the Fruited Plain." A clever homage to the actual 1893 views Katharine Lee Bates had in mind when she penned "America the Beautiful." We had been attending the church for only a couple of weeks when word got out that I was a preacher of sorts. Shortly thereafter, I was asked to fill the pulpit (made entirely of antlers) for their own Reverend Nolan Masterson from Gunnison, Colorado, who was at a pastors' fishing retreat somewhere on the Platte River. When I arrived all prepared that morning, I went directly to the sound booth at the back of the chapel to get "miked up." With the wireless microphone firmly adjusted over my right ear and curving downward like some space-age mouth guard, I returned to the foyer to greet people as they arrived. I had just finished saying "Good morning" to a couple from Palmer Lake when I turned to find a gentleman of medium height standing right next to me. His appearance was crisp and his suit neatly pressed. He had an authoritative bearing that was clearly military in background, which was ratified by his painfully firm handshake, angular chin, and close-cropped haircut. He reminded me of one of Dr. Banning's bodyguards. His name was Dave.

"Are you the speaker today?" he asked assertively, careless of the wireless microphone bobbing in front of my mouth as an obvious clue.

"Yes," I answered, with an ingratiating smile. He got right to the point, which I suspected was always.

"Just to let you know, I will be sitting in the fourth row on the left-hand side."

I stared at him. A deadpan expression reached his face, as if I should know exactly what he was talking about.

"O.K.," I said with a questioning inflection, prompting him for further explanation.

"If I stand up and say something to you, do as I say!" I gave him a look of incredulity, which goaded him further.

"If I run up on the stage while you're speaking and tackle you, roll with it! Or, I might just grab you by a belt loop and the back of your collar and carry you off myself."

"What?" I exclaimed. I, too, wanted to run, like Onesimus, right out of the building. Instead, I stood there, shaking my head vigorously and giving him my best puzzled look, but trying not to show my discomfort and that I now thought he was crazy.

"I'm on the Safety Team here at the church."

"The what?"

"The Safety Team." He leaned in, looking at me, searching my face in hopes that I would understand something so common. Then a light seemed to dawn on him, and his stiffness relaxed. He almost smiled.

"You're not from around here, are you?"

I shook my head again and said self-consciously, "California."

"Ahhh." It was as if Dave suddenly had gotten the punch line of a joke or correctly sized up a Delta Force special-ops mission objective.

"You know that we're 'concealed carry' around here?" Now it was *my* turn at enlightenment. "Ahhh! You mean guns!" He nodded, triumphantly.

He continued properly placing my puzzled pieces together. "The Safety Team keeps an eye on the congregation because many in the audience are probably carrying—"

"Guns," I finished for him. It was then that I stated what I hoped wasn't the obvious.

"So if they don't like my speaking style or what I'm saying in my sermon . . . BANG!"

Another nod from Dave, with his almost-smile returning.

"I'm preaching in the Wild West, aren't I?"

A final nod.

"So you folks don't shout 'Amen,' do you? You simply fire off your guns at the ceiling!"

He completely smiled and walked away, as if that could be a possibility!

"God's Spokes"

January 27, 2016

Hey Diary! Remember me? Or, better question, "Do I remember you?" A few days back, I got into a bicycle accident. I was riding Flash (the adopted name for my restored Schwinn Stingray) down the Cherry Creek Trail when I must have hit a rock or something, according to some eyewitnesses (who turned out to be very clear-thinking, compassionate Samaritans). The back tire of the bike flipped upward, and I was catapulted over the handlebars. I performed a couple of cartwheels in mid-air before hitting the ground and skidding to an abrupt halt, prompted by my helmeted head slamming into a rock. The Samaritan bicyclists, who were riding in the opposite direction, immediately spun around, coming to my rescue. Upon helping me to my feet, they began asking me some basic questions, a test I failed miserably! I was talking gibberish and asking back nonsensical questions. They had the presence of mind to call paramedics, who took me via ambulance to the hospital, to run some precautionary tests. By the time a frazzled Maria arrived, I was somewhat coherent.

"It's a good thing you were wearing a helmet!" she admonished, couching her profound relief in a cautionary tale.

"I look like Atom Ant!" The timing was off, but my helmet-wearing vanity was worth commenting on. She looked on the verge of tears.

"I'm gonna be fine!" I added consolingly, while ironically lying on a hospital bed with nurses scurrying around me, connecting and re-connecting tubes to my broken body. "And so is Flash!" I added, thinking Maria would also like an update on my beautifully restored, purple velocipede. To my male surprise, she couldn't have cared less. As it turned out, it was only a minor concussion and a fractured left wrist.

When it was time to make my hospital exit, she carefully helped the nurses lift me out of the wheelchair at the curb and place me in our Odyssey Van for a trip home, in which I was in no shape to drive. Maria held my hand the entire way, and I knew why.

"We could have lost you!" she said to me later that night, while she was smoothing out a cold cloth on my forehead. My helmet was somehow still sitting on the kitchen counter, with the sizable dent very visible from where we were sitting. A perfectly sobering visual to her, "What if?"

"I don't remember a thing!" I said, for the umpteenth time. The soft-hearted part of a hard-headed concussion is that it oftentimes spares the victim any recall of the dreadful incident. My out-of-body experience lasted nearly three hours!

"It's so strange," I explained to Maria. "You're riding along, not a care in the world, and suddenly life just disappears. The next thing I remember is talking to a blurry you from a horizontal position in the hospital!" My rambling took a turn a little too dreary for Maria's liking, especially so soon after the ordeal. "It's as if I died and came back! Or, at the very least, it would have been a perfect time for Him to take me. I didn't feel a thing!"

"God's Spokes"

"Or," Maria jumped in, correctively (*her* powers of recall were operating on all cylinders). "It is proof positive that God still wants you here, with us! There is obviously more that He wants you to do . . . through you . . . for Him!" She was tearing up at all the other possibilities that she had been spared, so we let the subject drop while she continued nursing her patient.

JOURNAL "ISM": The Flexy Flyer is a sinister wooden sleigh on wheels, with an apathetic front braking system much like placing a dried leaf on a blacksmith's spinning whetstone. You could ride the Flexy in either a knee-bent, sitting position—awkwardly steering with your feet—or, on your stomach, with your chin inches from the potentially epidermis-peeling, grinding asphalt that is rushing underneath the slats at G-force, ground-level speed. I would find myself on many afternoons, with the dismissing school bell of the John Adams Elementary School still ringing in my ears, racing Flexy Flyers with my friend Gene at his home just east of my own on Vista Street. Gene's driveway reached their garage at a steep incline, as, fortuitously, did the double-dare driveway exactly opposite on the other side of the street. This made for our very own 1960s cement skateboard park. The only problem was that there was a residential street going right through the middle. It never occurred to either one of us that, due to tall, manicured hedges marking off the property lines of each opposing driveway, coupled with our under-the-radar size and sledding positions, any foreseeable, windshield visual of us from oncoming cars in either direction was nearly impossible. What with only sparse traffic servicing the occupants of this particular neighborhood, the dueling concepts of danger and safety were the furthest things from our minds! We raced our Flexy Flyers back and forth across the street, making sweeping bank turns up and down each driveway, sometimes on only two of the four rubber-rimmed, metal wheels.

However, our carefree race-course pattern was interrupted one afternoon when I, from my sitting position, had just leaned into the embankment of Gene's driveway and was shooting past the protective hedge, gaining essential, significant speed, as I plunged over the sidewalk in preparation for the opposite slope ramping up a street away. It was then that I heard the deafening sound of screeching brakes. A lady driving a large sedan, who was fortunately dancing with the speed limit, caught in her peripheral vision just over the hood horizon, a towheaded shape like the hump of a duck in a shooting gallery, darting swiftly into the street. I remember the horrifying sound of the squealing brakes, as my pre-teen reflexes told my All-Star Converse high-top sneaker heels to drag the asphalt in an adrenaline-rushed attempt to stop. When I did, there was the gleaming chrome of the sedan's grill, just inches from the left side of my head. The lady burst out of the driver's side, her panic stumbling on high heels as she made her way past the deep, black skid marks to the front of her boat-of-a-car in order to look down at child endangerment. When she saw me intact, she shrieked, "ARE YOU ALL RIGHT?" I looked up and said with manufactured nonchalance, "Sure!"—a supreme effort to maintain my cool and dignity in front of Gene. I waved off the churning panic in my stomach, quickly stowing it in a psychological hope chest to be made sense of later, as an adult.

After two blue-baby blood transfusions at birth, and now a Cadillac's bumper kissing my left cheek, it was clear to me that I had been put on this Earth for a reason. It has been said that, thanks to God's sovereign measuring rod, we are invincible until He calls us home, whether on a Flexy Flyer or a Schwinn Stingray!

"God's Spokes"

January 28, 2016

The next day, I limped out to the garage to inspect Flash. Miraculously, the bike had only a few scrapes, considering. Then I looked at my skinned-up arm, felt the contusions on my back, and imbued my woozy, forgetful self with the same bullet-dodging prognosis a concussion provides, even a minor one.

We two "miracles" had that in common. In both cases, bike and I couldn't for the life of us wrap our minds around how either one of us had got here!

"Taste and See"

February 4, 2016

Dear Diary: tonight Maria and I celebrated our 32nd anniversary! We went to a highly recommended Chinese restaurant in Lone Tree, with a spectacular view of the Rocky Mountains. The majestic picture out of the restaurant's plate glass windows was yet another clear indicator that everything in my world had changed. The many pieces of my old life were suddenly gone. But, as I found myself seated across the table from the wife of my youth, there was simply no place in the entire world that I would rather be. Our dinner conversation traversed a variety of subjects. First was news from California. Maria divulged that she had talked to Candice Carlson that morning; O.F.E. had announced that Grayson Pomeroy was, in fact, making a lateral move and stepping aside to become the Associate Pastor once again. Given church culture these days, this was nothing short of heroic, and I said as much, "Attaboy, Grape!"

After some time of silence and chowing down sweet-and-sour pork, beef and broccoli, and fried won-tons, Maria asked, "Do you like it here, Ian? Or do you want to walk back to California like you tried to walk back home from the Cheyenne Christian Conference Center?" I looked up at her, rather surprised by the question, and its comparison. All circles were unbroken to Maria's way of thinking. In the grand scheme of things, we had not been here that long. But we had made a good life for ourselves, and our family was all together. For crying out loud, we now even had a "starter" farm with a dog, three spasmodic goats, thirteen flouncing chickens, three ducks, and a penal colony of feral barn cats (a Grayson Pomeroy paradise)! I deflected from the heart of the issue, "I like riding Flash on all of the celebrated bike trails here in Colorado!" I said, as I held up my splinted left hand.

"You know what I mean!" she pressed, with a slight tinge of scolding. I was skirting too close to a subject she did not want to talk about specifically, namely, my mortality. But, generally speaking, it was only a couple of years before my sixtieth birthday (minus two or three hours of complete amnesia), and I could feel a "Road of Life" evaluation coming on!

"You miss your life back in the old Monument, don't you?" she questioned. Without waiting for an answer, she fired again, "I know you miss your church!"

"Yeah, where they don't shoot guns at you!" I responded, trying to lighten my "Road of Life" with some sarcastic levity.

"Are you living in the past, Ian?"

Guilty as charged! As if paying my last respects, I looked out of the restaurant windows at the panorama beyond. I used to think that "the old Monument" in California at Christmas time rivaled the most picturesque, alpine ski resort in Colorado, but here I was still wrong even a month *after* Christmas.

"I am not sure I miss the life I actually had," I finally answered, oscillating back to her eyes. She looked puzzled.

"The old Monument in my head is seen through rose-colored glasses." I had given this admission to my mawkishness some thought. I discovered that I was playing the victim of two, sightless issues. First, the glasses I was wearing presented a glorified past that was always better than the present. One that was just as dreamed up as the sumptuous meals upon which the Israelites apparently gorged while in Egypt. All-you-can-eat "pots of meat," the "catch of the day," along with "cucumbers, melons, leeks, onions, and garlic"! But there is no mention of bringing in the sheaves for this bountiful buffet in the actual slave narrative—only brick, mortar, and hard labor! How did 430 years of bondage turn into a Carnival Cruise line in just two and a half short months?

The second issue was my looking at life through a dark crystal ball at an unknown, dreaded future that would surely harm me! God has led me into change just so He can terrorize and annihilate me! So said the Israelites while still toweling off from Red Sea spray—their current plight was actually a calculated plot so that they would shrivel up and die in the wilderness.

I surmised that this might all just be from insecurity, and I could relate. After three moves—from Vista Street to Chestnut Street, to Hollywood Heights, and now this—it seemed that God was trying to tear away the roots that have entangled me to *terra firma,* giving my feet more opportunity to find their way . . . home!

"Your memories of California are becoming more fantasy than fond?" That was clever of her. I nodded. Sometimes, even when I try to talk myself into enjoying the rugged beauty of the Rockies, I can't help guiltily imagining the ludicrous image of Jacob after seven years of hard labor, finally staring into the face of beautiful Rachel and still wanting to go back to a bespectacled Leah.

"Is it my parents?" I was surprised at this from Maria, but it was a legitimate question. As planned, octogenarians Paulo and "Ya-Ya" had sold their home in Southern California and had come to move in with us. But Nicole was now in the throes of Alzheimer's disease (like Esmeralda Barrington fourteen years earlier) and was requiring more and more care—a level of attention that even Maria's sister Angela did not have the time, space, or inclination to provide. But old Grandma "Ya-Ya" was a beloved daughter of the Ancient of Days, and when you count the birthday candles in eternity, that makes her just a kid. Once again, for one becoming more and more introverted as the years went by, the basement-dwelling, in-law arrangement was a bit of a stretch for me. As a result, I was homebound with cabin fever, literally!

"It's all about the journey, Ian!"

I had heard that sort of bromide many times before!

"And it seems that you're 'Drifting unseeing through a time of divine opportunity.'" She was quoting someone, although I couldn't remember who.

"How about you?" I didn't change the subject necessarily, but I wanted to flip the roles of questioner and answerer.

"I love it here!" she pronounced. "And we're supposed to be here!"

I could not agree more with this assessment. In my darkest, doubting days, I had often tethered myself to the bizarre series of divine encounters that we had experienced confirming that we were in fact "released" from California. It actually helped my spiritual objectivity to turn the whole experience on its head, imagining that, if we had refused to go, then we would have been—

"Disobedience takes just a few minutes to pull off; obedience takes a lifetime." Another quote from somewhere. But that's what staying in old Monument would have been—disobedient.

Again, Maria had read my mind, or at least stayed on topic. She still wanted to get to the bottom of this!

"I know you enjoy being close to your grandkids," Maria offered.

This was true to the bone. Josiah and Annabelle, the next generation of "Buds," were a joy to watch jumping and playing in the wide-open spaces that only Colorado could provide.

"You keep yearning for a comfort zone from the past, which is making it hard for you to recognize the life-giving blessings that are right here in front of you." She smiled compassionately, as her droll sense of humor provided the punch line.

"Just like that silly alligator of yours!"

JOURNAL "ISM": Her name was Audrey, my pet alligator—when pet alligators were legal. To give the Animal Rights folks the slip, they were called "caiman." As a teenager, I doted on Audrey, removing her nightly from her watery terrarium in my room, so that she could lay on my chest while I watched T.V. I gently stroked my finger down her boney snout, and she fell fast asleep. I was not told by the Monument Pet Store that, for a week or so, Audrey should be left alone in her new surroundings in order to acclimate. If she did not have time to properly adjust, she would not eat the bounty of small fish and insects I so generously provided on a daily basis. Instead, she just floated there, insects spasmodically bouncing around her bulging eyes just above the water's surface, while delectable fish below swam about, ignorantly exploring the perimeter of her jutting jaw. Her nightly diversions of taking siestas on my chest had set her back from ever feeling at home, and she starved to death within weeks.

I grimaced at the thought and sighed, "I loved her to death!"

"The bottom line is," Maria pressed, "that there is no place I'd rather be than in love with you, Ian! And I'm not going anywhere!" In response, I decided to put it another way, in honor of both the occasion and the location.

I picked up my water glass, inviting Maria to do the same, in a non-alcoholic, celebratory toast.

"To our rocking chairs pointed toward the West!" I proclaimed, as our glasses clinked together, referring not only to a country song by Tim McGraw but also to our own log cabin porch-seating arrangement. Additionally, I was thinking fondly back to two other rocking chairs that were pointed in the opposite direction more than a hundred years ago, occupied by my great-grandfather Adam, who was trying his best at being transparent to my great-grandmother Emiline. *Some things never change,* I thought, *and if they do, it's as 'slow as molasses'!* to quote my grandfather Colby.

With that, Maria slid an envelope across the table, sideswiping the small plate of fortune cookies. I looked down at it and then back up to her. She smiled. This time, I put on "Rose of Sharon"-colored glasses and pulled out the card from its envelope.

The cover photo was a serene picture of a snow-capped mountain range at sunset. Inside was the stuff of marriages, families, friends . . . and churches!

"Love does not consist of gazing at each other, but in looking together in the same direction."

RAISED!

May 19, 2035

*"Since my youth, O God, you have taught me,
and to this day I declare your marvelous deeds.
Even when I am old and gray, do not forsake
me, O God, till I declare your power to the next
generation, your might to all who are to come."*

—Psalm 71:17-18

Hello, Diary: I'm not sure how to start this. It has been quite some time since I last scratched your underbelly with a ballpoint pen. Decades, maybe. Grandma and I were going through a bunch of old boxes that had been stuck up in the rafters of our garage for many years, all for a charity auction we were going to be having at our church here. Mostly kid toys and games that the grandkids have all outgrown. Now that they're all grown up, you see. Grandma came across this here light-blue notebook in one of the boxes. It has surely seen better days. I thought this would be as good a time as any to try my hand again at journaling. My writing is a little shaky. I'm not the scrivener I used to be. But, as protester Marty Luther used to say, "The devil hates goose quills." So here goes. I was thumbing through this dog-eared diary and was so surprised at all that had gone on in my life. And this diary is even missing a decade or so of adventures!

We got two more grandkiddos, this time from Colton and Samantha! First things first, they had a boy, Teddy, named after our 26th president and Rough Rider cowboy. He takes after his

May 19, 2035

dad! He was quite the shot even as a youngster! So much so that I gave him my Red Ryder BB gun just in case there's a barkin' dog in the neighborhood. Then along came their little girl, Cheyenne! Samantha insisted on naming her after the Christian Camp that had started me on my spiritual journey! As Grandma Maria would say, I was "tickled pink" when they told me, after announcing that they were expecting. Colton and Samantha are getting on fine. They seem to be made for each other. On the other hand, Jackson had more personal work to do since he and Sharayah had "plighted their troth," and he found it. . . . well, too challenging. So he disavowed his truth pledge, opting to swim in shallow waters on his own. But, back on shore, Sharayah and her kids also seem to be made for each other.

Our lives are full of abundant living and daily dying, rugged crosses and morning mercies, snares of devilry and shouts of divine deliverance, disinherited here below but joint-heirs up above. And all with the constant joy of the Lord shining through the beaming, delightful faces of those Four Grand-musketeers: Josiah, Annabelle, Teddy, and Cheyenne! They are the pleasant surprise in my story, the sweet refrain in my song. I hope, Diary, that all of these crazy recollections are not just hand-me-downs, but hand-*Him*-down, once and for all.

After more than fifty years of marriage, Maria and I are still plugging along. We have had our share of health issues (some scary, some just aggravating), dealt with the loss of our parents—with both fond, photo-album recollections and difficult, unfinished graveside puzzles.

We never did cross paths with the rest of the Block family again, not even anthropologically.

We have watched the changing times go by (in a blink!) as well as everything and everyone grow up or move away all around us, but always with our two rocking chairs still creaking on Beulah land, pointed toward the West.

A few years back, I was invited to speak at the better-late-than-never, one hundredth anniversary of Our Father's Evangelical Church back in California. Old Grayson (although he's just a kid compared to me!) was still mounting up with "ings like weagles" as the Associate Pastor after the Senior Pastor search had been scuttled some years before. Well, "Grape" called me and told me about the big ta-do they were planning for the anniversary, and he wanted me to be what they call a keynote speaker. Keynote speaker! Not bad for someone who locked himself into the bathroom as a little guy, refusing to come out on that first Sunday morning our family was going to try that there church. What do they call it? Oh, yes, O.F.E.! I was a bit gun-shy about making the trip to the West Coast at my age, what with the long distance and all. But Grandma lit a fire underneath me and said that I should do it, and she came along for the ride!

My, how the town of Monument—*oops*, "Vista Pacifica"—had changed! It was not the little hamlet it used to be and was growing like a weed. But when we drove up Valentino Avenue and I saw the church perched up there on the hill, I admit my eyes started watering. The sanctuary was packed with so many new faces *and* some of the old-timers that I remember, many of them proud grandparents like myself. We got a chance to chew the fat before Grayson had everyone sit down for the ceremony. In my little speech, I wanted to get across that, from my perspective, nothing in life is wasted (not even Father Abraham thinking for thirteen years that his man-maid son, Ishmael, was "the promised one"). Through all of its lessons, its ups and downs, life finds a way to make its point. Which is to say, *God* finds a way. God makes a way. God always knew the way. And, oftentimes, it is through His church, *this* church—which has a unique life of its own—that we all get the point from a good Daddy who is raising us *up right*, and *upright*. In other words, our *up*bringing is a full-time ministry, in both directions!

Grayson gave me a fine introduction, ending with "Please welcome back to his home church, Ian Colby Block!" and I was on!

Thankful to God for every step of the way, I got up the stairs to the podium a little winded, but I spread out my wrinkled notes before the Lord, just like good King Hezekiah did with that "love note" from scoundrel Sennacherib. I looked out over all the people; Maria was already tearing up in the front row.

I cleared my throat a little too close to the microphone and jumped right in.

"I saw a bumper sticker many, many years ago that said,

'Jesus is coming. Look busy!'

"It was one of many plastered all over the SUV in front of me, as if the driver considered his vehicle merely a motorized piece of old luggage that needed to account for every spiritual tourist trap he had visited on his life journey thus far.

'Jesus is coming. Look busy!'

"I had to think about that one, as . . ."

"The Father was playing the 'Shell Game' with the Son and Holy Spirit. Underneath one of the three gigantic coconut halves was hidden a ball—planet Earth. The Son and Holy Spirit nodded in readiness to start the game, as the Father cupped His hands over two of the coconuts and began to shuffle the halves among themselves. He first spun the outside two and then the middle one. Switching hands with lightning speed, He grabbed the right two and then the left. Occasionally, He would change the direction of the frantically dodging and shifting coconut halves in order to throw the other two Trinity members off track. At last, the whirling, fuzzy brown blur ended when the Father fake-reversed a figure-eight pattern of the outside two halves and exclaimed 'It is finished!' He looked at the Son and Holy Spirit for their guesses on the whereabouts of the coconut-concealed planet Earth. After some thought, the Son pointed to coconut number one on the left. Having no choice, the Holy Spirit agreed with Him. The Father lifted up the guessed half shell. No planet Earth! He then lifted up coconut number three on the right side. Again, no planet Earth! The entire Trinity looked down suspiciously at coconut number two in the middle. The Father upturned the remaining coconut half. Still no planet Earth! The old ball had completely disappeared! Questioningly, the Son and Holy Spirit looked up at the Father, who looked back at the two of them. Then, with a winning smile, He winked . . ."

"Turn to First Corinthians 15:52."

THE END

About the Author

Brad Brown graduated with high honors with a Master's degree in Theology from Talbot School of Theology in La Mirada, California. He also graduated cum laude from Biola University with a degree in Speech Communication and a minor degree in Biblical Studies and Theology. He was voted the Most Outstanding Student of the Speech Communication Department for 1981–1982. *Raised!* follows *Upon This Rock.*, *Rightly Dividing?* and *This Is The Church . . .* , the completed four "seasons" of Our Father's Evangelical Church.

Brad lives with his wife, Cindy, in Franktown, Colorado.

Milton Keynes UK
Ingram Content Group UK Ltd.
UKHW040257291024
450401UK00014B/204/J